OUT OF THE DARKN... W9-CDL-540

The psychiatrist leaned forward as Andrea began to talk in hypnosis.

"Little Andrea-Ellen is scared, she's afraid to talk to people," she said.

"But can't I talk to her?" the psychiatrist asked.

"She can't. She won't come out of the closet. She is too small, too hurt . . ."

"Hurt? How?"

"She is very young. Just a sad little child. Her dress is covered with blood."

"How many others are there in the closet?"

"Lots . . ."

Now for the first time that closet door was opening— to shed the first light on the most fascinating and horrifying human drama of multiple personality ever—to show the tricks the human mind can play and the torment it can inflict . . .

PRISM
Andrea's World

"EXCEPTIONAL . . . AN ABSORBING BOOK!"
—*Colorado Springs Gazette-Telegraph*

"EXTRAORDINARY . . . THIS IS TRULY SERIOUS READING."—*Detroit News*

"SENSATIONAL . . . INTRIGUING . . . DESERVES SPECIAL ATTENTION!"—*Bestsellers*

"A DRAMATIC, OBJECTIVE TRUE STORY."
—*Library Journal*

IN THE MIND'S EYE

☐ **ONE FLEW OVER THE CUCKOO'S NEST by Ken Kesey.** Randle Patrick McMurphy is a boisterous, brawling, fun-loving rebel who swaggers into the ward of a mental hospital and takes over.... What starts as sport soon develops into a grim struggle for the minds and the hearts of the men, into an all-out war.... (143426—$3.95)

☐ **AGNES OF GOD by Leonore Fleischer.** Based on the screenplay by John Pielmeier. A nun indicted for manslaughter... a dead baby... an arrest. And now, if the court-appointed psychiatrist found her sane, a long sensational trial would follow. But how did you judge a 21-year-old girl who wasn't even sure where babies came from? Who didn't even remember having one... or what happened to it?   (138260—$3.50)

☐ **I NEVER PROMISED YOU A ROSE GARDEN by Joanna Greenberg (writing as Hannah Green).** The extraordinary bestseller about a sixteen-year-old girl who hid from life in the seductive world of madness. "A novel that reveals deep truths about mental illness... a rare and wonderful insight into the dark kingdom of the mind."—*Chicago Tribune*
(137477—$2.95)

☐ **DEAR THEO: THE AUTOBIOGRAPHY OF VINCENT VAN GOGH edited by Irving Stone.** A powerful self-portrait—the artist's intimate letters to his brother reveal a desperate man whose quest for love became a flight into madness. "A great book, the greatness of a man in his own words."—*The Nation*   (140982—$4.95)

Prices slightly higher in Canada

Buy them at your local bookstore or use this convenient coupon for ordering.

NEW AMERICAN LIBRARY,
P.O. Box 999, Bergenfield, New Jersey 07621

Please send me the books I have checked above. I am enclosing $_____
(please add $1.00 to this order to cover postage and handling). Send check or money order—no cash or C.O.D.'s. Prices and numbers are subject to change without notice.

Name_____

Address_____

City_____ State_____ Zip Code_____
Allow 4-6 weeks for delivery.
This offer is subject to withdrawal without notice.

PRISM
Andrea's World

*by Jonathan Bliss
and Eugene Bliss, M.D.*

AN ONYX BOOK

NEW AMERICAN LIBRARY

PUBLISHED BY
THE NEW AMERICAN LIBRARY
OF CANADA LIMITED

First Onyx Printing, August, 1986

2 3 4 5 6 7 8 9

SIGNET TRADEMARK REG. U.S PAT OFF AND FOREIGN COUNTRIES
REGISTERED TRADEMARK — MARCA REGISTRADA
HECHO EN WINNIPEG, CANADA

SIGNET, SIGNET CLASSIC, MENTOR, ONYX, PLUME, MERIDIAN AND NAL BOOKS are published in Canada by The New American Library of Canada, Limited, 81 Mack Avenue, Scarborough, Ontario, Canada M1L 1M8
PRINTED IN CANADA
COVER PRINTED IN U.S.A.

Contents

PART III

Prologue

This account is taken from many hours of interviews, more than 700 pages of transcripts, and a patient journal (kept at the doctor's request as part of the therapeutic process) on a case concerning a patient we have called Andrea Biaggi. We have changed her name and certain of the places where she lived, but in all other respects the story of her life and the words she has used to describe that life are unchanged.

As for the psychiatrist, Dr. Eugene Bliss, his name as well as his thoughts are unretouched. Throughout the research and writing of this book, both patient and physician were very helpful, contributing not only their time, but what was more important, their notes and observations. Most of the words and all of the events pictured here are presented as they happened. In the second and third sections Dr. Bliss and Andrea are left to tell their own story without unnecessary narration or commentary, for it seemed to both of us that the story stood on its own merits without excess embellishment. We believe most readers will find the story of Andrea Biaggi a fascinating one.

PART I

1

Separating

ANDREA had been only dimly aware that there was something wrong before she entered the Franciscan convent. That's when the serious separating began.

It was her first time away from home, traveling from a small town in Northern Illinois to the outskirts of Chicago to begin her career as a nun. It was 1965 and Andrea was 17, just graduated from high school. The convent sat at the middle of a 40-acre estate, a post card advertisement for serenity where the devout could take up their vocations. Surely in such a surrounding, problems would make way for peace.

The entire family had been ecstatic about her decision, and they all came on visiting days, treating her like an adult, calling her "Sister," already falling into the ancient custom of deference. She in return wrote the appropriately "nunny" letters, filled with piety and wisdom, assuring all she had discovered her "true home on earth." They were happy, secure in the knowledge there was someone to pray for them, someone to "save" the Biaggi family. It stood to reason, she must be happy.

But she wasn't.

Not long after entering the convent, Andrea began to experience an overwhelming sense of fear and confusion. She realized that her feelings centered on her violent, insane father.

Her fear, she thought, was naturally spawned by a logical anxiety over the safety and stability of her family.

Her misgivings became so great, however, that she arranged a special visit with her eldest brother, Michael, to discuss the situation.

Her brother's words did little to allay her fears:

"It's like a powder keg ready to explode," he told her. "You just pray it doesn't."

Prayer. That's what they required of her. Yet her sense of fear and confusion was increasing daily. But she mustn't show it. She was intensely aware of a need to hide her emotions behind a mask of tranquility as one classmate after another was summarily rejected and sent home for showing signs of instability. A nun, after all, had to be perfect.

And so Andrea chained her terror to silence and became the perfect nun. The initial training was almost entirely a matter of discipline, rigid and exacting—a boot camp in a cloister. Tasks like making a wrinkle-free bed with hospital corners and washing the walls of your room with a toothbrush were prized accomplishments, designed to weed out the "chaff" from the masochists. Andrea Biaggi passed with flying colors. Her behavior was exemplary. She became a model of the promising novice, and the Novice Mistress recognized this fact by assigning her the room at the beginning of the hall with the glass wall through which visitors could see the model in all her serenity and perfection.

In other activities she also excelled. She was always first to chapel in the morning before sunrise, always the most fervent in her prayers, always the most enthusiastic and ardent in her chores . . .

Yet it was a sham.

She had learned the formula for utter resignation from watching her mother, Dara Biaggi: hard work, discipline, zealous acceptance of all pain, complete avoidance of leisure. It was what Andrea called her "Joan of Arc complex": an overweening willingness to toil until the body sagged and the mind swooned.

Still, somehow, tranquility resisted her. The quieter the external world became, the more hectic her private world seemed. Time fled. Moments that should have been spent in work or contemplation were lost in labyrinths of dread. On their heels came a malignant panic that fed on her fears.

She was working in the convent laundry, a large industrial building filled with steam machines, when the first urges to hurt herself came. She'd been assigned a job on a mangle—one of the large presses used to iron sheets. She would place the sheet on the lower plate and bring down the upper one. A hiss of steam, and the plate would ascend again. She'd been doing this same thing for hours, working in silent concert with her sister novices, never speaking, never raising her eyes. She'd been looking intently at the machine, the way it closed and hissed and opened again, like the jaws of hell. She'd been looking, staring, but had seen . . . nothing.

A terrible, mordant terror consumed her, surrounded her, taking the breath out of her, making her heart pound in counterpoint to the rising and falling of the mangle. Soon the strange anxiety had grown to overwhelming proportions.

In the next moment, without thinking, she had reached out and pressed the back of her left hand flat against the hot surface of the upper jaw. There was a sizzling noise, the smell of burning flesh. She felt nothing, remembered nothing.

The wound was never seen by anyone. Other burnings followed. They also escaped scrutiny. Andrea kept her secret abuse to herself, safe even from the confessional. Only the severe wounds on her hands did not go unnoticed, but these, too, were never questioned. Such things were excused as accidents, moments of carelessness. In a convent it was easy to keep secrets. There existed such contempt for worldly concerns that intimacy, even among the novices, was hindered. It was essential to ignore physical injury in the face of so much virtue. Physical injuries were, in a sense, testaments to faith, mortifications of the flesh, and were silently condoned as signs of special piety. St. Francis, founder of this sisterly order, inflicted many wounds upon his own body in various tests of his loyalty to God, including throwing himself onto the thorns of rose bushes for the slightest unclean thought.

Andrea's self-abuse continued and grew more vicious. She could not stop herself, and when she tried, her sense of fear and confusion increased exponentially. In a strange way, the act of hurting herself drained off some portion of the teeming emotions she harbored, but no wound could wholly excise the dread. It was a festering that would not heal.

The self-injury grew more serious and happened with ever greater frequency. While working in the kitchen one day, cleaning the industrial ovens, she gave in to a sudden craving to pour oven cleaner over her hand. She remembered no pain, was conscious of no shock at her action. She was an indifferent observer, watching someone who looked like her pour the caustic over her hand, and she saw, with only a feeling of relief, the skin redden, crack, and then bubble.

These injuries she could not hide from the Novice Mistress because they required medical attention. For the first time the Mistress was compelled to ask how the injury happened. Andrea said it had been an accident, no more. She'd simply allowed one of her gloves to fall off, and the cleaner had gotten on her hand. Never mind that such severe injuries must have been neglected for many hours to get so bad. The Novice Mistress accepted her story without comment.

The need to burn herself grew greater as time passed. She would sneak down to the kitchen at night, ripping the fresh bandages from her healing hand, and pour still more oven cleaner on the wound. This happened three more times, yet no word of it was mentioned. It was simply taken for granted that the injury had gotten infected.

With each fresh injury, her panic would recede for awhile and then, like the tide flowing in, would overwhelm her again, forcing her to ever greater acts of self-wounding.

Still the Novice Mistress maintained an aloof silence, choosing not to interfere with Andrea and her ''meditations.''

It wasn't to be wondered that in such an environment, barred from any conventional avenues of expressing or admitting her terror, and with the panic accosting her like a tempest, Andrea's faith began to falter. Like many Italian children, she had been raised to believe the two most important things in life were God and the family. Religion was more than a concept: it was a way of life. She clung to God in times of turmoil; she prayed for His mercy every night; most, if not all, of her activities outside the home centered around religious and church occasions. So now, in the midst of this apprenticeship, which was supposed to bring her into closer communion with God, she was distressed to find herself instead slipping further and further away from certainty. Lost in nightmares, she felt suddenly abandoned by God. How could He allow her to do these things to herself? How could He bring her so much doubt in this place where faith was most needed?

Desperately, she sought answers but found none; just more injuries and greater panic. She contemplated leaving the convent then, but it was not a real option. Home was the only other place she might go, and right now it was the last place in the world she wanted to be. Like it or not, she felt she *had* to stay.

She was on the very edge when she met Sister Theresa. Perhaps sensing the young girl's deep distress, the older nun gravitated toward Andrea, seeking her out during study sessions, spending long hours talking to her. For Andrea it was the first real human warmth she had had in years. Through her friendship, she began to recover some of her faith, discussing various theological questions with Sister Theresa, probing into some of the more obscure and baffling questions that had so impinged on her faith. She began losing weight, becoming thinner and more fit than she had been for a long time. The panics receded; she felt in greater control again.

Sister Theresa introduced her to the writings of the great scientist and Catholic theologian, Teilhard de Chardin, and Andrea quickly became absorbed in his teachings. Here was a more rational approach to Catholicism, here were tenets and beliefs a person could think through. Here was logical validation for a renewed understanding of her church. She consumed his works, reading everything she could find by or about him. Her outlook brightened, and she began to enjoy the convent existence. Many patterns began to change, including the vicious compulsion for self-destruction. Not only did Sister Theresa give her the spiritual guidance she so desperately needed, she also provided the mothering that Andrea craved.

She had begun writing a large study of de Chardin when the convent announced the institution of a new program of psychological therapy, to be led by a Boston psychologist adept in the problems of the acolyte. When Andrea heard about the new program, it excited her. Here was something else that might help her work through the terrible uncertainty and anxiety under which she'd labored for the past year and a half. She signed up for the therapy group and waited impatiently for the first session.

The session was scheduled for the hour following individual study, but Andrea was so intent on finishing her paper on de Chardin that she had to hurry to make the beginning of the first meeting. She was a minute late, and as she walked into the room, twenty-six pairs of eyes looked up to watch her. The sharpest and most accusing were the psychologist's.

"Why are you late?" she demanded in an angry tone.

"I was just finishing my research paper—," Andrea began.

"That's *not* the reason!" snapped the psychologist, her face flushed. "You did it intentionally, just to sabotage this group meeting. You wanted to keep the rest of us waiting!"

"That's not true."

"Of course, it's true!" The woman rose to her feet. "Anyone can see it's true. Just look how fat you are. No one with any discipline at all would be that fat."

Andrea couldn't fight back. For the next hour the psychologist bullied her. It was a senseless, brutal skirmish; even the other participants in the session looked uncomfortable, but the psychologist was unrelenting. Exactly why she was singled out for such abuse, Andrea was never able to find out. But day after day, week after week, throughout that long summer, the bile spilled out of the psychologist, and most often it was aimed at Andrea. Other people in the group came in for punishment, but they wouldn't put up with it and left. Andrea, inured to punishment and survival, weathered the storm, perhaps more to show she could than to gain anything from the therapy, for certainly such a leader could contribute nothing to Andrea's stability. The reverse, in fact. As the summer went on, Andrea's new-found confidence began to disintegrate before the psychologist's attack. Everything Sister Theresa had tried to do was rapidly undone.

Only later, while living in Boston, did Andrea learn more about this woman psychologist. A disciple of confrontational therapy, which was sweeping the country in the late sixties, she had been dismissed from several similar jobs at convents in the Boston area for her combative approach to mental care. It was Andrea's bad luck that the woman had chosen to resettle in the Chicago area. She destroyed the delicate balance that Andrea had so painstakingly achieved.

By the time the summer was over and the "therapy sessions" had ended, Andrea was in serious trouble. The only thing that kept her from collapsing completely was a solemn oath she had made not to give the psychologist the satisfaction of seeing how much pain she'd caused.

Soon after the sessions ended, Andrea again began losing time and gaining weight. The panics returned and increased, the periods of lucidity decreased markedly, and the self-destructive acts proliferated. She wasn't unaware of what she was doing; she couldn't control the course of the incidents. After all, she wasn't really there. Something was happening down at the end of a very long tunnel: there was someone there who looked like her, and there was a lot of nonsense with oven cleaner and fires and the like, but there wasn't any pain attached to the events—nothing was really going on. It was something projected on a screen, like a movie or TV, while she sat back, part of the audience, and watched, uninvolved in the action.

A few weeks later she had broken into the convent pharmacy and had swallowed a large number of pills. Nothing of note had happened; she had been put in the convent infirmary where she was looked over, judged okay, and released to recuperate in the convent infirmary.

A few weeks later she had renewed her attacks on her arms and wrists using the mangle in the laundry room. This had happened three times. Finally, she had "fallen" down two flights of marble stairs. Semiconscious and unable to speak, she had been taken to a local hospital where she was detained several days for observation. Though the Novice Mistress was aware of this rash of injuries, no step was taken yet. She was merely patched up and allowed to go back to her duties.

Her family, meanwhile, knew nothing of this. Andrea continued to send them a steady diet of happy mail telling them how well everything was working out and how happy she was.

However, there came a time when even the Novice Mistress could no longer ignore what was happening. Andrea's bouts of self-injury had become so frequent and violent that she was in constant danger of permanently maiming or even killing herself. Finally, after three years of this casual mutilation, Andrea was told to leave the convent in the morning. The Novice Mistress offered the girl only one piece of advice: she had best see a psychiatrist.

Andrea's family was never told anything of this. They were told, and had no reason to doubt, that she was leaving because she had been found too immature for the profession. The convent officials were of course aware of her father's condition and perhaps did not wish to aggravate an already dangerous situation.

As Andrea stood outside the convent, her suitcase beside her, waiting for her mother and father to pick her up, her trepidation grew. Though she loved her father and mother very much and could remember many happy times during her childhood, a strange, uncomfortable dread grew in her. Something was wrong. She wasn't looking forward to the reunion at all.

2

Beginnings

THE first sixteen years of Andrea's life were wild and turbulent. She, along with her three older brothers and three younger sisters, always lived near the precipice. In typically Italian fashion, meals often devolved into screaming matches, debates degenerated into fights, emotion was barely beneath the surface. Family reunions were bulky, disorganized affairs with more than two hundred aunts, uncles, cousins, and assorted strangers. Because discussion was rarely possible, decisions were most often made on the basis of ancient precedents, according to a rigid code of obligation and responsibilities within the framework of an archaic system, complete with castes where women always occupied the lowest rung. The Catholic Church and the father of the family were usually the arbiters of debate, and violence was the enforcer. Food was the cultural glue that held the antique engine together.

Amid the clamor Dara Biaggi, Andrea's mother, was the calm center of the family. Despite a lifetime of poverty and emotional uproar she had survived and in the process had raised seven children. But not just raised, for the vital lesson—that education would lead to a better way of life—had been inculcated thoroughly by her. Of her seven children, five acquired advanced degrees. For Dara, working hard was more than an ethical precept; it was a financial necessity.

Dara had been born in a small town in Northern Italy. She had two sisters and a brother, a very small family by Italian standards. Her mother was a gentle, sensitive soul who worked long, hard hours as a housekeeper but maintained a sense of humor and passionate regard for her children and husband. Her father had been a stonemason, a very respected occupation in Italy. They had moved to Northern Illinois near the turn of the century, and her father had resumed his career, providing enough food for the table and sufficient clothes to dress the children at a time when most immigrant Italian families who could boast of such things were envied for their "affluence." Sometime around Dara's fourteenth birthday her father died. Many years later when Andrea asked her mother how he had died, the answer was evasive—Dara made some reference to pneumonia.

It was from her cousin that Andrea learned the real truth: Dara's father had been implicated in a scandal after one of his buildings collapsed. His business had declined rapidly, and there was some allusion to "family troubles" as well. He was found by one of Dara's sisters one afternoon in his barn, hanging from the beam. The suicide had been hushed up, of course, but the rumor of scandal had remained.

Dara went on to complete high school—a great achievement by the educational standards of her family—and met her future husband. She was eighteen when, against the wishes of her mother, she married Joseph Biaggi. He was twenty-three.

Joseph Biaggi's life was shrouded in dark beginnings, primitive emotions, half-glimpsed ferocity. He'd been born in a small mountain village on the island of Corsica and had spent his first fourteen years there, living in a society that had changed very little in a thousand years. Corsica is a mystical land, more alpine than Mediterranean in its aspect, with rocky coves and high mountains, a land dotted with small villages where few outsiders ever venture. Here are found the megalithic soulstones, the "menhirs," wrought by a mysterious race and left in numerous sites around the island. A primitive spirit emanates from these ancient roots and pervades the life of the islanders. Corsica has always been a country of feudal customs and primeval rituals, which have had a sobering effect on the Corsican character.

As described by many travelers, the average Corsican appears to be an aloof, passionate, vengeful creature, loyal only to his family and suspicious of all outsiders (which often includes the Corsican family next door). It was on this island that the custom of "vendetta" was born, from whence it spread to Sicily. The concept of "omerta," or code of silence, was also spawned here and has such a grip on the minds of the natives that few of the many murders committed there each year, results of ceaseless blood feuds, are ever reported—or if reported, ever investigated. There are no witnesses, no murderers—only victims and corpses. Life is savage, lived under a patriarchal feudalism where the head of the clan still wields life-and-death powers over every other member. Child and wife abuse are accepted norms; the occasional death of a wife or child under mysterious circumstances is taken for granted. Perhaps no place in all of Europe resembles the medieval world more than Corsica.

Into this violent world Joseph Biaggi was born and no doubt suffered all the rites of passage common to most men reared in the Corsican society. He had been allowed to attend school only through the third grade before he was called home to work on his father's farm. Then, at the age of fourteen, he was shipped off to America, to the iron mines in Northern Wisconsin. He was the first in his family to go, and he worked hard to enable the rest of his clan to join him. The first to come was his father, a massive, violent man who believed in physical discipline to "train" his wife and children. Anything he had wanted, the elder Biaggi felt no compunction about taking, whatever it was, in the time-honored Corsican tradition. When he had fancied a particular woman in his youth, he had simply abducted her, thereby setting off a bloody feud between the two families. He had proved equally as peremptory in all other areas of his life.

Two decades after settling in this country, Joseph's mother had died after a self-induced abortion, and a few years later his father was arrested on charges of raping several of his own daughters—charges brought by a visiting social worker. He was summarily convicted and sent to jail. Cursing his victimized daughters for an imagined betrayal of him, he hung himself in his jail cell. Joseph Biaggi borrowed the money he needed to give his father a Christian burial. Ever after, Joseph kept alive his father's delusion and his anger, cursing his sisters for their "betrayal."

With this background and father, it was scarcely to be wondered that Joseph was himself a violent man. There was, in fact, immense menace in his presence. A muscular man like his father, Joseph was also subject to fits of convulsive fury bordering on homicidal rage. Andrea could remember that several times he had held his wife and children at knife point, threatening them with death. There were frequent fights between Dara and Joseph from the very beginning of their marriage, and almost always these degenerated into wife-beatings. Dara stoically bore the scars of many battles with her husband, believing the worst thing she could do was let someone outside the family know the truth about Joseph's violence.

But, there was another side to Joseph: he could also be a friendly, charming, loving man, a hero to every child in the neighborhood, a hero especially to Andrea. Perhaps in the beginning of their marriage, it was the only side of Joseph that Dara saw or wanted to see. It was only later, around the time of Andrea's birth, that Joseph Biaggi began to show this darker nature.

What triggered Joseph's decline is not obvious. Perhaps it was the grindlng poverty that threatened him and his growing family. After leaving the mines, he had managed no better than a handyman's job at a local hospital, and his wife had been forced to get work cleaning houses. For a man of Corsican upbringing, pride was the most important element in life. Perhaps the knowledge that he had been unable to provide for his family as he had wanted, that he had been reduced to a state of constant penury far beneath the relative affluence his wife had enjoyed in her childhood, had eaten away at his self-respect. Almost certainly of greater importance, however, was his personal history of a childhood filled with violence. Like poisons circulating in the blood, accumulating over years until they reach virulent proportions, the atrocious precedents Joseph learned in childhood altered his naturally kind and friendly disposition to something quite opposite.

Joseph's slow disintegration was noticed by his wife and his relatives but was not remarked upon. It was forbidden to talk of such matters within the clan; how he conducted his own affairs was no business of theirs. But slowly, as the years passed, the Biaggi household became a scene of many fights and arguments, witness to Joseph's malignant rage that at last breached even Dara Biaggi's sense of reserve. At the age of fifty, when Andrea was only eight, Joseph Biaggi was committed to a state mental institution. He was placed there under court commitment after a series of "attempts on the lives of the family." It was done with the utmost reluctance by Dara after years of silent suffering. Indeed, so complete was her veil of secrecy that Joseph's own sisters and brothers did not know of the commitment or the troubles at the Biaggi house until after it was done. Inevitably, Dara was blamed by all the relatives for her "betrayal." Why couldn't she keep quiet? Why did the outside world have to know of the Biaggi's little problems? Joseph himself carried his sense of betrayal—reinforced by memories of his sisters' betrayal of his father and the sinful death of his mother—to the institution, where he swore to break out and kill his wife if he could. In fact he did manage to escape no less than three times, but each time was caught and brought back before he could carry out his threats. Through four years of institutionalization, he was subjected to electroshock and insulin shock therapies in addition to various other forms of psychiatric intervention. They seemed to do little for him, only aiding to justify his rancor toward Dara. Diagnosed finally as a paranoid schizophrenic and incurably insane, the hospital psychiatrists remanded him to the care of his wife, despite his many threats on her life. The rationale for this action as explained by his doctors was that Joseph Biaggi would prove less dangerous to his potential victims if he were actually living with them, rather than nursing his hatred in a hospital. Also, they had noticed a change in his behavior over the last few months, and the doctors optimistically proclaimed him stable.

To no one's surprise, least of all the family's, he returned a man still dangerously deranged, now devoid of even those periods of lucidity and kindness that had before served as counterpoint to his psychosis. Never again was he able to hold down a job. He haunted the house, a grim presence.

Always poor, the Biaggi family had sunk into destitution when Joseph was committed. Dara finally succumbed to the necessity of accepting welfare—thereby shaming herself and her family in the eyes of the entire Italian community. As hard as she worked, she could not hope to support her four daughters. And now with Joseph's return there was another mouth to feed. They sank more profoundly into poverty. To his irrational sense of injustices inflicted on him by his wife and family was now added the very real fact that he had become a burden. This was soon twisted by his mind into a certainty of female collusion—a conspiracy by his wife and daughters to strip him of the last vestiges of his manhood. The remaining ten years of Joseph's life were filled with poverty, alcoholism, and violent madness.

Andrea was 12 years old when her father returned. It was during these final ten years that she finished high school and went off to the convent. In her mind she blamed herself for having caused the commitment of her father, though exactly why, she could not say for sure. She felt guilty but couldn't remember how she'd come to feel that way—why her mother seemed to blame her for her father's insanity, or why her father seemed to curse her above all the other members of the family for sending him away. Andrea accepted the guilt heaped on her and learned to survive under its weight as she had survived the trauma of so many other family troubles, but that guilt had not been made supportable without considerable penance.

Penance had led to a plan of sacrifice by which she might expiate her sins. She had been responsible for making her father crazy, for having him sent to an institution, for making her mother and her whole family unhappy. That was the truth as she saw it. She had much to make amends for. What better way to repent than to take up a vocation for which she felt least called and for which she had the most revulsion. She had decided to go into a convent and join the order of nuns who had educated her in the Polish parochial school where the poor Italian families had been forced to send their children. Because of these nuns she had formed a deep and abiding contempt for the Poles; because of these teachers, she had lost all interest in education. So many of them were cruel, or hypocritical, or just uncaring. Leniency was unknown, forgiveness never practiced, education little more than a series of perfunctory catechisms. It seemed to Andrea that there was no happiness or kindness in these sisters. Becoming a nun was the last thing in the world she had wanted to do and therefore the perfect means of atoning for her many sins against her family and her father. To become a nun was to gain some measure of personal salvation and would also help save the family.

When she tried to think of the past, of her childhood, it was unspeakably painful. She panicked, she couldn't see clearly. It brought on a feeling of nothingness, of numbness, even though those years—as best she could remember— were for the most part happy ones. Most, if not all, of her memories were associated with her father, a man whose actions were inconsistent. At one moment he was taking her out for ice cream, splurging on treats for her, demonstrating his love, and the next moment he would be trying to hurt her. From a laughing playmate to a screaming madman. He was a Jekyll-and-Hyde personality, a creature caught in unpredictable fluctuation between extremes. And still, Andrea had loved him. After all, Joseph had never hurt her worse than he had hurt himself or the rest of the family. As she riffled through her memory, she could only dredge up one peculiar and vaguely alarming footnote from her past, an event incongruous with her memory of childhood. At some point around the age of four she had deliberately run out into the middle of the street in front of her house as a car sped by. The car had almost hit her. But then, that had been the point. She had wanted to be hurt . . . she had wanted to die.

She had always been of a sensitive, even moody disposition. She had caused both her parents a lot of trouble. Her mother was constantly screaming at her in those early days. She was always to blame for some ruckus in the house; it seemed that Andrea of all the children could anger her father the most. She couldn't remember exactly why this was so, but surely her mother's anger was not earned without good cause. Obviously she had been a very naughty and disobedient child.

Nor had Andrea been much of a student. In grade school her performance had been downright abysmal: Cs, Ds, and Fs were the norm. Moreover, she was disliked by most of her fellow students who found her moody, aloof, absent-minded, and Italian—which in a Polish Catholic school was no small indictment. In only one respect was she consistent: she was inattentive. She was often punished for this lack of attention by her teachers, but it didn't stop her. It wasn't just daydreaming. There would be lapses when the whole world seemed to grow very small, even disappear, and she was left alone in the silence, trying to make herself as small as possible.

Perhaps it was because of all this wrongheadedness that her mother always maintained a distance from her. There was no love in Dara Biaggi's behavior toward the fat little girl who was her eldest daughter; all her affection was directed instead toward the three younger daughters, Dalia, Rose, and Lucy, and her sons, two of whom had moved out of the house by the time Andrea was eight or nine. Dara seemed always to regard Andrea with suspicion and a secret, festering blame, as if the girl had been responsible for some great and unforgivable evil. Though desperately in need of love, Andrea was denied everything but the most perfunctory attention from her mother. There was only civility on the best of occasions, a civility that could be colder and more distant than any actual show of anger. Andrea never understood.

Her father, despite his sudden and perverse shifts of mood and personality, could be far more affectionate toward Andrea. On weekends he would take Andrea to the hospital, where he would have the nuns watch her; either that, or he would let her stay with him while he worked in the furnace room. A talented handyman, Joseph would spend hours working on the house or their car while Andrea watched. He could take apart an engine and put it back together again in a matter of hours without forgetting even one of the many parts; he had built the house they lived in from scratch; around the neighborhood he was regarded as a jack-of-all-trades, the idol of every kid. Nothing involving machines was beyond his understanding. Andrea marveled at his ingenuity. And he, in turn, focused much of his affection upon her. Whenever she scoured her memory trying to recall her role in the event or events that had precipitated her father's breakdown, she could recollect nothing.

Never mind: she knew with absolute certainty that she was responsible. She would sacrifice herself for his sake. It was a pact she made with God when she was eight years old: her father's life in exchange for her own. An oath once sworn was not one that could be withdrawn. So, when her father returned from the mental hospital, Andrea secretly finalized that pact she had made with God.

As the oldest daughter in the family, Andrea took on the role of baby-sitter for her three younger sisters while her mother was working. It was a role she enjoyed no more than being a student. It was a hard task, and somehow she always seemed to do something wrong for which she was punished. Nothing ever went the way it should when she was around: something would get broken or one of the girls would hurt herself or there would be a fight. Whatever the altercation, Andrea was always blamed for it and sent to her room.

When she was thirteen, two events occurred that changed her outlook. The first was her entrance into high school. Because of her family's poverty, they couldn't afford to send her to a Catholic high school. It was the only time that Andrea was actually grateful for being poor. Instead, she entered the public high school with a new set of classmates and teachers who didn't know of her family or her former performance in grade school. For the first time in her life Andrea began to enjoy school. Out from under the cloud of accusation and suspicion that had tainted her grade school experiences, she began to prosper. Her grades rose. Her teachers applauded her progress and encouraged her to excel as the nuns in her grade school had never done. She responded with even greater dedication to her studies. Where in grade school she seemed numb and distant, here in high school she was cognizant of a new Andrea—a bright, high-flying, energetic person who was never tired, was always cheerful. Her conversations with other people sparkled with laughter and wit; she acquired friends effortlessly, charming them with her breezy, happy manner. The lumpish, recalcitrant failure, Andrea Biaggi, had now become a gay, outgoing girl. By her senior year, she had become a straight-A student and was very near the top of her class.

The second event that encouraged her new perspective on life was her part-time job at the local hospital where her father had once worked. Here from the age of thirteen through seventeen, she worked in the cafeteria—the first year for nothing, and thereafter for the modest sum of 80¢ an hour. Generally she worked nights during the week and all day Saturday and Sunday. More important than the work itself was the time it gave her away from home, away from her father and the clamor that arose because of him. Between work and school she could avoid most of the tempests which nightly raged in the Biaggi household. As her contact with her father and her mother became less, her ability to cope with life and improve in school increased. In addition, her vow to join a nunnery after graduation allowed her the excuse she needed not to date, though exactly why she was afraid of boys, she didn't know. But then she could reason, *who* would have taken her out anyway? A fat, dumpy teen-ager with large, sad eyes, she knew she was too unattractive for any young man to ask her.

It was with a mixture of relief and apprehension that she finally graduated from high school and made good her vow. In the fall of 1965 she entered the Franciscan convent outside of Chicago.

3

College

HAD Andrea lived five hundred years before, her self-inflicted wounds might have been regarded as compelling evidence of saintliness, but this was the twentieth century. In such an age, the convent saw Andrea merely as a girl in trouble, someone for whom therapy was advised.

Although the sisters had not divulged the truth of her problems to her parents, Andrea knew the explanation they had provided would serve as sufficient pretext for one of her father's tirades.

She couldn't have been more right.

As soon as the car pulled to a stop at the curb, she realized that she was in for a long trip home. Her mother sat there quietly, looking pale and plump in a cheap house-dress; in the driver's seat was Joseph, his large dull eyes glowering out of a round, swarthy face. His body was still big, but hunched now and bloated from alcoholism and inactivity. Large pouches underscored his eyes.

Even as the car came to a stop and the door opened, he was already screaming at her.

"Immature! That's what the sister told us. It's unbelievable. You're not mature enough for the convent? Goddammit! Anyone but you. Immature!" He was just warming up. Within a few miles he had launched into a steaming harangue. Andrea sat silently in the back seat, staring at her shoe tops, not daring to say anything. Even if she could have, it would only have made him angrier, more violent.

Dara did not intervene. She said nothing the whole way home, she just looked straight ahead.

Her father could not stop talking about her "immaturity." In fact, his indignation seemed to increase as the miles passed. He fixed on it and wouldn't let it go.

"Immature!" The volume rose. "You're twenty years old! You've shamed the whole family. Made us the laughingstock of the neighborhood. You know that! The laughingstock! Our daughter was goin' to become a nun, make us proud. Sure. Yeah. And then, zip, just like that—'Come and pick her up, Mr. Biaggi, she's not mature enough right now. Maybe in a few years'!"

He ranted, his fury spilling over into his eyes. His face grew mottled and quivered with anger, while he beat the back of the seat with a big hand.

Was she listening to him? She couldn't be sure. It was like a tempest raging about her. How could she control it? How could she survive it?

The house was like a place of mourning. While her father's fury increased with his obsession, her mother and sisters stood by and did nothing. They had all been so pleased when she'd gone away to the convent. Now that she was back, it was as though she'd been excommunicated. They tried to smile, but behind the eyes and the empty words were looks of disappointment. She had failed again, this time in her holy mission. The family had been shamed by her conduct.

Her brothers, predictably, turned out to be more censorious than her sisters. Raised rigorously with Italian mores, the boys all believed that a woman's place was either in the home or in a convent. To them, Andrea was a blot on the escutcheon of the Biaggi family. Not that they sided with Joseph, either. They all had reason to dislike his tyranny, particularly Larry, the youngest, whom his father had tried to convince was illegitimate. But some part of the basic Italian ethic kept them from taking Andrea's side either.

Even before she had left the convent, Andrea knew she could never survive at home. Her father prowled the small house, his low-lidded looks giving way to volcanic accusations of betrayal. Her mother and sisters were working during the day, and when they returned, there was always tension followed by fights and sullen silences. Joseph's mind had given way completely; he was now obsessed by the infidelities and treacheries of all women, particularly of Andrea's. One day in the house was enough to convince her she had to get out. Within hours of coming home she'd contacted her oldest brother, Mike, who was a professor at a university, having earned a Ph.D. through pure hard work. The natural leader of the clan, he felt a keen sense of responsibility for keeping the Biaggi family together, and he'd gone to great lengths to do this. He'd even kept his father at his house for the first year after Joseph's release from the hospital and had supervised his behavior ever since.

"What can I do for you?" he asked her. He sounded distant, as usual, and slightly uncomfortable.

"I want to go to the university, Mike. Fall quarter begins in a week or two and I was wondering—"

"What do your grades look like?" Brusque.

"Well, about a B+ average, I guess. Maybe a little higher."

"Good enough." There was a brief pause on the other end of the phone, then, "I'll see what I can do." He hung up.

Three days later Andrea packed and left home on her way to attend her freshman year at college. Somehow Mike had even arranged a student loan for her. Her hope was that she was leaving all her problems behind her, that all the craziness she'd experienced in the convent was tied to her fundamental unwillingness to become a nun. Now, away from home and convent, she was beginning a new life, one that appealed to her far more than the old one.

From the outset, though, something was wrong. It wasn't the strain of adapting to university life. It felt as if a storm had been triggered in her mind and she was at a loss to quell it. How much of the time she was aware of where she was or what she was doing never became clear to her.

She was ruled by intense periods of depression interspersed with fear, confusion, and now a new emotion,
anger. There were things happening inside her that she
couldn't understand. She tried to will the storm to abate,
but it didn't work. The self-destructive acts resumed: burning, bruising, overdosing with drugs. As in the convent,
she could even *see* herself doing it, inflicting this punishment on herself, but it was as if she saw it through the
wrong end of a telescope or played on a stage a mile in
front of her. Though she lived with roommates much of
this time, she managed to hide the wounds from them, or
if they saw them, conceal their cause.

In despair after several months of this, she sought help
at the University Counseling Center. It was her first contact with a psychologist since the convent, and it did little
to change her original estimation of their competence. She
was treated as a neurotic—allowed 50-minute sessions
once or twice a week, where daily fears and frustrations of
life were routinely discussed in an ambience of coffee and
normality. But her mind screamed insanity. During and
immediately after the sessions she would experience a
brief interval of relief, but these were followed inevitably
by a complete collapse. The interpretations and feeble
support the Counseling Center could provide did little to
help. She continued hurting herself and "blanking out."
Nothing seemed to alleviate her turmoil, and there was
much to exacerbate it.

She seldom went home, but when she did on special
occasions the visits always took a heavy toll. Her father
grew more and more abusive toward her. He became
increasingly irate at the memory of her dismissal from the
convent. His anger was fed by an obsession, itself a facet
of the mental disease that sought to fit all actions, all
people into a complex pattern of conspiracy in which he
was the victim and all others schemers: he saw Andrea as
the most powerful of the forces allied against him. In
consequence his wrath could not be stifled when she was
there. His denunciation of her became more vicious with
each visit. Already alienated from her family, Andrea

became still more resentful of these gatherings, not only because of her father's ravings but because of the docility of the rest of the family. They would not defend her; often, they pretended it wasn't happening at all.

The Christmas before Joseph's death was a perfect example. Her father sat at the head of the dinner table, cursing at Andrea as he drank. His anger became so intense at times that his swearing got completely out of control. Every word was an obscenity, and all of them directed at the small, plump figure. No one raised a hand to help her; everyone indulged his madness. It almost seemed to Andrea that they were in secret agreement with him since they let it go on.

Andrea's sisters-in-law finally ended the ordeal by taking away all the food and dishes. But still the brothers acted as if nothing had happened, as if it were really Andrea's fault. There were no words of comfort from any member of her family. The next morning she took the bus back to college. Her anger sustained her for a month. For perhaps the first time in her life she had been truly and completely angry at him. She had forgiven him so much, but the humiliation at the dinner table was the final straw. However, after her Catholic conscience had had a chance to churn away at the anger, she found it directed inward once again. She had wanted to kill him, she had actually wanted to hurt him. Surely no good Catholic could have felt such things. Obviously she was a potent sinner: first shunned by Mother Church, now ostracized by God Himself.

Despair set in with guilt and assured her that she would only get worse. Her mind could no longer retain the pain that emanated from that combination of anger, guilt, and desolation.

So the cycle of panic and punishment began anew. Her mind shattered at regular intervals and was glued back together again with only the greatest difficulty. Huge fragments of time mysteriously disappeared, and she would suddenly "come to" in her apartment, not knowing what time or day it was. It was the beginning of her sophomore year. In confusion and terror she sought out a school counselor who soon diagnosed acute depression and recommended psychiatric hospitalization.

The idea of entering a psychiatric hospital so appalled her that she resisted the notion with all her strength. Anyone who had ever watched television or gone to the movies knew what "those places" were like. Bedlams. Miasmas of abuse and neglect, with dingy, rotting walls, choruses of demented screams, a darkness made visible by sadistic attendants and endless, purposeless hours. But more than that, once she entered that place it would be proof of her madness. There was a difference between lost days in a corner of her apartment and a waking death in a hospital; it would certify her hopelessness.

And yet, the episodes were getting worse, not better. She was burning herself, hurting herself, driving out reality. She had to do something.

At last she went to a priest friend for advice. After a short time, listening to everything she had to say, he was forced to agree with the school counselor's assessment: Andrea needed psychiatric hospitalization. He offered to drive her to the hospital, an hour's ride from the university.

It was like riding in a hearse. Her friend, feeling some overwhelming compulsion not to speak, maintained a determined silence. Was it compunction on his part, she wondered, or something akin to uneasiness? Did he harbor some fear of her, now that she had revealed herself to him as mentally unwell? Was he perhaps even a little frightened of her?

He dropped her off at the front door of the hospital, making awkward excuses about how he had to get back to the school for some pressing engagements, and sped away. She made her way alone to Ward 2B.

It took a surprisingly short time to register, admit herself, and get a room. As she passed into the ward, the door swung locked behind her. She was suddenly gripped by an overwhelming desire to turn and run, trying to get as far away from the hospital as she possibly could. But it was too late.

She expected to find a scene from *The Snake Pit* being

played out in front of her: wild-eyed men and women in tattered uniforms foaming and cackling in the halls, filth and decay everywhere. But it was just another building. The corridors reminded her more of a university dorm than a hospital, complete with sterile, cinder-block decor and linoleum floors of an indifferent off-white. Her room was an empty rectangle, containing four beds, next to an ancient bathroom. There was of course no privacy, but at least she had the bed by the window from which she could look out at the Illinois winter. With the weather so close and the temperature of the room kept so very cold, she often felt as though she were outside rather than inside. There was no one else in the room at the time, so she whiled away the hours peering out from under her blankets, exploring the perimeter of her allotted space, numbed to all feelings.

Much of the reality in her life had been provided by television. She spent many hours now watching attentively, never questioning its truth. The people she saw on it were real, their jobs real, their lives normal. It never occurred to her that television might misrepresent the doctors and nurses of this world. Wasn't it true that all physicians and health care professionals wore white, were friendly and compassionate, always correctly diagnosed diseases, and always cured whomever they treated? It would be easy to recognize these ministering angels, wouldn't it?

The first person to enter Andrea's room was a young woman dressed in street clothes who extended a brisk welcome, assured her she would be fine, then walked away without another word. While Andrea was trying to figure out whether this was her doctor, another person entered the room, an older, very distinguished gentlemen in a brown, three-piece suit. Sitting at her bedside, he began to ask her questions about what had brought her to the hospital, how long had she suffered from the present symptoms, and what he could do to help her.

They talked for quite awhile, the whole time the gentleman smiling and nodding his head and occasionally giving Andrea acute looks. Then, unexpectedly, the brisk young woman reappeared, and with hands on hips, began to scold the well-dressed gentleman for leaving his room and not taking his medicine. Sheepishly the man excused himself and left the room.

It was Andrea's first lesson in reality: it would often be very difficult to tell the patients from the staff.

The young woman, who was the head nurse, took Andrea on a tour of the three corridors that comprised the ward. The first thing she was aware of was the smell: a noxious combination of stale cigarettes, overcooked food, and rancid sweat. She retreated to the comfort of her room, which by now had a thin coat of ice on the *inside* of the window. No matter how cold the room became—and it never ceased to amaze her how cold it could get—it was easier to endure this frigid tedium than the offensive odors outside.

Soon another man entered the room. He was young, bearded, wearing blue jeans and cowboy boots. He proceeded to ask all the same questions that the old gentleman had asked. Not feeling terribly sociable, and a little suspicious, she asked the man to kindly leave her alone and go back to his own room.

There was a pregnant pause, and the easy smile on the young man's face melted away.

"I beg your pardon?" he said.

"If it's okay with you," Andrea repeated, "I've just gone through this number once today, and I'm not really up to it. Please, it's nothing personal, but just go back to your room and stop annoying me."

A chill radiated from the young man's eyes. For several more seconds he stared at Andrea.

"I, young lady, am a doctor—your doctor to be specific, and if you expect to be helped by me, you'll have to try a little harder to cooperate."

Andrea gasped. "You're a—"

"Yes. Who else were you expecting?" Acid, humorless.

"Oh, I'm sorry. It was just—"

"Yes. Well then. If you don't mind, we'll get down to business here."

As her carefully constructed images of doctors and hospitals melted and the ice on her window thickened, she decided to leave the hospital. It was at this juncture she ran headlong into another truth that television had failed to teach: the Catch-22 of voluntary patientdom. It's a folly to believe that just because you check yourself into a hospital voluntarily and submit to treatment, you may exercise the same volition to get out. When Andrea signed those papers committing herself to the hospital's care, she had lost her freedom to make such decisions.

In the affable manner characteristic of all her dealings with the outside world, she asked the head nurse if she would kindly unlock the door so she could leave. The nurse's reaction was immediate and, to Andrea's way of thinking, objectionable. Without explaining why she was not free to go, the nurse simply directed two orderlies to escort Andrea back to her room where they were to stand guard until further notice. Five minutes later the nurse returned with a large pill on a small tray, and told Andrea to swallow it.

"It will make you feel better."

"I'll feel all right if you just let me out," Andrea pleaded.

"That's not possible."

"Why?"

"Take the pill, please." The voice was cool, testy.

"But I don't want to."

It is not wise, Andrea soon learned, to disagree with a nurse and two orderlies when you are the patient. The pill which was supposed to make her feel so much better did not fulfill its purpose. Nor did subsequent pills of the same sort. They only made her feel worse; in fact, they fed not her sanity but her growing confusion and silent anger at the way she had so far been treated by the hospital and its staff.

Her anger was further reinforced that evening when, still groggy from the drug they'd given her, she was taken down the hall to undergo a medical examination. Perhaps if she hadn't been so cold, so afraid, so lost in dreams and premonitions, the examination would have been okay because she hadn't been feeling well for a long time and had, several times, experienced a compelling need to hurt herself. She slipped docilely into the patient gown and sat on the examination table, trying to be the model patient. And for the first part of the examination she was. In this way she hoped she might speed up the odious procedure so that she could get back to her room.

She soon learned, however, that medical personnel suffer from the same lamentable ignorance concerning patients as she had experienced concerning doctors. It must have said somewhere in the textbooks that all 21-year-old women had long since undergone a pelvic examination. Doctors in general, or at least those doctors assigned to her case in the psychiatric hospital, had obviously never heard of the strict Italian family or the strict Italian Catholic family doctor who dispensed with pelvic examinations until after marriage. It was information this examining physician learned after two hours of struggle and three shots of valium.

Andrea had never encountered cold metal stirrups on the side of the examining room table, and she had most decidedly never seen a speculum.

"What's that," she asked, frightened. "What are you trying to do?"

"Now just relax, relax," said the doctor. "I'm just going to . . ."

That was enough for Andrea. Here were several nurses and a doctor trying to violate her on a table—trying to pry her legs apart and insert some steel device.

Something inside her mind clicked. Her brain exploded with panic and anger.

"No!" she cried. "No!"

The room tilted and began to wheel around. There were hands reaching toward her and leering, ugly faces.

"You're not cooperating," came a voice from thousands of miles away. "You must relax. How else can we continue the examination?"

"No!" The world had turned syrupy, thick and resisting. She couldn't fight. She *mustn't* fight or she'd get hurt.

She did not resist. She couldn't even yell. From long experience, from ancient buried memories came inexorable laws to guide her conduct. She closed her eyes, praying that the cold steely sensation wouldn't last long. The speculum entered without warning, and her whole body went into spasms.

Again from far away came the disembodied voice:

"Now if you don't relax, this is going to take a lot longer, Miss Biaggi."

"Please . . ."

She tried to relax, she really did, but somehow the signals weren't getting through. Her body had gone rigid.

What seemed days later, the speculum was withdrawn. For a moment she had a sense of security. She'd survived once again.

Abruptly, fingers entered, probed her. Another explosion went off in her head. Memories stirred and wailed. Synapses fired. Her body began to buck and gyrate convulsively.

Sharp voices pierced the ether around her, voices more remarkable for their disapproval than their comfort.

". . . a classic anxiety attack . . ."

"But was it caused by the examination?"

"No, just simple hysteria."

"Do something."

A needle pricked her wrist, and a coldness seared her arm, passing up, invading her shoulder, her chest, her head. She felt herself resisting and then her body slumped. But her head continued to rage. She could hear voices, arguing, contentious and angry, as her body slept. But where were the voices coming from?

She opened her eyes, but there was no one except the window and the winter scene beyond. It had begun to snow again. Immediately around her was a shore and ocean of blankets and sheets, a bed, a sterile room. Now she remembered. She closed her eyes again, and voices returned. Arguing, always arguing. What had they done to her? What?

The night passed with the evenness of an eternity. Did she sleep? She couldn't remember. There had been darkness—great pools of it—and then, finally, after a time that took a thousand years, she recalled the dawn, a gray, relentless cloak bearing the skeletons of trees, a leaden horizon.

That morning she tried to escape again from Ward 2B but once again was thwarted. The nurse and her orderlies escorted her back to her room and deposited her in bed. To demonstrate her displeasure she decided not to talk to anyone. This tactic, of course, was calculated to impress no one; since she had done so little coherent talking anyway, they could hardly appreciate the alteration in her behavior. Soon after, they began medicating her with large quantities of drugs: tranquilizers, sedatives, antidepressants, unidentified pills.

If she did as she was told and took the pills as directed, things ran smoothly, and she spent most of her waking time in a stupor little different from sleeping. But if she sought to rebel, or tried to free her mind from the numbing effects of the drugs, she was medicated still more stringently. Pills gave way to injections and suppositories, and nurses' instructions became orderlies' restraints. Lost in a wordless frenzy, disoriented and confused, it took her a long time to learn this was the standard procedure for treating all recalcitrant patients. After a while, she managed to comprehend that if she wished to leave the institution, she would have to play the game—learn the correct strategy—for it soon occurred to her that this place could never offer her the help she really needed. It could only quiet the body, not the mind. The madness was still there. What she had to do was *hide* the madness, smile and nod and act appropriately. Never let on that her mind was a vortex of dark rage and frightening images, that she was almost constantly losing time and hallucinating. She could never admit to this.

She learned stealth and cunning, how to blend into the

normal world, to accept the protective coloration of sanity like a chameleon. She was taught these valuable lessons by fellow patients. The doctors and the nurses didn't understand; they were no more helpful than wardens and guards. She had to camouflage her disease, to suffer in silence, greet the outside world with rosy smiles and friendly handshakes. The patients taught her how to cooperate with the staff, how to ''get better,'' how to answer the psychiatrists' questions in a manner that flattered their own definitions of sanity. While the tumult and madness raged inside her, while every nerve in her screamed with panic and her body sought a way for her to destroy herself, she would smile with the doctors, laugh with the doctors, agree with the doctors.

But her family didn't make it easy for her. Mike had been keeping tabs on her and had been informed when she checked herself into the hospital. Now he came forward and, having notified the family of her condition; took it upon himself to enlist the services of a nationally known psychologist to treat the case. This psychologist in turn, having interviewed Andrea, decided on an ''innovative'' therapy—family counseling.

To accomplish this, Andrea's mother, sisters and brothers were brought to the campus to participate. The plan from the outset seemed a bad one to Andrea. Her family didn't need therapy—she did. But the psychologist insisted and, buoyed by that weighty determination, her family agreed. There was no way out, once again, for Andrea. A quiet, sensitive young woman who hated any confrontations, what chance did she have against the bullying of three brothers and the solemn theorizing of a new-wave psychologist?

''For the honor of the family,'' Mike told her. ''You have to do it.''

''But why?''

''Just do it.'' His eyes darkened with anger. ''You don't have any decision in the matter.''

''But I . . .''

That cold, direct gaze would brook no argument. She acquiesced, still filled with trepidation and confusion.

The session, when it came, was worse than any she could have imagined. She was marched into a large auditorium and was asked to sit down by the psychologist, who sat in a chair facing her. To her dismay, she immediately discovered she was on a small stage with a crowd of some fifty or sixty students sitting attentively below her, watching with notebooks and pencils poised. Turning away, she caught a glimpse of her family behind her, encased in a glass booth, looking like observers from another planet.

"What is this, a game show?" Panic rose like bile.

"This, Miss Biaggi, is a family therapy session," the psychologist pronounced in even tones.

"You didn't mention them!" She pointed to the audience.

"Just pretend they aren't there." A patronizing smile.

"Are you kidding?" She swiveled nervously in her seat, looking for an escape. "This is ridiculous."

"The only thing ridiculous about it is your overreaction."

"But . . ."

"Listen, why should it matter what's around you? The real thing is happening right here, between us. Who cares about what's out there?"

"*I* do!"

For the next two hours she barely survived. It was half interrogation, half dogmatic presentation to the class—a freak show. It was bad enough she had to go through it at all, but that she had to do it while her family was right there, looking at her humiliation. It was too much.

It was not an enlightening experience. It was a tribunal, a rigged trial, a public flogging. Over and over again she kept asking herself how a psychologist like this man could justify such a callous and insensitive exhibition. What kind of a sadist was he? Had it even occurred to him there was more at stake here than just another forum to promote his latest psychological theory? Had he cared in the least about the mind of the young woman? Were all mental health experts equally as uncaring? If so, she would never be well . . .

Soon after this ordeal, the psychologist made his diagnosis: paranoid schizophrenia, just like her father, only hers was still in the latent stages. But it would blossom, given time.

"You are a very seriously ill woman, Miss Biaggi," the psychologist intoned. "I very much doubt whether any institution can do much for you."

Her sense of isolation, depression, and rage deepened with each passing day. Now she had only one objective in mind: to get out of the hospital. But how?

Finally, she learned.

It was in a casual conversation with several patients on the ward that she learned how she could get a legal discharge. "Didn't anybody tell you nothing?" an old-timer asked. "Getting out is easier than getting in, once you know the trick. You signed yourself in this place, didn't you?"

"Yes."

"Well then, there's no one to stop you from signing yourself right out again. They'll hate to do it, of course, but under the law they have to."

The next day she filled out a standard hospital release form at the nurse's station. The old-timer was absolutely right. There was no legal way they could stop her from leaving. Three days later she was released with a document in her pocket saying she was neither a danger to herself or to anyone else.

Without consulting anyone in her family she took a bus back to the university. They wouldn't have approved, she knew that already. And in fact, when told what she'd done, they strongly disapproved, arguing she should have spent more time in the institution. Andrea knew differently. She would never get better in that place.

But neither would she improve on her own. Though she somehow managed to do her work, even did well at it and became fairly popular, immersing herself in the anti-war and anti-racist movements of the late sixties, her emotional and psychological life was a disaster. The periods of panic and despair, accentuated by loneliness and an intense feeling of isolation from the "normal world," grew worse and more noticeable. Arm-in-arm with her comrades in demonstrations against the Vietnam War, her mind continued to grow more erratic. The nights were the worst. Then the part of her she thought of as "Mr. Hyde" would come out. Those were blank hours when her conscious mind relinquished control to some other agency.

Over that next year she experienced three more psychiatric hospitalizations. Each time she tried to conceal her problems from her family. But Mike Biaggi knew; each time she entered the hospital, he was informed by the university. He never visited her, never spoke to her, but he was kept abreast of her problem. Andrea had no inkling of this, however. Every week her mother would send her a short note, filled with news about the weather, her flowers, her arthritis, the latest babies born to the family, the success and manifold blessings of Andrea's brothers and sisters, but not a single word about her condition . . . or her father's. Not that she didn't understand her mother's reticence to broach that painful subject. It was like having an alien presence in the house: an incubus turning the small house upside down.

It wasn't until she came home for a short vacation in the summer of her sophomore year that she discovered the truth. Her father was dying. Cancer riddled his intestines and had metastasized. He had also suffered a stroke, which left him partially paralyzed. But the madness was still there. It shone in his eyes, manifesting itself only occasionally in speech, but always there.

Seeing her father lying in bed, so vulnerable and helpless, gave Andrea neither pleasure nor particular pain. Only a strange kind of numbness and a sense of security—for he couldn't talk easily, and that saved her from the agony of his raving and invective.

Over the next four months Joseph Biaggi clung tenuously yet tenaciously to life. Andrea would be called in to witness his death several times during the next two months, only to watch him escape at the last moment. Three recoveries followed three vigils, and somehow he lingered.

After a while the doctors changed their tack and seeing

no certain death on the horizon, looked forward instead to Joseph's recovery. Soon, they told his wife, he would be well enough to go home.

Within two weeks he was on his deathbed once again. For the fourth time Andrea hastened to the bedside of her father. As she looked down into the emaciated face, she saw eyes stark with death, and heard a soft gurgling in his throat. For many minutes he didn't move at all; then, suddenly, as if registering her presence for the first time, he beckoned her nearer. His lungs were so riddled with cancer that he could barely speak, and Andrea had to bend still closer to hear him. The words that came out then took every last ounce of the energy he had obviously hoarded for this one occasion, and even then it was no more than a soft whisper:

"Your mother . . . she did a terrible thing . . . you aren't my daughter."

It was the last thing Joseph ever said to anyone—one last demented thrust at a world that had become a dream of vengeance to him. Did he know that those words would resound in her head forever? Did he understand the additional burden of pain he was heaping on her? Or was he so utterly divorced from reality that he understood nothing? She would never know.

She didn't cry at the funeral; there were tears enough from others who hadn't known him well. As she stood there looking down at his grave, she cursed herself for being Italian: the gratuitous emotionalism, the false sentiment, the hypocrisy of mourning for a death everyone welcomed as a blessed relief. She particularly hated the funeral ritual that dictated she stand by her mother's side in front of the casket. Why beside her mother? Why in front of her father?

Friends passed her with looks of condolence, empty words of comfort telling far more about what they didn't feel than what they did.

What could she do? She tried to emulate sadness, tried to look appropriately grieved. But she wasn't grieving for her father, she couldn't make herself do that. Instead she was mourning for herself, for the malignant insanity spreading in her mind. She was going crazy, just like her father. It was the family curse. From generation to generation, one member after another had succumbed to a hideous, deforming, incurable dementia. And now, like a cancer, she felt it growing in her skull, taking her bit by bit, stealing every vestige of reason from her.

As the senseless ritual continued, she found herself singing "Songs for Aging Children," by Joni Mitehell—an elegy to her own spiritual death.

When the priest had finished his service at the graveside and her sister-in-law had counted the cars in the funeral procession, it was time for the final ritual—placing a flower on the grave. As her turn came to drop the red rose on her father's grave, her hand clenched tightly shut. Try as she might, she could not make her hand release the flower. She was frozen over the grave, staring numbly down.

For a full minute the whole ceremony stopped, suspended while friends and members of the family focused on her, staring. It was a tableau set around her reluctant hand. Her mind was storming, raging, out-of-control, and her body was in complete rebellion.

At last, her sister-in-law leaned over and forced Andrea's hand open. The rose dropped to the grave. It was only then that Andrea began to cry. Everyone thought it was just a simple grief reaction.

But they were wrong. Her tears were not for her father, but for the rose. She loved flowers.

4

Breaking Down

ANDREA could hardly conceive of the extent of her madness that followed her father's death. In fact a strange insanity seemed to grip the whole Biaggi family. Now that the curtain had been lowered on the archantagonist, the three brothers rose up to lead a vigilante raid against all the "forces of evil" in the family, hoping perhaps to exculpate Joseph's name, to rationalize the protracted time of travail, to show the world the Biaggi family was regaining its health.

During the first two years of her college career, Andrea had had generally good grades. But after her father's death she began to receive grades that represented the extremes of success and failure. The average quarter brought perhaps three As and two Fs as her biphasic world oscillated. She did not prosper. Soon education, like the rest of her life, became a question of survival, a desperate effort to avoid detection as a defective individual. She played her role indifferently, however. Her sophomore year had seen a slow deterioration. And the last two years were a dance with insanity. Most of her days became "problem days," and she retreated to her apartment where she rode out the worst of the storm alone. In her own mind she identified the diametrical poles in terms of the Jekyll-and-Hyde metaphor she used to describe her father. As heir-apparent to that malady, she now fought the madness until its force subsided. Then once again she would emerge to take up a "normal" life. At the best of times, this normality would last for weeks with only an occasional panic to be over-come. During these intervals the world was a reasonable place to live in; she made friends, kept up with her classwork, was possessed by the same drive for achievement that had dominated her high school years. But then, with a crashing finality, the veil would drop again and she would descend into a nightmare world. The doctors called it "dissociation" and "psychotic episodes," but these were benign labels for the horror she experienced. She had hallucinations—visual, auditory, and tactile. Her thoughts were crazy, wild. She was lost in a labyrinth, "blacking out" for days at a time. When she emerged, she would pull the pieces back together and go about her business as if nothing had happened, hoping desperately the episodes had passed permanently, but knowing they hadn't. Somehow through the last two years of college she staved off the demonic force that she knew was chasing her. Two years of subterfuge and pretense. Two years of telling her suspicious brothers she was all right. But near the end of her senior year, her world caved in.

She was spending whole weeks huddled in her apartment, inert, unreachable. But even in the nadir of her madness she somehow found ways to avoid detection, knowing that her brothers were waiting for her to collapse so they could blame her for everything that had happened to the family. For a while—she scarcely knew how—she managed to put up the necessary defenses when they were needed. However, there was no place to hide when she started to inflict really serious injuries on herself. The burnings began anew and soon increased in severity. She spent more time in the mental health ward. Her panic grew as she realized what was happening to her, but it only seemed to increase her craziness. Desperately she sought the reasons or origin of her problem, but she found only the old explanation: she had inherited the family curse.

It was at this point, only a few weeks before graduation, that two of her brothers stepped in to invoke their own form of justice.

That justice took the form of Mike Biaggi, arriving one

morning unexpectedly at her apartment. His attack, when it came, was vicious.

"We've come to a decision," he announced straight out.

"About what?" she said.

"We've decided that either you get your ass out of this state and away from this family or you check yourself into a mental hospital, permanently. No more of this conning the doctors into letting you go. Once you're in, you stay in."

"I don't understand."

Mike screamed at her, "It's not a proposal, damn it! It's an ultimatum!"

"Why?"

"Why? You know why. You're crazy, nuts, bonkers! Anyone can see it. Look at you. Just look at you." He was almost out of control with fury, his eyes staring, his finger pointing at her. "Just like Dad. Making everyone else around you nervous and uncomfortable. Making the whole family sound like a bunch of loonies! We don't need any more of that. No more! Now that he's gone, we don't need another one to replace him!"

Words and arguments strangled in her throat. Against such apparent hatred she had nothing to offer but her manifest confusion.

"That's all! I have nothing else to say to you. Either get out or check in. That's our final decision."

"I don't understand," she said again, feebly.

But Michael had already turned to leave.

"Jesus! Crazy just like the old man. Do everyone a favor, will you? Commit yourself."

Her head swam. She couldn't even talk as the door closed in her face. Mike was gone. Two minutes of yelling and then he was gone. The family had decided—either commitment or exile. Not much of a choice.

In the confusing days that followed, Andrea found that the special teaching internship she had worked so hard to get had mysteriously been withdrawn. The heads of her department had decided they didn't need a graduate student like her around to teach children.

Mike had blown the whistle on her, had convinced them she was incompetent. It took all her powers of persuasion and some tears to convince them to allow her to finish even the conventional six-week student teaching program—funded at her own expense. It took all her energy to get through, besieged as she was by the Education Department, her brothers, and a number of clinicians convinced that the only place for her was a mental institution. She fought them all and somehow earned her certificate.

The six-week period went by in a flash—she was practically unaware of the interval, only of the diploma awarded by a reluctant department. After that she packed her bags. Faced with the choice of leaving the state or accepting a protracted period at a mental hospital where they would only fill her full of drugs, she felt she had no choice. She decided to leave. For a while she flirted with the idea of remaining in Illinois against the wishes of her brothers, finding a job for herself and setting about her own life, but soon she realized her brothers would never allow her to do such a thing. Like their father, all three men could be violent, particularly when crossed, and she didn't feel up to testing their anger.

How she avoided total collapse she couldn't say. Some stouter force seemed to reinforce and refresh her, infusing an energy and outgoingness she could only marvel at from afar. It had seen her through the worst. Now she girded herself to survive the adversity ahead.

The day after the Education Department awarded her the teaching certificate, Andrea climbed into an old Mercury Comet she'd bought for three hundred twenty-three dollars and set out for the East Coast.

5

Boston

SHE picked Boston. It was a question of closing her eyes and pointing at the map. She knew nothing about the place except that it contained a large number of good colleges and universities and one of the most progressive Catholic dioceses in the country. She made a few contacts before going, sent an application to a graduate program in school counseling at a university, and was quickly accepted as a part-time student.

Once established at the university, there was still the sticky question of money: she didn't have any. She'd arrived in Boston with little more than the clothes on her back and one hundred dollars. There would be no help from home. She was in almost every sense of the word an exile, trying to make a new life for herself in an alien world.

In 1970, Boston was convulsed by a wave of political and cultural unrest that saw the creation of hundreds of different organizations espousing thousands of separate causes. The chief podium for this was Harvard Square, where flower children mingled with religious cultists, philosophical dissidents, political activists, and various intellectual hangers-on. It was a disruptive atmosphere for someone like Andrea—a place where her isolation was emphasized and exaggerated by the ephemeral displays of unity and community around her. Worse still, when she arrived it was Thanksgiving, a time of traditional family gatherings, and here she was in a strange city, without any home to go to.

Finding a place to live was the first order of business. This she managed through the help and under the auspices of an organization she had become involved with in Illinois: the Institute. It had, in the beginning, been an act of idealism for her to join. As a proponent of an international community of religion, the Institute had the avowed intention of joining all the Christian faiths together into one large, brotherly movement and, in taking on Andrea, they were trying to recruit one of the movement's first Catholics. A friend of hers in the movement had arranged for her to be quartered in the Institute house in a poorer part of Boston. She was only one of two single members living in the large house and was immediately given two jobs: first, to serve as the chief liaison between the Institute and the Catholic Diocese of Boston; second, to get married. The first she did gladly; the second, she felt constrained to avoid.

After finding a place to live, she found herself a full-time job as a secretary at the University Hospital to support her part-time career as graduate student. What with the cost of living in Boston and the workload in graduate school, she could not hope to do both on a full-time basis. Money came first.

From the outset, nothing went well. In school and at work she was trying hard but not succeeding. Graduate school, she soon decided, was little more than an assembly line for turning out education majors in bulk, without particular regard to the qualifications or appropriateness of the candidates. There were more than a hundred and twenty graduate students pursuing the same course of study as Andrea, all of them competing for the advice and attention of a small number of professors who maintained a dignified distance from their charges. Andrea soon found she could not work effectively in such a vacuum. Sensing that the faculty cared very little about the students and feeling no particular stimulation from the graduate program, she rapidly lost interest. Work was little better. While she got along well enough with the other secretaries and doctors, the confusion of her personal life inevitably began to seep into her working life. Associates eventually would begin to notice all was not right with Andrea.

She tried to retreat from the problems she encountered in her job and at school, hiding in her room, but it was a strange room in a strange house in a very strange city. She felt lost and, more and more, was acting lost.

One factor contributing to her problems was the group she lived with. As she came to know the Institute better, she realized it was, by and large, a narrow-minded group, comprised primarily of Southern Baptists and Methodists, bent not on unifying the Christian faiths but on bringing all the other sects around to its own form of fundamentalism. All money earned by the members of the house was pooled, all children and property shared. It didn't take long for Andrea to see her days in the Institute house were numbered: she didn't fit and wasn't particularly appreciated. Her contacts with other people in the house were only superficial. Her only real acquaintance was the other single girl, and in a house that stressed the importance of religion, the difference between a Catholic and a Methodist became an insurmountable gulf. Her only personal contact came from the people she was meeting through the Boston Diocese, particularly Father Henry, the abbot of a progressive seminary near Framingham. He seemed to recognize in Andrea a certain quality he liked—a bright, troubled soul in search of answers. He was ingenious enough to make his answers tantalizing and, if nothing else, his friendliness was genuine. Andrea, in her loneliness, found herself attracted to him and his group. It helped fill some portion of the void. As a ''missionary'' from the Institute to the Boston Catholic Diocese, she found herself more appreciated by the latter than the former. Her qualities of frankness and evenhandedness won her friends if not disciples. In truth, she soon ceased to want disciples. The Institute did nothing for her. Often, on her way to work in the morning or going home from work in the evening, she would stop at the small Catholic Church across the street from the hospital where she worked and sit down in a calm, cool place near the front just beside the votive candles. It was quiet there and safe; though she had long since repudiated orthodox Catholicism, she found this church a place of real comfort in her increasingly chaotic world.

It was, of course, not enough. She had made a big mistake in choosing Boston—there was nothing here she knew or liked.

She spent Christmas Eve wandering Boston Common, crying and raging silently at the family who had cast her out. But it wasn't just the loneliness. There was something else wrong, something that inevitably made a bigger difference. She was unraveling, splitting into contentious fragments of consciousness. ''Separating,'' she called it. ''Going 'in between'.''

During these times, she saw glimpses of things she didn't want to see: dimly perceived images from another person's life on an old black and white TV. There were figures, familiar but tenuous. It wasn't logical or believable, and yet she couldn't shut them out. Nor could she exclude the voices. They haunted her. There were many of them and always fighting, divided roughly into two camps: some raised in support, others in opposition and anger. They filled her room with noise, and yet part of her knew there was no one physically with her.

Sometimes she would recognize the voices. They were familiar and, though vexing, she accepted them. After all, she wondered, didn't everyone have voices inside them? To be human was to share consciousness with semi-autonomous spirits. The truth had begun to dawn on her in college and gained credence as she lived more away from home and began to see that not every family was like hers. No, she learned, other people might have consciences, hungers, and sexual drives, as she did, but most did not house in their heads a congress of voices.

Such a realization brought panic, which in turn inflamed her need to forget, to burrow into that dark, cool place where memory never went.

But awaking from that place was never happy. Several times she emerged from this Lethean world to find her clothes torn, her body bruised as if by some struggle. But how and where? Considering the mystery brought panic and started the cycle of amnesia anew. Where had she been? What had she done? She didn't know . . . she didn't want to know.

By springtime part of her was still working effectively at her full-time job. But as if governed by a separate rudder, the other part of her life glided toward the brink. Away from the office, she was beginning to contemplate suicide.

It would be so easy. It would solve so many problems. She was submerged in feelings of confusion, fear, self-loathing. She wasn't any good. She was irreparably crazy, just as her brothers said; she was her father's legacy. They'd been right to throw her out; she'd always be a problem to anyone who helped her. She had always been overweight, but now she began to binge, stuffing chocolates into her mouth as fast as she could, sneaking and gorging, spending every penny she had on candy. Soon her body became distended and swollen. She waddled, fat quivering as she moved. For the first time in her life she had to face the fact that she was very obese: over 250 pounds on a frame made for 125. Her face was attractive, her skin was lustrous, but her body was grotesque. Her ungovernable and irrational hunger was devouring her. She tried to stop but could not.

Physical grossness only increased her self-hatred. It was just as the convent psychologist had said: how could anyone care about someone so fat?

Detesting the crying, the confusion, the isolation, most of all the panic, she finally determined to end the pain. Working at the hospital made it easier to expedite her plan. Over the next two weeks she was able to secure a lethal dose of Seconal. Then she waited. She was able to calculate a time of the week when the house would be empty and everyone away, long enough for the drug to take effect. She didn't want to be saved in midcourse. It wasn't a cry for sympathy. She wanted to end her life and went about her preparations in a calm and methodical manner. Strangely, she found the ritual of arranging her affairs and putting everything in order soothing. On a Friday night she wrote a farewell letter to her mother and placed it next to her bed. It was ten o'clock. Everyone was either asleep or out. She took the pills and lay down. No one would bother her: the housemates were used to her habit of sleeping late on Saturday mornings. No one would suspect anything until it was much too late.

She'd put clean sheets on the bed that afternoon. Clean sheets had always made her feel more comfortable and better rested. As she lay down, she felt a sense of total peace. She closed her eyes for the final time. She felt better at that moment than she had in many years. The worries and confusion evaporated and she drifted away joyfully. Her tormented soul was at last peaceful.

A warm, yellow light surrounded, buoyed her, completing her serenity. She was floating out to sea . . . losing sight of shore, waving farewell to pain and self-hatred.

Then the light changed. It dwelt on darker themes, it adopted a more somber hue. Unexpectedly, she felt discontentment. Here the tide was taking her out and she was feeling doubts. The dim light intensified, bringing with it a chorus of dissenting voices. Later she would remember it as bloody fighting: an escalated version of Biaggi family dinners. Screaming, yelling, fists pounding on tables, and all the time Andrea trying to avoid or ignore the anger. She quailed before this attack on her plan. What would they have her do? She was too weak to confront life, she was too much of a coward. What possible good would it serve to keep her alive? She was a worthless, wicked madwoman.

She sensed the anger on the tide, heard the confusion of voices raised against her. Above them all a single voice—commanding, definitive—thundered out an accusation: it was a mortal sin to commit suicide. The offender would go to hell most assuredly. No questions asked.

Hell for Andrea was a very real place. More than many Catholics, she felt she had a good idea of what it was, what violence and pain awaited the unrepentant. With dismay she backed away from the grave, from the certainty of damnation. She didn't want to hear it; she didn't want to feel anything ever again.

"Please, don't let me feel," she pleaded under her breath. "Just let me die."

But in her confusion she did something she hadn't done since childhood: she prayed for guidance. Suddenly the gabble of voices diminished, and through the static Andrea heard a single voice, quelling the arguments inside her, bringing back the peace. It was a familiar voice; she hadn't heard it for years, not since her schoolgirl days. Yet she knew instantly it was the Virgin Mary.

"Why are you doing this thing, my child?" the Virgin asked.

"I don't want to live anymore," Andrea pleaded. "Please, Mother, do I have to?"

"You must live. You are wrong in dying."

"But I have nothing to live for."

"Of course you have, my child. You have much to do yet in your life before you are ready for death. You are worth a great deal and must fight on. I will not let you die, Andrea. I will not."

Andrea remained stubborn. She couldn't stand the limbo of her private reality. Better death than a place for lost souls. But the voice was insistent. The world was only a limbo if she made it so. Andrea was capable of much more, said Mother Mary. She must fight for her sanity.

For hours, or so it seemed, she vacillated between life and death while Mother Mary counseled her. Andrea wept as Mary spoke. In desperate solitude she fought through the night, until finally, beside herself, she struggled to her feet and told one of her housemates what she had done.

She was rushed to the emergency room where they administered ipecac. Nothing happened. They examined her but nothing appeared to be wrong. At last the attending nurse angrily announced to Andrea's friend there was nothing wrong with her. She had obviously made the whole thing up. No one who had taken as many pills as she said she had would still be alive.

Had it all been a gigantic, grotesque hallucination? Had

she imagined the whole thing? Was it some pathetic play for sympathy? If so, it hadn't worked. Her one close acquaintance in the house began to avoid her, and the others became still more distant. But it didn't bother her anymore: she'd already decided to leave the Institute. Her friend, Father Henry, had counseled the change and suggested an alternative.

"Get out. You don't belong with them. They don't understand anything about you or your problems." He looked at her. "Imagine a good Catholic girl like you mixing with a bunch of holy rollers like them. I just happen to know about a little apartment in town for a decent rent . . ."

"I don't belong with anyone. I don't believe anymore. It just doesn't make sense to me. Not Catholicism, not life, not anything."

"So? There are lots of things about The Church I'd gladly change, too, lots of things nobody in his right mind could believe. That's part of the fun: trying to make changes from within the system. Give it a try. Money-back guarantee if not completely satisfied. May return purchase within sixty days for a complete refund. Yes?"

"Yes."

The next day she announced her intention to leave the collective and was summarily anathematized. Her last few days in the place were spent in utter solitude. No one would talk to her, no one would look at her. She'd become a nonperson.

Father Henry proved as good as his word, helping her find a nice apartment nearer to her job in Boston. She shared the place with several other people—all friends of Father Henry and members of his noncomformist group—but even this new sense of belonging couldn't cut through her isolation. She took to prowling the Boston Common at odd hours, particularly after midnight, looking for . . . something . . . she wasn't sure what. Most of this time was lost, and she came away from these absences with feelings of self-loathing and terror. Where had she been? What was going on?

The arid armistice that followed her mysterious suicide attempt brought little comfort. The membrane holding back the hordes, pictures, and voices was growing thinner, becoming more brittle. Occasionally there was leakage. Compulsively she attended to it, patching where she could, sweeping up the debris where she couldn't, hiding most of the time in any case.

Soon after moving, she began to shatter again. Whole days were spent crouching in a corner of her small bedroom, rocking back and forth, entangled in endless nightmares, battling imaginary enemies. The hallucinations increased and the terror they caused drove her into deeper levels of fear; in such a state she was immobilized by her insanity, incapable of helping herself. Sleep was unattainable, unthinkable. Eyes wide, unseeing, shivering and pale, she fought desperately for some shred of reality, but whole days would pass without the least sign of it.

The voices and the visions grew more insistent; they taunted and screamed, forcing her down into ever-darker regions of her own consciousness. Perception was a many-storied hell with dark labyrinths to trap and disorient.

Her certainty grew that she was exactly like her father, dangerous, destined to burden the lives of anyone who tried to help her. Wouldn't it be better, she thought again, just to end it, saving herself and the world all that anguish? For it *was* anguish. While the mind raved, a portion of her could still understand what was happening. That was the worst part: *knowing* she was utterly crazy and yet not being able to do a single thing about it. It was a strange kind of paralysis, in many ways just the reverse of quadriplegia. The body and the spirit were willing but the mind was uncontrolled.

She took to climbing up to the roof of her building and looking over the edge. But something would always stop her from jumping. Something inside her refused to give up. The voices railed—at least half wanted to die, craved for an end to the fighting. But some calmer voices always prevailed. This brought on its own frustration. She felt trapped, unable to live yet unwilling to die. Like the

Flying Dutchman she moved in a mid-world where neither real life nor real death were permitted.

She sought and gained some respite from the terror and the despair by hurting herself. In some way the self-injury relieved her anxiety, helped to expiate her suffering. It was sacrificial, as it always had been. But now the hurting took on a more virulent form. No longer content to burn her wrists and hands, she now began pouring caustic oven cleaner into her vagina, fascinated by the sight of it, intrigued by the lack of pain that should have been associated with the act, afterward oblivious to the episode. She was a frequent visitor to the emergency room and seemed perpetually to be bandaged or sutured or anointed with some foul-smelling antiseptic cream. But the appalling sight of these injuries didn't seem to have any power to deter her actions. No matter how ugly or vicious the attack, it didn't placate her festering madness for very long. How could any injury serve to punish her for the mortal sins of waywardness, ugliness, and uselessness that an inner voice told her she possessed in unnatural quantities? She was wicked. She had to be punished.

And there were other, deeper sins she had committed and for which she sought redemption. But for these acts of wickedness there seemed no comfort in petty acts of inward-directed retribution. The voices continued to scream for an end to such folly, for a truer, more sincere dedication to complete annihilation. Only that way lay true redemption—in a perfect act of death. Slowly she was giving in to these voices.

6

The S.S. Bedlam

"**S**TRAP her down."

The voice sheared through the darkness that surrounded and buffered her. She was a prehistoric fish swimming toward the surface after a millenium at the bottom; she was a cave dweller emerging into the open world after a lifetime in darkness.

There was the sound of metal buckles clicking, tugging at her hands and legs. Then the groan of leather as her body weaved back and forth. There were people around her—people in white uniforms. She squirmed and moaned, her head still full of amber syrup, her vision muddled.

It hurt. Whatever it was, it hurt. A disembodied cry—had it come from her?—brought the stooping nurse upright, and she pointed to Andrea's hands. Andrea moaned again.

"Loosen the restraints," the nurse said. "I think they're a little too tight."

Thank you, nurse, Andrea thought. Compassionate woman. A good, compassionate woman.

"I don't want the supervisor yelling at us for putting more marks on her than she's already got. God, what a mess!"

She felt a hard prick. A needle and an ensuing coldness creeping through her body. The thorazine stunned her. Her body melted away, leaving only the head in confusion, floating in the air. The S.S. *Bedlam*, a ship of madmen.

In single file, the nurse and the orderlies left the room

after a final check of the locks on her restraints. Andrea was alone.

The stench of urine and excrement overpowered her. She began to cough and gag. The world decayed around her: all was putrefaction and death. Her body gave a sudden shudder—head to toe, toe to head—and abruptly the smell was over, shut out, exiled to another part of the universe. Calm descended, reigned.

There was only a single light: a small pane of glass in a steel door. Through that pane, eyes intruded occasionally, examining her.

Except for the leather restraints on hands and feet, she was naked. They'd stripped her before putting her in here. There was no way she could cover herself. She had to focus on something else.

She chose the walls. Originally they'd been painted green, but that had been years ago. Now they were crusted with dirt, feces, urine, blood. Graffiti was scrawled on them too—random, crazy words. The drugs and exhaustion blurred her vision, but there was still one word she could read there, larger than the rest: MAMA.

She must have moaned aloud, for abruptly there was the sound of the door opening and a white-robed figure came in. Another needle pricked her skin. Another shot of thorazine.

What was this place, she asked herself? Where was she? How had she gotten here? The answers didn't come clear quickly. It took hours of wandering in a drug-induced fog before the truth occurred to her. She was in an observation room on a psychiatric ward of a Boston hospital. She'd obviously checked herself in. Either that, or someone had found her wandering and called for help. That wasn't important now. What was important was living through the next few hours, the next few days. Every hour they came for her with needles and blood pressure cuffs. They took away her body and left her mind floating in the room. Even in her stupor she knew what was going on. It was a favorite method used by most psychiatric wards—using superhigh dosages of tranqulizers to quiet the patient and subdue the craziness. The patients called it "snowing" and denied it was anything more than a professional punishment for misbehaving. How could they not misbehave when they lacked control?

The thorazine and restraints could numb her body, but it left her mind intact and spinning out of control. The restraints themselves were enough to whip her into a frenzy. She was imprisoned in this place as long as her captors cared to keep her there.

Her mind wandered, embracing elements of the past, present and future without distinction. She began to pray to a deity she didn't believe in any longer, praying for Him to save her. She felt she was dying. Her pulse sped up wildly. Her body bled out its spirit, shrank, became smaller.

Sometime during the night, she learned later, her blood pressure fell perilously low, and the nurse on duty had to discontinue the thorazine injections.

After twenty-four hours of this "observation" in the Treatment Room, Andrea was transferred to a bed where she was once again bound hand and foot, this time in leather shackles they called "four-point restraints." There she lay, now assigned a bed among many other beds in a small dayroom. What with the overflow of patients, it had just been turned into a coed dormitory with beds jammed together. It was something out of a war movie: the wounded soldiers stacked like cords of wood in halls and closets while the overtaxed, understaffed workers labored amid the human suffering.

A man to her left tried to climb on top of her, and she screamed. The man skittered off, wide-eyed and filthy, back to his own bed where he crouched, waiting, watching her patiently. She shivered, trying to pull herself together. But the restraints and the drugs only increased her confusion. The only medical attention she had had in those three weeks came from people with needles, pumping her full of thorazine, mellaril, and valium. At least before she'd landed here there had been some coordination between body and mind; but now the body was dead, paralyzed by drugs. The mind raced on, unchecked, unmoored, driven from nightmare to nightmare. The doctors didn't understand. The hospital was so overburdened—they had no time. But even if they had known, could they have helped? Never had Andrea felt so profoundly alone. Of all the hospitals she'd been in, Andrea could never remember anything as bad as this. The conditions were deplorable—even she could recognize that. It was supposed to be one of the main psychiatric teaching hospitals for the medical school, a place preeminent in research and advanced in psychiatric treatment. So where was the miraculous intervention? Where were the advances? Their method for treating Andrea consisted of giving her another needle every time she groaned. So she languished, getting no better; indeed, if she could judge by her confusion, she was getting a good deal worse.

This is how Father Henry found her after four weeks of "therapy." He was so appalled by the conditions that he instantly had her remanded to his custody. He left with her that day, stopping just long enough at her old apartment to pick up what few possesions she had. From there he drove out to Waltham.

She didn't know where he was going, and she didn't care. After insanity and incarceration, her senses were no more acute than a lump of lead. She didn't even notice when the car pulled off the main road and started up the driveway of a large house.

"Everything's going to be all right now, Andrea," Father Henry kept assuring her. "We're going to see that you get better."

The big, warm woman who opened the front door gave her a hug and a kiss on the cheek. Andrea, in her stupor, could not understand the gesture or even where she was.

Tidiness was not one of Joan's strong points. With fifty pet animals—including twenty cats—and five active, often unruly children dashing around, there was little time or reason for cleaning. She had been Father Henry's special friend for many years, and after divorcing her husband she and her children had become his special charge. As his newest charge, Andrea was placed under Joan's care. She was given a room of her own, a bed of her own, and privacy. For a while anyway, the change was salutary. But all the attention and kindness of Joan's family could not mitigate the fact that Andrea was still ill. The turmoil continued, the episodes of hurting herself did not greatly diminish and often grew much worse.

She returned to her job at the hospital, but after—and even during—her working hours she would lose time and find herself walking the Boston Common or crouched in a corner of her room. She was constantly disoriented, continually blacking out, breaking into pieces.

Then there was suddenly more to repent, more than ever before. In a dim, conscience-stricken way she remembered. A new curse had overtaken her, a new and more monstrous aberration. It had happened just before her commitment. It had involved a cat.

She had always liked animals, had thought of herself as a nature-lover and a child of flowers and sunshine. There was a part of her that danced through meadows, talked to unicorns, laughed at the wind, at perfect peace with all of the world. It was her happy side. But one day a cat had wandered into her life, yowling and pleading for a bite to eat. She had found it outside her building and had snuck it upstairs. She had fed it milk and watched it purr. She had stroked it, feeling the soft fur under her fingers. What had happened? It was something about the cat. Suddenly it was more than a cat, it was a mortal enemy. Its small body was endowed with all the anger in the universe.

She grabbed the first thing at hand, one of her father's old shirts, and snuck up behind the animal. With a sudden motion she pulled a sleeve of the shirt tight around the cat's neck and began to twist. Her pulse raced. It was a punishment and a purgation. The harder she squeezed, the better she felt.

How long the struggle lasted she could not remember. The cat had been strong and desperate. After some time, the animal hung limp from the noose. She had seen it all happening, but it was far away, separated from reality. Someone else had carried out the cat's execution and had left her to handle the burial. The sight of the corpse repulsed her. She sought desperately for some clue to the act. The anger was gone, only the guilt remained. Why had she done this?

In and out she went. In and out, diving into unconsciousness only to be yanked back by a reality she couldn't cope with. For a long time she simply stared at the dead cat and did nothing. Then, at last, she looked for a container. She ransacked the house until finally she discovered a shoebox in the closet. It served as a coffin; at least it hid the fact she had murdered the cat. She stuffed the corpse into the box and then put the box into the back of her car. She'd get rid of it somehow, maybe throw the thing into the river, box and all.

But it wasn't that easy. Like the telltale heart in Poe's short story, the memory of the cat lingered. Driving the car became a horror to her. As the smell of decay became more offensive she panicked. Her mind reeled when she recalled what she'd done. She could forget while the evidence was out of sight. She could hide in her private closet, but the smell and the car reminded her, and she would experience the episode all over again, as if for the first time.

She did not last long in Joan's house. There were too many things pulling at her, too many voices yelling out their execration and vengeance. The house was too confused for her, filled with commotion at a time in her life when she most desired tranquility.

She moved into a one-bedroom apartment and maintained some semblance of stability, at least for a while. But soon the terrible panics could not be kept down any longer. She was wandering again, coming out of her spells miles away from where she'd been only a moment before. She was losing all track of time. Most of her daily activities at the office were being handled by some bright, efficient part of her she christened Super Andrea, who didn't seem affected by the constant ebbings and flowings of her private life. When it came to doing work or talking to people, this other part of her took over. How she did it remained a mystery to her, but somehow it was done and she wasn't willing to investigate the reason for it too closely.

But as the days went on, Andrea often didn't go to work at all. She was habitually tardy, and hard working though she was, she could not cover up for the recent time in the mental hospital or all those other, odder times when she had mysteriously been somewhere else when she was supposed to be at work. It cost her the job. After less than a year working at the University Hospital, she was let go. Father Henry was there, once again, to help.

Andrea had worked diligently and with excellent results for the Archdiocese, and now Father Henry was in a position to offer her a job as a Religious Education Director. Andrea jumped at the chance: it meant more prestige, more money, and more challenge. It would take her mind off all the craziness and restore her to health, or so she hoped. And, in fact, for a while she *did* flourish. Life was uneven. The bad times were so bad, but the good times would almost make up for them. Not that the episodes of panic and self-injury ceased completely, but she had a way of keeping the lid on them now. She had backstops. Father Henry was successful at keeping her spirits up and convincing her there was still hope; and when she moved back out to Waltham to live again with Joan, that good woman provided some essential mothering which helped also to stabilize her.

Perhaps more important than any other factor, however, was her introduction to a private psychologist, Jack Holt. A few months before she could never have afforded such an extravagance, but with medical insurance and further financial assistance afforded by her new job, Andrea was able to pay for the once weekly sessions. Holt was a Gestalt psychologist. He was neither as confrontational as some of the trendier practitioners (for example, the one who humiliated her in the convent) nor as hidebound and conservative as the traditional psychoanalysts. He sought instead to provoke recollections through informal theatrics, restaging and thereby reliving the present and the past as realistically as possible.

The therapy began harmlessly enough. After a few weeks during which she and Dr. Holt warmed to each other, Andrea began to feel a sense of real hope that she might be curable. Perhaps together they could uncover the origins of her disease and cure it. What would it be like to live a normal life? Could any word sound as sweet as the word "sanity?"

Soon she grew to depend on him, to believe what he was doing and saying. And the sessions gave her a vehicle to investigate some of the pent-up secrets of her inner life. But not too fast: she was still terribly inhibited, seeking always to bind over the pain, to bottle up the panic so that no one, not even Holt, could see it. If only this procedure could be done in a mannerly and discreet way, then maybe she wouldn't be so frightened. She'd started in the traditional way, describing what little she could remember of her recent life. There were large spaces she couldn't really account for, and trying to fill in the blanks always panicked her. She told him about her experiences in the convent, her self-inflicted wounds, her flight from Illinois. She even dared the bold step of describing to Holt one of her more elusive nightmares, a recurrent vision of herself on a white table, getting a gynecological examination from a doctor while her father held her legs open. It was an unsettling dream, subject to several interpretations. Holt apparently didn't know what to make of it either.

Then there was the information, gleaned ever so slowly, about her parents. She continued to represent her parents to Holt as troubled but kind. She was particularly warm about her father. Sure, he'd had his problems. He'd had something wrong with his brain, but that had been an organic thing. For the most part, Joseph Biaggi had been kind and wonderful and fond of everyone. She'd idolized him. That much she could clearly remember.

"Could you ever remember him being unkind to you?" Holt had asked.

Andrea had thought about that for awhile. "No more than

the others. It was his temper, you know. Everyone accepted it. Maybe once in awhile it got out of control . . ."

"Is that why they sent him away to the State Mental Hospital?"

"It got too much for Mom. She couldn't handle him any longer. You know how it is."

"What was he like when he got back?"

"About the same. A little worse. But he always treated me really well. You know, buying me candy, playing with me. The kids in the neighborhood really liked him. He was good to everyone."

"How do you feel about your mother?"

"She's all right. A little distant maybe, but she writes letters every week. I never really got as close to her as I did to my Dad. I never understood exactly why." Holt noticed that Andrea's eyes tended to focus and unfocus rapidly while she talked. Sometimes there were long pauses in her conversations. Occasionally he even had to prod her to finish her thought. Naturally he attributed this to shyness. Andrea was too inhibited. He had to find a way of relaxing her. Maybe changing the surroundings a little would help. For several of his patients, having them lie on a mattress had helped calm them, helped them reach back. But when he suggested the idea to Andrea, he was met with immediate resistance:

"Why? What will it prove?"

"I just thought it would make you feel better. Maybe take away a little of that tension you've been feeling."

He could see she was fighting with herself, looking out into some middle distance with a combination of starkness and blankness.

At last she acquiesced. His office was in the basement of his house, warmly furnished, comfortable, secure. In such an environment how could anything go wrong? Despite warning voices, the part of her that was calm overcame the part that was panic. She lay down on the mattress and tried to relax. As if by some reflex, her eyes closed and she began to drift.

Through a thick fog she heard Holt say, "Now I want

you to remember back. I want you to remember that nightmare you've been telling me about—the one where you're on a gynecologist's examining table.''

She was drifting, leaving Holt's office, floating away from his voice, slowly sinking. "Where am I?" she heard herself ask. "It's my parents' bedroom. What am I doing here?''

She started to gyrate on the mattress.

"Where . . . where are my clothes? I can't find my clothes. There's a terrible weight on me. I can't lift my arms or legs! Something's on top of me. Something I can't . . .''

She began to hyperventilate, her legs and arms spread wide.

"My God! It's my father! He's pushing down on me. He's suffocating me. He's . . .''

"Yes?''

"There's such a pain . . . such a hurting, pressure . . .''

"Where, Andrea?''

"Down . . . down there. It's hurting me. Please. Please don't let him hurt me. I mustn't scream. He'll hurt me even more . . . He'll . . .'' More crying and trembling. Then, "What's that? A noise. Someone at the front door. Someone coming this way to save me. The footsteps. My God, it's my mother! MOM! MOM! HELP ME! PLEASE!'' She convulsed in tears, curled into a ball on the mattress, screaming at the horror. "No!'' she sobbed. "No!''

"It's all over, Andrea,'' Holt soothed. "You're going to be okay now.''

"No. No. No.''

"Now you know and now we can really begin to work.''

"No.''

For the next half hour Andrea said nothing else but "no.'' Her eyes were closed. Occasionally she would blink, her mouth agape, but Holt knew she wasn't there. And he couldn't escape a sense of discomfort. He was used to treating neurotics, but he had not dealt with people whose problems threatened their own or other's physical existence, and he sensed in Andrea a major problem.

There was no communication. She flitted between several different levels of excitement and consciousness; in Holt's view, Andrea had slipped over into psychosis—flipping around on the floor, babbling, crying, curling up in a ball.

For Andrea the events of that day broke everything wide open. The membrane that had, for years, served to insulate her from her private chaos was suddenly and dramatically rent, and through the opening poured nightmares populated with members of her family. The tide descended upon her, overtaking and drowning her. There was no escape, only the tried-and-true expedient: to curl up like a child and retreat inside her mind.

Somehow she managed to function at the office. But her job was demanding and there were great sections of her that were missing, crouched and trembling in that small psychic space. Most of her, in fact, was not there. The nightmares persisted and grew more frightening; as they increased, the amount of time Andrea herself was conscious decreased. Her supervisor at work, a nun, noticed the change but at first did nothing about it. Andrea was such an extraordinary worker that even a portion of her was better than the whole of most other workers. But her work with Jack Holt ground slowly to a halt. She was never there when he was in the room. To Holt it was like trying to communicate with an autistic child. At the first mention of her mother or father, at even the suggestion of her past, she would flee back to a world where her eyes blinked, her mouth opened and closed spasmodically, her body trembled and flipped about uncontrollably.

She was a rabbit, frightened by the slightest event, fleeing constantly back to her warren, scurrying for shelter at the merest breath of wind. Words came from her, but only in fractured bits—disjointed, indecipherable snatches of conversation:

"It's like . . . lots of fighting . . . angry . . . wanting to kill, wanting to die . . . dying inside. Screaming, yes. Lots. Just like him . . . yes, just wildness . . ."

Holt couldn't reach her, couldn't get enough of a purchase to allow himself access to her shattered world. She couldn't hear him, and she wouldn't listen.

"Andrea? Andrea? What do you mean? Can you talk to me, please?."

The frustration increased on both sides. At last after a month of deadlock, Holt admitted defeat. One-on-one wasn't working out at all. Maybe another strategy would work better. He decided to start her in on his therapy group, hoping other people would help draw her out. Andrea's reaction to his decision was predictable: she felt that he was deserting her, trying to disentangle himself from a tough situation. And in a sense, he was. He felt terribly uncomfortable with such a difficult case and was trying to stabilize her before she did something really dangerous. She'd mentioned suicide several times, and then there were the hints of other things, other killings, other fury. The few fragments of sense he'd dredged from her random, patchy monologues suggested a personality capable of real violence, and whether that violence was merely self-directed or not, he couldn't take any chances.

She tried the group sessions for a while, but they didn't seem to do much good. Actuated by her morbid sense of abandonment, she sought to command Holt's attention, and the frequent, brooding silences she fell into intimidated the rest of the patients. It was an uncomfortable situation for both Holt and the group as a whole. The sessions degenerated. At last Dr. Holt couldn't tolerate it any longer.

"Andrea, what are you doing? I can't talk to you, and yet you're demanding so much from me. What do you expect me to do? You're like a leech draining the life out of me. Don't you see what you're doing to me and this group?" The comment was made less in anger than frustration, an attempt on Holt's part to prod Andrea out of her stupor. But it was an ill-timed, ill-conceived outburst. Andrea did not understand—how could she in her state of mind?

She fell into a panicked silence, her eyes all but turned inward.

"I'd be real hurt if someone said that to me," one of the group members said. "It'd really bum me out to hear you say that."

Holt did not apologize.

Andrea left that session in silence, most of her lost in private darkness. She never went back. Nor did Holt make an attempt to recall her. To Andrea it constituted rejection, pure and simple; to Dr. Holt it was an untenable situation—trying to cure a patient he deemed far too sick, and far too frightening, for his kind of therapy. After a few desultory attempts to collect past-due money for Andrea's sessions, he gave up, perhaps feeling guilty about his inability to help her. For Andrea the question wasn't what had set Holt off, but rather what had she done wrong, why was she so bad? Given the assumption she now shared with her brothers—that she was irreparably crazy—she quickly deduced the failure of her therapy had more to do with her than with him. Blame-taking came easily to her. She was so used to thinking of herself as handicapped, unloveable.

Her life went totally to pieces after that. Any semblance of internal government had been sabotaged, and now she could no longer protect herself from the horror of visions. Most of them, of course, she couldn't remember. Her life became a continuous nightmare of panic and amnesia. There was always fighting now, and unhappiness. A consensus of the voices seemed to urge her abdication. She was no good, she was a whore and a lunatic, a subhuman creature undeserving of love.

Soon after the fiasco with Dr. Holt, Andrea tried to commit suicide again. This time she almost succeeded. She had slit her wrists, swallowed a large quantity of Valium and Seconal, and, just for good measure, some oven cleaner. However, Joan had found her in time and had rushed her to the hospital where she recovered despite herself. She could recall nothing of the incident afterward.

The craziness didn't relent. Whole weeks disappeared without trace. She rarely went to work. The outside world had become unbearably painful to her, bringing with it all those intimations of madness, and frightening disorientation.

She killed several more cats, and inflicted second-and third-degree burns on her arms and vagina. She became a frequent visitor to emergency rooms throughout the Boston area. She was prowling the Boston Commons again, finding herself at the end of the night with torn and soiled clothes, unable to remember where or what she had done. Occasionally while driving, she'd begin to scream and wail uncontrollably, and several times barely avoided crashing her car.

About that time Dalia Biaggi appeared with her new husband. Dalia was the second oldest of the sisters and the most beautiful. There had never been much rapport or sharing between Andrea and Dalia. They'd always fought, even come to blows on occasion. But now, for some reason, here was Dalia at Andrea's front door, asking for a favor. Living near the rest of the Biaggi family, explained Dalia, had become intolerable, and Andrea's new beachhead in Boston now offered the only sanctuary for Dalia and her husband.

Andrea obliged by lining up Dalia and her husband with a caretaker position at Father Henry's seminary.

From the outset things had not gone well. For one thing, Dalia's new husband was a long-haired, dull-witted young man who spent all of his waking time trying to reach various levels of drugged stupor. As a human being he was a pathetic spectacle, and as a mate for Dalia he was a disaster. But it wasn't just him; the main problem lay with Dalia herself. Andrea tried not to notice, but it was too obvious to ignore. Beautiful though she was with her long, black hair and her svelte figure, Dalia Biaggi was terribly troubled. Soon after her arrival, she started acting strangely. She took to walking at night in her negligee around the seminary ground, sneaking into the church at two o'clock in the morning and playing the organ, losing her temper at the slightest provocation, becoming violent and abusive to anyone who got in her way. In a talk with Father Henry she talked about her father ramblingly, alternately expressing love and hatred for him. The situation reached a critical point soon after their arrival when one night she tore apart a seminary classroom and wrote gibberish on the blackboard. Andrea was called in to help. She found a screaming, knife-wielding maniac backed into a corner by a group of Catholic fathers and several policemen. It took several priests and a whole team of emergency medical aides to restrain her. By then Dalia was moaning over and over again:

"They're after me! The Mafia—you're the Mafia! After me! You can't kill me! I won't let you hurt me . . ."

As they were taking her away, Dalia looked up at Andrea out of wild eyes and in a low voice said, "You understand, don't you? You know what it means. You're the only one who *really* knows."

Andrea stared after her. What had she meant? What did she understand? What was this great secret that had driven her sister crazy?

Right then Andrea began to split again. If she'd been well enough to maintain any sort of concentration, she might have concluded that Dalia had also inherited the family curse, that Dalia was even sicker than she.

In the weeks that followed Andrea tried to get some help for her sister, but finally Dalia and her husband opted for a return to Illinois. Dalia's visit could only complicate matters. And it did.

The Archdiocese and Andrea's supervisor had been keeping track of her and her problems. She'd lost so much time at work, she was almost never in the office—and even when she was, more often than not she was preoccupied and staring. At last and with the utmost reluctance, the Monsignor called her to his office.

"We'd like to keep you on here, Andrea, but you know the way it is. We need someone around all the time and you . . . well. It's not that you haven't been a good worker when you were here, but the stress of the job has obviously gotten to you. You're a very high-strung person with a lot of brains, but maybe you'd be happier in some kind of secretarial position where there would be less stress on you."

To the original rejection by her family had been added

the rejection by psychologists, employers, and church. She was no good; she was destined to alienate everyone who came into contact with her.

Soon afterward she moved out of Joan's house, despite that special woman's protests, and found a very small apartment in Boston. She wanted to be alone, no matter what came of it. Peace and quiet was what she needed, peace and quiet.

Without a job Andrea could no longer afford private therapy, even if she had found a psychologist who was willing to treat her. Yet she couldn't afford to just go about her life without some kind of assistance. She was in too much trouble for that.

She sought out the only resource left open to her—a public mental health facility, a new building made completely of concrete and steel where, it was said, brave new directions were being taken in psychiatric treatment. For Andrea it was only more of the same. The building itself seemed so anonymous and dispassionate that it scarcely surprised her when the staff turned out to be the same way. There was no Treatment Room, that was true; but there was most certainly an overworked staff and the usual phalanx of physicians with the same old diagnoses and old ideas, except when it came to drugs. Rather than the traditional range of mind-numbing pharmaceuticals, her new therapist prescribed a new drug, Prolixin. Its chief benefit to medical science, in Andrea's view, was the ease with which it could be administered. A one cc injection would last for two weeks at full potency. In Andrea's case, as in so many others, Prolixin had the effect of transforming her into a zombie. She had no energy for anything, least of all work. Her walk became a loose-jointed shamble; her face took on the slack-jawed, black-eyed gaze of the mentally retarded; her words were always slurred, and when she tried to think, everything was vague and confused. Inevitably no one, even the most saintly of employers, would hire her. One look at her was enough. She went on twenty-seven interviews for jobs over the next two months and was rejected every time. Her finances became less than dismal, and yet she couldn't bring herself to go on welfare; her mother had always warned her: *"Never go on welfare."* So she stayed away and starved.

At her weekly therapy session she pleaded with her attending physician to take her off Prolixin and told him what it was doing to her. He refused. She then attempted to avoid her biweekly injection, but her therapist had prepared for that eventuality, having supplied the administering nurse in advance with a pre-signed commitment form should Andrea refuse the injection. It was either take the Prolixin as an outpatient or have it administered forcibly as an inpatient. This blackmail only increased her psychic despair and made it even harder for her to recover.

At last, bowing to the financial necessity of her position, she was forced to compromise what little dignity she had left. Demeaned, desperate, hungry, her spirit broken, she sought out public assistance. Now twenty-four, Andrea Biaggi had become a ward of the State of Massachusetts.

7

Two Years of Madness

FROM September 1971 through November 1973, Andrea was hospitalized in Massachusetts six times, amounting to more than ten months, the last time for half a year. With regularity she would find her old therapist gone as hospital rotations changed, and she never felt any kind of confidence in the young, inexperienced psychiatrists assigned to her. Nor did she ever voluntarily sign herself in for care at the hospital; each time she was committed against her wishes. Not that she didn't need help. The occasions she chose to call "panic episodes" grew ever more frequent, and the periods between these episodes grew shorter. Cats and her own body became the two focuses for her destructiveness. She was driven to strangle cats as an alcoholic is driven to drink. She couldn't control herself. And, after these acts her despair always turned into a suicidal frenzy. The guilt was awful, and it fueled her burning and cutting. The doctors who treated her saw no alternative to hospitalization, and the last tenure of six months was maneuvered through a court commitment.

Andrea, of course, fought the commitment. It symbolized to her not only the loss of freedom but also the dire nature of her insanity. In a 15-minute hearing she lost her plea and was placed in the hospital. That night she set fire to her bed, apparently in a suicide attempt, and was saved only because an attendant smelled the smoke and was able to rescue her and the other patients on the ward before the fire spread. The fifth floor of the hospital was gutted.

She remembered none of this. She dimly remembered being angry after the trial, seething at what she saw as the injustice of the commitment. But had she really set that fire? Why would she do anything like that? People could have been hurt. She might be crazy, but she had never hurt anyone before except herself and a few mangy cats.

When faced with this newest proof of her insanity, she cracked up again. For more than a week she lay in a bed without moving, catatonic. She'd given up, resigned herself to madness, retreated to her inner space forever. Rarely now was she aware of the outside world. That was all behind her. Occasionally she fought her way to the surface long enough to look around, but having to face the reality of her predicament so appalled her that it sent her screaming back into that space again.

It would have been so very easy just to lie there and slowly die—a vegetable cared for by the state. But the world inside her head was still a living hell, and no one could live with what she saw there. She at least had to try to escape.

She learned of an educational opportunity offered for the benefit of special "handicapped" people and applied for it. She was accepted in the program and chose a course of study leading to a Master's Degree in Women's Studies with emphasis on community mental health. The combination of her college records and her resume were sufficient to convince the admissions committee, and she soon found herself attending daily classes at the Boston college, away from the hospital. It proved a turning point in her rehabilitation. The panic episodes decreased, and during the months that followed she was able to leave the hospital altogether, returning only once for a period of three days.

She prospered there. She formed friendships and came in contact with a number of fine teachers. She was luckiest in her choice of advisors, Betty John, a warm, understanding woman who helped her reestablish a measure of pride in herself. Instrumental also in this rebuilding process was Andrea's development of a program she had first suggested to her advisor as a means to help other people like herself. Ever since her first commitment to a mental institution, it had occurred to Andrea that a halfway-house system might be useful to help reintroduce former patients to the outside world. There just weren't any places for recovering mental patients to go after discharge, and some kind of support system could help immensely in keeping them out of the mental hospital again. It sounded like a good plan to Betty, who helped Andrea fill out all the necessary applications for federal funds and state assistance for the project. It took almost a year to get everything ready, including finding a suitable building for the project and a support staff to aid in counseling the residents. The House opened in 1974, and for more than a year Andrea served as volunteer coordinator and administrator for the project. It was an immediate success and became the only residential treatment program in Massachusetts for discharged mental patients. Despite a battery of caseworkers, all of whom had told her she was hopelessly deranged and non-rehabilitative, she was beginning to prove them wrong.

While at the House, she got to know the two young psychiatrists who had volunteered to help lead support groups and provide personal therapy for the residents. The male psychiatrist had learned of Andrea's condition firsthand and, after reviewing her record, suggested that maybe her problem wasn't schizophrenia at all.

"It sounds awful strange to me," he told her. "You're too good a worker when you're functioning, and those panic attacks—they don't jibe either with the classical patterns. At least there's a measure of doubt."

"So?"

"Well, I can't be sure, but it could be something neurological."

"You mean all these years I might have been walking around with a brain tumor or something?" Her interest was suddenly piqued.

"A possibility. Like I said, it's worth a shot."

"So what are you suggesting?"

"There's this group over at the University looking into

temporal lobe epilepsy. They say it mimics many of the symptoms of schizophrenia, and they've worked out a protocol for it. Up for it?''

"Are you kidding? That's like offering a miracle cure to a terminal cancer patient. Where do I sign up?''

The arrangements were made for her to meet with a team of physicians at the Medical School, and she subsequently under went a battery of tests. The tests were all seemingly positive for temporal lobe epilepsy. Andrea was overjoyed. Here at last was a chance to shed the stigma of incurable schizophrenia; here was a hope for ultimate recovery. She was immediately started on a series of anticonvulsive drugs the staff felt sure would ameliorate the symptoms of her disorder.

But as the months passed she was no better, no matter what drug was administered. She was still experiencing bouts of intense anxiety and panic mixed with periods of amnesia. After months of careful examination and treatment, one of the doctors finally pronounced his judgment: Andrea was "only one-quarter of a normal human," she heard him say; she would never be able to work or live effectively outside a sheltered environment; she would almost certainly end up on permanent disability, in and out of hospitals for the remainder of her life.

This she took for the final, dismal prognosis. Such an opinion—for that was exactly what it was—did nothing to aid her recovery. It catapulted her into a deep and sustained depression. Once again, and now from the foremost authorities in the field, she had been assured of the worst. She was incurable. As if to reaffirm this sentence, she was committed twice more to psychiatric wards—bringing to thirteen her number of hospitalizations in the last five years, during which time she'd been interviewed and treated by innumerable staff and doctors and subjected to a plethora of drugs. No fewer than five diagnoses had so far been rendered in her case: a character disorder, borderline personality, undifferentiated schizophrenia, anxiety neurosis, and temporal lobe epilepsy. Would it have been any wonder if she wanted to give up hope?

The real wonder was that she did not. Something inside her refused to believe she was incurable. Despite despair and depression she sought out the other psychiatrist who had befriended her at the House, a woman named Dr. Nancy Good.

Dr. Good offered to see Andrea in accordance with the patient's own wishes: first, they were to meet *more* than once a week; and second, there was to be no medication or hospitalization, no matter how out of control Andrea appeared. Dr. Good was caring and bright, and her sessions often lasted two hours if she felt Andrea needed it. With patience she started to work at the roots of her problems, picking up at that tumultuous point where Dr. Holt's Gestalt therapy had left off. Patience was needed, for at critical moments when a breakthrough looked imminent, something would suddenly happen to Andrea; she would freeze, become unfocused, start to babble and stutter, even change the timbre of her voice, and finally drop into some kind of a limbo state that Dr. Good didn't understand.

Even Andrea had to admit: after one year of therapy with Dr. Good, little real progress had been made; panic episodes were less frequent now, but they were still happening with alarming regularity. What had been gained, though, was a sense of friendship—a quality almost as precious to Andrea at this point as a final solution to her problem. Therapy with Dr. Good was nurturing, comforting, friendly. Even in the absence of real progress, Andrea did not feel capable of leaving the only person in the world who really seemed to care for her. And when Dr. Good left her job as a psychiatrist at the hospital for a similar job in Salt Lake City, Utah, Andrea couldn't turn down the offer from Dr. Good to keep on seeing her—if she was willing to move to Salt Lake City.

With no job, no prospects, and few friends, there was nothing to keep Andrea in Boston. She believed that it had been the worst decision of her life to move there in the first place, and after six years she was willing to make a change. What did she know about Salt Lake City? What had she known about Boston before her move? There were

Mormons in Utah and mountains and maybe a job for someone willing to work. And maybe Dr. Good could find something, eventually, that would free her from this terrible, debilitating curse. Despair could be a liberating thing, and, anyway, Andrea had nothing left to lose.

8

Salt Lake City

SALT Lake City was no worse than Boston. But no better, either. There were beautiful mountains and long, dry summers with cloudless blue skies. It was a clean city, too, with wide streets and an encompassing sense of safety. But it was perhaps the largest small town Andrea had ever seen. It was not a city alive with entertainment—despite its ballet company, opera company, live theater, symphony orchestra, and several professional sports teams. There never seemed to be a lot to do. Nothing was ever hectic. And there was the clannishness of the Mormons to contend with—their private vocabulary of terms like "ward house," "Mutual," "Primary," "testimony," "friendshipping"—as well as their righteousness, the dependence of their women, the unison of their opinions. And the winters. They could be so long and so very hard.

She had transferred her disability claim from Boston to Salt Lake and was unemployed, with few or no prospects for work, and living in a city even stranger and more distant from her home than Boston had been. She spent most of her time either waiting for her appointments with Dr. Good or going in and out of panic states. The move to Utah hadn't changed her behavior in any basic way. She was still hurting herself (they were becoming predominately sexual injuries), killing cats, and losing time. The same pattern kept recurring: the guilt and anger would build up to pressure-cooker levels and then explode into some act of self-mutilation, either of the vagina or the hand. She still frequently contemplated suicide, finding respite from such thoughts in the completion of these punitive actions against her own body. The oven cleaner and the knife she used were not felt at all. Even hours after the attacks, when she was brought to the emergency room, there would be no pain. The nurses and doctors would wonder how she managed to deny the pain, but in her wide-eyed, unseeing way she had somehow blocked it as effectively as if she had taken morphine or heroin.

The part of her life devoted to dealing with the outside world had become so infinitesimally small that she was always surprised when she had to confront it. The rest of her time was spent . . . nowhere. It was disorienting. All she knew for sure was that in those few moments each week when she was actually cognizant of the real world, she was terrified by it and its demands upon her.

Even when she met with Dr. Good there was trouble and despair. Often she would wander—Dr. Good could see it happening, though she didn't know how to stop it. The eyes and face would seem to fade away, and suddenly Andrea would mouth a confusing jumble of words. "There's a lot of fighting. They're not happy. Cheap, dirty, evil . . . I'm . . . I'm so evil. It's like . . . like wanting to die . . . wanting to hurt and punish . . ." Any attempt on Good's part to bring Andrea back proved futile. She wasn't there.

So when her psychiatrist friend called Andrea from Boston, urging her to come back for more tests, she was interested. She was ready to grasp at anything then. She managed to scrape together enough money to make the trip back for more tests to determine whether she'd be an acceptable subject. In Boston, several members of the medical staff tried to convince her that a temporal lobotomy would relieve all her symptoms, and she came within a hairsbreadth of consenting to the surgery. At the last moment, with the advice of Dr. Good, she demurred and returned to Salt Lake feeling dissatisfied and confused. It was the idea of someone operating on her brain in the hope of finding something wrong that she couldn't justify to herself—not yet.

After almost a year in Salt Lake, Andrea finally secured a full-time job as a clerk at a small store, and, owing to her immense energy and tireless dedication, she soon was promoted to store manager. She was good with people, and the job suited her. But not long after, the owner decided to close the shop—not because business was bad but because it bored him. Once again, Andrea was out of work. But there was still an indomitable spark in her. She wouldn't quit. She found a job working at a Referral Center in Ogden, 34 miles north of Salt Lake and, despite her terrible bouts of self-injury and cycles of forgetfulness, she somehow managed to impress everyone in the office. How this was accomplished was largely a mystery to her. Often she wasn't particularly aware of working. She was a doppelganger learning over the shoulder of someone else, half remembering conversations and interviews, aware of the ebb and flow of her attention.

More often than not, she wasn't really there at all, or rather, time continued to be discontinuous for her. On weekends when the facade could be lifted, there were huge blank spaces and personal injury; cat-killing; nocturnal walks that led to torn clothes and a vague memory of male trespass. She hadn't been there, yet she had; or else that part of her that she *thought* hadn't been there had been dreaming, and the nightmares had really happened; or perhaps, rethinking the problem, the whole thing was a hallucination and she hadn't done anything except go in and out of elaborate trances.

To the normal person there is little doubt about the nature and texture of reality. But for Andrea there was every reason to suspect reality as being counterfeit: how could she learn the truth from her blighted perspective?

Her mind, no less than anyone else's, needed a centerpoint from which to investigate the world around her on sure grounds, and this she didn't have. Without anchor or moorings she drifted, feeling habitually disoriented and confused.

Now, adding to her confusion, was a new and disturbing event. Dr. Good had been offered a better paying job in California. She had accepted and planned to move almost immediately. Once again she offered Andrea the opportunity to move with her, but the offer was less wholehearted this time. There had been very little progress. Andrea felt no better.

Neither physician nor patient fought the inevitable separation.

"We've gone as far as we can go," Andrea admitted to Dr. Good one day.

"Which wasn't very far to begin with," Good responded ruefully. "I'm sorry it didn't work out better."

"So am I. Sometimes I feel like nothing is ever going to change."

"Don't say that. There are other therapists in the world— even in Salt Lake. Some are excellent people. Maybe one of them can help. It's worth a try."

"Yes, but who?"

Good shrugged. "I wish I could tell you. But all my work has been in Ogden. I'm just not familiar with the people in Salt Lake City. I can't even give you a recommendation."

For a while, Andrea's job search kept her busy. The Referral Center had served as a useful first step for her, but after several months she had formed enough contacts and sufficient reputation to secure another job with a better salary. There was also the problem of her boss at the Center who had begun to form certain suspicions about her. She had seen Andrea in a few of her panic states and had afterward kept a gimlet eye on her. The woman was too close to discovering the truth, and Andrea had no intention of divulging it.

Her new position was with a nonprofit agency in Ogden as its personnel director. She proved surprisingly good in the role. She was a good public speaker, an accomplished public relations person, and an inexhaustible worker, putting in eighty hours a week and more without ever seeming to flag. No one could have guessed from the way she conducted herself at work that there was anything wrong with this pleasant, aggressive, hard-working woman, except perhaps for a persistent weight problem and occasional remoteness. But while at home, or driving in her car, or behind closed doors with no one else around, there were panics and craziness and the usual jumble of auditory and visual hallucinations that she could bottle up only with the utmost willpower. She tried to keep busy, living with a succession of roommates in an attempt to keep herself surrounded and preoccupied. But that never seemed to work well; the terror and the amnesia would always return, whatever she did. Even at committee meetings occasionally, when her participation wasn't necessary, she'd blank out. Who would suspect? Meetings were made for daydreaming, and who could tell the difference? The fact that at such times her eyes went dull and lightless, that her whole countenance seemed to slump, didn't attract more than momentary notice. Whenever her opinion was asked, there she was again, all bright and full of useful comments.

More to the point, her success in her duties was incontestable. No one had ever done the job better. Within a short time she had made herself virtually indispensable, and when the job as Executive Director for the agency opened up, she applied. There were more than sixty applicants for the job, and the board chairman, a rigidly conservative woman, was thoroughly opposed to the idea of a woman as head of the organization. But such a prejudice was overcome. Andrea was the best person for the job in the opinion of the board's majority, and she was given the directorship. No one yet suspected the nature of her disorder. As long as she could keep the condition under control, she would prosper in her job. It gave her hope.

With that expectation in mind, she went about the task of finding a new therapist. Recommendations from friends brought her interviews with two woman therapists. Since she had felt comfortable with Dr. Good, she reasoned that another woman therapist might be the ticket. She sandwiched these interviews between meetings at work and managed to keep the whole process very quiet. Unfortunately, neither therapist would take her. Both were sympathetic to her problem, but after a single interview they could see her case was much too complicated. However, they both gave her referrals, and she applied to several more therapists. They also declined, citing the severity of her symptoms and the unusual nature of her complaints. Daunted but resolute, she continued making the rounds of therapists in the Salt Lake area. There was nothing else to do. She knew that her panic states were still happening, that she was blanking out frequently, and that she was having a hard time controlling their onset, even in the office. No matter how much she might dislike the idea of seeking out a therapist, no matter how little respect she'd formed over the years for the profession as a whole, she still needed to search out one on the off chance something might be done to help her.

After several more rejections, she finally heard of a "feminist" therapist who worked at the counseling center and had an excellent reputation, according to several of her trusted friends. In fact, the therapist was quite positive on the phone when Andrea explained her circumstances and assured her she was perfectly capable of handling her case.

"No commitments? No hospitals?" Andrea asked.

"I promise. Nothing to harm you at all. Just you and me." The woman's voice sounded pleasant and self-assured.

"Okay then. What time?"

"How about tomorrow? Ten o'clock."

She was there.

It was a Saturday, and Andrea had already begun to slide down into her usual weekend despair. The voices and the nightmares were there, clamoring for attention, and it took her a while to get out of the car and find the right office. The therapist seemed nice enough and listened patiently as Andrea recited her story; the smile never left the therapist's lips. Andrea, feeling that here at last was someone willing to help, let it all spill out. There was much that was straightforward, but much else that was spoken haltingly between whole minutes of staring and silence.

"It was like . . . there were . . . cats. Killing cats. Having to kill the cats. You see, it helped . . . it . . ." She writhed and gyrated in her seat, eyes bulging. "I was cursed. My father and . . . well . . ."

After awhile the therapist excused herself saying she had to go to the ladies' room. Five minutes passed before she returned and the session continued. But ten minutes later, there was a knock at the door, and the therapist sprang to her feet and opened the door.

Two security guards stood there. "Is this the one?" asked one of the guards. "Yes," answered the therapist. "Take her up to the hospital and . . ."

"But you promised . . . " Andrea burst out.

"This is the best thing for you, Andrea. Trust me. You need to be in the hospital."

There was a scuffle then, and Andrea momentarily broke free, only to be caught in the parking lot. Outraged and crushed, Andrea still knew enough about hospitals and therapists—she'd become an expert in how *not* to get admitted. Within an hour she was free— over the strenuous objections of the irate therapist, who confronted Andrea.

"You know you should be here, don't you? I don't know how you managed to talk them out of admitting you but—"

"How dare you try to have me committed after promis-

ing me you wouldn't?'' Andrea tried to keep her voice
even.

"You're a sick woman, Miss Biaggi,'' countered the
therapist. "You shouldn't be out on the streets."

"That isn't true. I function well enough to hold down a
very responsible job and live like a normal human being.
Besides, you betrayed a confidence between patient and
doctor. That's unethical.''

"That's just the way you feel because you're not thinking straight. You're obviously not responsible for what
you're saying. Anyone can see that,'' the therapist
said.

"What a wonderful argument! Always so easy for you
people to say. If I disagree with your ethics or your judgment, then *I'm* the one at fault because I'm insane by
definition."

"Well, under the circumstances—''

"You never even consider it might be *your* problem, not
mine?"

The therapist looked at Andrea with a mildly shocked
expression on her face. "That's just the kind of reasoning
a person in your condition would use to justify her problem. Can't you see that, Andrea? It's perfectly obvious to
me."

The episode exacerbated her problems. She subsequently
stopped searching for a new therapist, all but certain now
she would never find anyone willing to treat her.

It was during this period that her mother wrote to her,
saying she was very ill. Andrea quickly arranged a trip
back to Illinois to coincide with an administrative conference. She asked for, and was reluctantly given, a few extra
days to spend with her mother. As soon as she saw her,
Andrea knew her mother was dying. She had waited to go
to a doctor until Andrea arrived, a fact that the daughter
found surprising. But over the years, Dara Biaggi had in
some mysterious way drawn closer to her eldest daughter.
That week spent together was the happiest of Andrea's
life. Dara made some of Andrea's favorite meals, and

Andrea took care of the small backyard and cleaned the house. When they talked about death, as was inevitable, her mother made Andrea promise not to use any extraordinary means to keep her alive: she wanted to die with dignity and peace—even if she'd never been able to live that way.

Between the doctor's visits and hospital tests, they spent many hours talking, sharing their sense of the sad world into which both had been born. There were memories of happy times and forgiveness for the bad ones. Dara shared with Andrea secrets she had never divulged even to Mike, who (Andrea had always thought) was her confidant. The conversation inevitably came around to Joseph, and for the first time her mother revealed the hell of her marriage. He had never been an easy man to live with—tender and tyrannical by turns, going from gentle to brutal without warning. But after Andrea's birth the madness had grown worse. He became enraged at the slightest provocation. He beat her many times and threatened her frequently with death. At times, Dara told her, she was not sure he even recognized her during his outbursts. She was merely an object of anger, a symbol to punish and rail against. She never knew what set him off and could never predict when he would flare again. She had been at his mercy, finally, a victim of his sick mind as surely as his sons and daughters.

"He was crazy, Andrea. Crazy. Always screaming and yelling. It was very frightening. I wanted to do something . . . to help him to help myself and you kids, but what could I do? I was trapped here. Who would've helped? Who wanted to hear? Such a sick, angry man, your father."

Dara had never talked to Andrea like this before. Now, all of a sudden, they were friends, loving friends: Dara was the mother Andrea had always wanted. When they parted, they both knew it would be for the last time, and it made their parting all that much more poignant. A few days later, Dara called Andrea to tell her the doctors had definitely diagnosed her condition as acute leukemia, and they gave her only a few weeks to live.

Both to forget the imminent death of her mother and also to prepare for it, Andrea began to work in the office at a furious pace. She was in the office a minimum of sixty hours a week and more, bringing her work home for another fifteen or twenty hours extra a week. After five weeks she was utterly exhausted, even more vulnerable to the panic attacks. At first she thought she could handle them and managed to keep them at bay while she was in the office; but once home, she found it increasingly difficult to avoid the swarm of anxieties and hallucinations that set upon her. As self-injury became the main focus of her anxiety, she knew she must finally find someone to help her.

Five weeks after Andrea's visit, Dara Biaggi died. Andrea survived her mother's funeral by keeping very busy. She flew to Illinois and helped make arrangements for family and friends coming to town. She managed the details of the funeral, and after the funeral took an inventory of her mother's meager possessions, packing all the unwanted items for St. Vincent DePaul and distributing the rest as her brothers had requested. She wrote the obligatory thank-you notes and finally returned to Salt Lake, more controlled yet more desperate than she'd ever felt. Caught in the grip of increasing terror, she finally telephoned the last psychiatrist who had been suggested to her more than a month before. Her case, he told her, was a special problem and, he felt, warranted a specialist. And there just happened to be someone up at the University of Utah who might fit the bill.

"Who is he?" she asked.

"A professor of Psychiatry at the Medical School. He handles a lot of intractable cases."

"What's his name?"

"Dr. Eugene Bliss. Used to be chairman of the department. Now he's doing research with difficult cases. Get in touch with him."

She didn't waste any time following the young psychiatrist's advice and called Dr. Bliss's office.

For Andrea it seemed to be merely the beginning of another vain effort, and she expected it to turn out just as futilely as all the rest.

This time, however, she would be wrong.

PART II

9

A First Meeting

DR. Bliss wasn't what Andrea was expecting. For one thing, he looked too much like what a psychiatrist is supposed to look like. An unkempt thicket of salt-and-pepper hair above a tanned, handsome face with sparkling, even mischievous eyes. A rumpled suit, ill-matched, with a tie so thin it predated the hospital. He was smoking a pipe—thereby explaining the constant puffing noises she'd heard on the phone—which habitually sent forth a redolent haze of smoke, or, when not lit, tinkled loudly against the side of a large glass ashtray as Bliss emptied its contents. He wore a pair of shoes that looked more like bedroom slippers and occasionally when in the act of interrogating or listening, he would put one foot on the desk and lean back in his chair. He was also a chronic throat-clearer, a noise that usually presaged a comment necessarily more profound or more important than the comment that had preceded it. And when he talked, he had a way of flourishing the fingers of his right hand.

Bliss looked fatherly, genial, and professional in a way that resisted pomposity but aspired to absent-mindedness. His educational and medical credentials were on his wall: Yale University, '39; New York Medical College, '43; the Menninger Institute after the war. Not on the wall was the information that he had had another stint teaching at Yale before becoming a professor of Psychiatry at the University of Utah Medical School. There were pictures of him with colleagues, children, friends (always smiling, frequently scruffy in a distinguished way); magazines and books on a bookshelf (several of which bore his name on their spines); one overstuffed chair in the corner; an undersprung loose-jointed desk chair and a capacious desk; and over the desk, a picture of a bearded Gene Bliss in parka and high-altitude gear below the Khumbu Glacier at the foot of Mount Everest.

The one window in the small office produced an uninteresting view: the Medical Center's first floor roof. There was little else to fix her eye on except for Dr. Bliss himself, and when she was nervous or not in a mood to look at him, she generally focused on his Yale diploma trying to figure out the Latin script, associating that dead language with her dead past.

"So." Dr. Bliss smiled. "I guess we should begin by your telling me a little about the problem."

"Like what?"

"Oh," Dr. Bliss cleared his throat again, "like what you think your problem is, where did it originate, your history of hospitalization . . . that kind of thing."

All right, she thought. Here we go again. She took a deep breath and dived in.

"Since 1965 when I entered a convent I've been experiencing episodes of self-injury. Hurting myself, sometimes feelings of wanting to die. I've tried to kill myself three or four times. I can go along for weeks perfectly normal and then just lose control. My mind goes wild or something, like it's been split in pieces."

"Any hallucinations?" he asked.

"Lights get brighter sometimes. Noises get louder. My depth perception goes to pot and there's dizziness. But that's only the beginning."

"Oh?"

"I can hurt myself badly and never feel a thing. A lot of it's very crazy. Like an overdose of LSD, only it lasts for a long time."

"Do you have any control over it?"

"None whatsoever. If it continues for long, I get real

scared and don't make any sense and finally end up hurting myself.''

''How long has this been going on?''

''Oh, a long time. High school? Maybe a little before. I don't remember things that clearly.''

''Are you violent?''

''Only toward myself and a few cats. I've killed quite a few of those. I can't help myself. But mostly I hurt myself. I silently scream and yell and break apart. But I wouldn't hurt anyone, not really.'' Her eyes, her whole face, shifted and changed.

''And when you commit these self-destructive acts, are you aware of doing them?''

''Well, yes and no. Part of me can see it all happening. It's not like a psychotic episode or anything, though lots of therapists have called me schizophrenic. It's more like I can see it happening but I can't do anything about it. As if I'm seeing it all happening from a long way away.''

''You've been diagnosed as schizophrenic, and yet you say you've usually held down responsible jobs?''

''I had to survive. That was the most important thing. I couldn't just fold up. I had to make money and I seem to be able to function pretty well except during the really bad episodes, when I'm panicking.''

''How would you describe these panics?''

''Something triggers me off . . . I don't know exactly what. My job, a letter from home, I don't know what else. Then I just begin to go crazy—things go wild inside my head. I can't do anything to stop it and that's the worst part—knowing I can't do anything to stop it. So the panic grows. Pretty soon the voices and the weird nightmares come . . . sometimes I just lose it altogether and don't remember a thing about what I do.''

''A kind of amnesia?''

''Well, maybe. Yes, I guess. That happens to me . . . it used to happen a lot in Boston. It's kind of uncomfortable waking up in the park or on a street somewhere and not knowing where you were the night before or where you are now.''

"What about your childhood. Any trouble you remember there?"

"Well, there is something I remembered when I was in therapy back in Boston," Andrea said. "It was one of those Gestalt therapy things and I was on a bed on the floor, acting out, and all of a sudden I start going into this number about how my father was lying on top of me, crushing the life out of me. I must have split really bad or something then . . . because I scared the hell out of the therapist."

"What does that suggest to you?"

"You mean the thing about my father?"

"Yes."

"Well, Dr. Good said it could be something to do with incest and all that. My father was a pretty sick man, especially when I was eight and after he came back from the hospital." She shrugged again. "He might have raped me or something like that. It's possible."

"Possible?"

"Well, I don't really know that for a fact, do I? I mean I have some crazy dream, but there's nothing to say it really happened. How could it be true? He always treated me so well."

"I wonder if you'd cooperate with me in a little experiment," Bliss said.

"What kind of experiment?" she asked suspiciously. Years of treatment had taught her to be wary.

"Oh, nothing dangerous. Just a thought experiment really. No pills, no shots, none of that. I just want you to look at that spot on the wall . . . that one over there." Bliss gestured toward a small crack in the brick. "Can you do that?"

"Sure, but I don't know what you're trying to get at."

"Humor me for a minute," Dr. Bliss said. "Now just concentrate on that dot. Look at it very hard . . . very hard . . ." His voice was low and strangely melodious. There was nothing demanding or dictatorial in it. "Continue to look at the spot. Now your eyelids are beginning to get heavy . . . heavy . . . heavier . . . your eyelids are becoming heavy as lead . . .''

A moment later she was staring at Dr. Bliss. Had any time passed? She wasn't sure. She examined the clock on the desk. She'd misplaced fifteen minutes in his office.

Dr. Bliss was still smoking his pipe, filling the air with smoke. ''I think I know exactly what's wrong with you, Miss Biaggi. And I think I can help you.''

Andrea sat quietly, disbelieving.

''I'm perfectly serious. I've handled dozens of cases like yours.''

''I don't know what to say.''

What kind of a doctor would make such rash statements, she wondered? It all sounded fishy to her. Like a barker selling nostrums.

''No need. Just be here next Wednesday at four o'clock. That's September seventh. Can you make it?''

''Do you really think you can help me?''

''Yes. I *know* I can, if you're willing.''

She was.

10

The Theory

IN his profession, Bliss was a maverick. Before it had been fashionable to espouse the physiological components of mental disease, he had been experimenting on the effects of stress on the endocrine system. Later he had investigated certain neuromediators in the brain.

His work on anorexia nervosa resulted in a monograph on the subject, the definitive manual on the disorder for a time. But that was years before the syndrome came to national attention and the disorder became almost epidemic.

After exploring a particular topic to his own satisfaction, he had the habit of moving on before the field became "hot," leaving the rest to others. He enjoyed splashing around in overlooked eddies of psychiatry.

His most recent investigations were proving to be a perfect example of this.

He had more or less stumbled onto the subject of hypnosis and multiple personalities. Always in search of an interesting case, he had been referred a patient, a nurse at a local hospital, who had suddenly changed personality in front of her supervisor. The patient seemed a possible multiple personality, and Bliss accepted her for therapy. He had never seen a case of multiple personalities, at least never recognized one in his thirty years of practice and teaching. He had no idea how to treat one but felt an obligation to accept the case.

He guessed or had a hunch—maybe it came from a dim memory of something he had read or speculated about in the past—that the nurse should be a good hypnotic subject. Up to that point he'd never really believed in the efficacy of hypnotic treatment. Hypnosis was something practiced by carnival actors, spiritualists, and charlatans. Only a few credible experts in the field used it. It was a field only slightly more legitimate than ESP, as far as he was concerned. But with this patient, he tried it. He hadn't used hypnosis since the days of his residency, and it hadn't been a spectacular success then. Untutored but willing, he muttered a few "hypnotic incantations," and the patient quite unexpectedly went into a deep trance.

For Dr. Bliss, what happened next constituted high drama. He urged her to look for someone inside herself and, after initial reluctance, the unexpected happened. From a quiet, even demure matron, his patient changed before his eyes into a gum-chewing, brassy-voiced slattern. Over the next months, through hypnosis he discovered that the woman's alter ego had been created when the patient was six and had been used many times thereafter during periods of stress and pain. Characteristically, she herself remembered nothing while the personality was in control.

Using hypnosis he had been able, after a relatively short time, to discover the causes of her illness. The experience exhilarated him and also made him curious, particularly about the extraordinary ability of his patient to enter a deep trance in half a minute or less, even on the first try.

His second multiple personality case was also exceedingly responsive to hypnosis, falling into a deep state within fifteen seconds, and through hypnotic probing Dr. Bliss soon identified no less than sixteen distinct personalities.

At that point, the syndrome was still a tantalizing puzzle to him. What was he to make of it? By the time he had encountered several more cases of the same sort, Bliss was certain he was on to something important. All the patients had proved excellent, not to say spectacular, hypnotic subjects, and none had been suspected of having multiple personalities.

One case, a woman who had been diagnosed as a classical hysteric with a plethora of physical complaints, had not been perceived as a multiple until Bliss saw her. He recognized the symptoms immediately: amnesia, panic, many physical complaints, frequent mood shifts, and a childhood history of upheaval and trauma. He couldn't be certain, of course, but he tried hypnosis just the same— and opened up Pandora's box. Not only did she go under with surprising rapidity, but out sprang a host of personalities, all with names and individualized functions. At one count there were more than fifty.

As his detection of these cases grew keener, he began to spot clandestine multiples hiding behind a battery of complaints and diagnoses. One patient had been diagnosed as a sociopath, another a kleptomaniac, several as schizophrenic, and another a hysteric. They came with every diagnostic label imaginable.

The more cases he identified and studied, the more certain he became that the key to the syndrome was hypnosis. Not just hypnosis, but spontaneous self-hypnosis. He ran a series of tests on the hypnosis potential of these patients. While the average person might score a five or six out of a possible twelve points on the test, his patients averaged over ten—a very high score indeed.

And there was another, a precipitating, factor that many of these cases but not all seemed to share—a childhood of brutality and neglect. Some of the women admitted under hypnosis they'd been raped by fathers and brothers when young.

He started reading back through the history of hypnosis, filling in his understanding of a method and practice he'd never studied until then. He found there was a rich literature of hypnosis with many examples of the phenomenon under many different guises going back to antiquity. Modern hypnosis had begun with Franz Anton Mesmer in the late eighteenth century. It had developed through the Marquis de Puysegur, the Abbé Faria, Depotet de Sennevoy, James Braid—and many others. Some devotees of hypnosis had pursued practices little different from alchemy and charlatanry; many more, however, had been ethical physicians who investigated the subject with scientific rigor.

The early commentaries piqued Bliss's interest, and he followed the trail into the last half of the nineteenth century, to the publications of Jean-Marie Charcot, Ambrose-Auguste Liebeault, Hippolyte Bernheim, Paul Briquet, and others. The material on the subject was voluminous, far more so than he'd ever suspected.

There were two investigators in particular: Pierre Janet (1859-1947) and Josef Breuer (1842-1925). Though Janet had never occupied more than a footnote in the official histories of psychiatry, it was he who in 1889 first discovered a *special* unconscious. He had noted in the case of severe hysterics the existence of what he termed "dissociated states," and used hypnosis to treat these cases. Through this method, he soon discovered that some patients could then divulge early forgotten traumas they had somehow managed to isolate and divorce from the rest of their experiences. These observations led Janet to the novel thesis that hysterical symptoms were due to subconscious "idées fixes" that had been frozen in time and forgotten. Unfortunately for these patients, while the bad memories remained forgotten, they frequently manifested themselves in many kinds of symptoms and illnesses. Janet determined that somehow—he wasn't sure quite how—his patients' minds had become "fragmented," breaking down into semiautonomous provinces, and that hypnosis seemed to aid the reintegrating process. Janet discovered numerous examples confirming his thesis, but the cases that excited his interest the most were a handful of patients who demonstrated alternate or satellite personalities existing in parallel with the dominant personality.

A few such cases had been previously reported by other physicians, but they were considered rare and bizarre conditions of limited interest and dubious credibility.

However, by one of those odd coincidences, at the same time Janet was conducting his studies, another physician, Josef Breuer of Vienna, was treating "Anna O," the most famous case in the annals of psychoanalysis.

At the time of Breuer's research with Anna O, he had a younger friend named Sigmund Freud, and together they often talked about this remarkable case, which helped alert Freud to the importance of the unconscious.

Anna was a gifted and well-educated intellectual, able to converse in no less than four languages. Later in her life, she became the first social worker in Germany, founded a periodical, espoused woman's emancipation, and labored to help orphaned children. But in 1890 she was a pyrotechnical hysteric with a whole sideshow of symptoms. At one time or another, she suffered paralyses, anesthesias, auditory and visual hallucinations, amnesias, neuralgias and tremors. And yet there was a perplexing twist to her case. At times, she would lapse into a state that Breuer termed "hypnoid" or "self-hypnotic." In this altered state, Anna would remember and reexperience on a conscious level all the events and emotions that had generated a symptom. Then it would miraculously disappear. This mode of treatment Breuer called his "cathartic" therapy.

In 1895, Breuer and Freud published a monograph on hysteria containing an account of this therapy and much more; it is probably, next to Freud's volume on dreams, the most important text in psychoanalysis. From Bliss's point of view, one of the most interesting aspects of the monograph was just how closely Breuer's findings agreed with Janet's observations, even though their interpretations differed. Janet, in his final arguments, had concluded that hysterics suffered from "split minds" because of some genetic weakness. Breuer had said that self-hypnosis created an unconscious in which traumas resided. Freud, however, had accepted neither verdict.

Freud flatly stated he'd never encountered a case of "hypnoid" or "self-hypnotic" hysteria. As far as he was concerned, most neuroses were caused by forgotten childhood traumas, and in his cases these were sexual offenses inflicted by fathers on their daughters. These abuses, he initially concluded, constituted the true causes of hysteria. Freud now discounted Breuer's theory of "self-hypnosis" and substituted "repression" for it. Repression relegated these sexual traumas to the unconscious, while the patient's powerful resistances prevented their liberation.

However, Freud soon experienced a reversal of opinion. He had been wrong. These childhood sexual assaults he now decided were not real experiences but fantasies produced by sexual feelings toward the parent, which violated the incest taboo and therefore had to be repressed.

It was a sensible deduction, or so it seemed. There were no census-takers, no statisticians, no researchers to point out the prevalence of child abuse and incest in the late nineteenth century; these were uncommon aberrations to the Viennese physicians—totems broken in only the most debased of homes. To explain neuroses in respectable middle-class Viennese families by such behaviors was unreasonable, so Freud consigned these reports by patients to the realm of fantasies.

The hypothesis of fantasies then led to many of Freud's favorite concepts: the Oedipal and Electra Complexes; the oral, anal, phallic, and genital states of psychosexual development; and castration fears. Much of what Freud later wrote was based on these assumptions—constructs that Bliss believed must be faulty.

After investigating many of his own hysteric patients using hypnosis, Bliss was ready to formulate a theory contrary to Freud's but consistent with Breuer's. In his view, the severe disorders he was treating originated through self-hypnosis. But what caused the hypnosis to take place? What had initiated the process in the first place? Not fantasies and the emergence of mother-or father-love, but *real* traumas. Bliss's patients and numerous statistics pointed to the conclusion that not only were such traumas present but were, worse yet, common.

Bliss proposed that Breuer had been essentially correct.

The mechanism Breuer had recognized in Anna O. as self-hypnosis was the key concept. Only hypnosis could have produced such an obliteration of memory as Anna O. had manifested. In Bliss's opinion it was the same hypnotically induced amnesia that Mesmer and other early pioneers had described. The old literature on the subject was filled with examples of what a person could do under hypnotic suggestion. Vision, smell, hearing, taste, touch, pain—all of these could be manipulated by the hypnotic adept. Hypnosis had even been used as an anesthesia.

After conducting some simple experiments with several of his excellent hypnotic subjects, Bliss began to see that almost anything was possible. He had induced hypnosis and transported people magically to another part of the country, another part of the world; he'd even sent one of his subjects to the moon where she described the cold, the darkness, and the cratered landscape. These were things he had merely suggested. The rest was embellished by the subjects themselves.

Pain could be eradicated or magnified; people could be reduced to the size of a mouse or inflated to the dimensions of a giant. An unwelcome guest could be vaporized or an apparition suddenly conjured up. Many of Bliss's patients could do these things under his direction when he placed them in a trance. But when questioned about past similar experiences, they recalled identical happenings long before they ever encountered a hypnotist. They had been performing such feats without any help from him or anyone else.

What made these patients such exceptional hypnotic subjects? Part of the reason was genetic; some people were born more adept than others. But practice makes perfect, and they had been going into self-hypnotic states since childhood. It had to do with old traumas so painful that the mind refused to accept them. It was akin, he felt, to the ancient reflex many animals resort to when cornered or under attack: an instinctive and self-induced catatonia meant to keep the animal absolutely immobile—''playing dead.''

In his patients this "instinct" had been raised to the level of an art. But whatever the physical seat of this ability, Bliss was also learning that this "refiex" was more than simply a means to shunt aside unpleasant memories, consigning them to deeper vaults. Paradoxically, the memories did not remain inert forever. Eventually they could erupt as personality disorders, schizophrenia, hysteria, sociopathy, hypochondriasis—there was a constellation of problems this mechanism could simulate or promote.

This was interesting enough, but there was a still more provocative aspect. The self-hypnotic process could take a collection of traumatic memories and mold them into personalities responsible for their keeping. Frequently, if the original mind felt the need, the offending memories could be divided among several personalities—it was a matter of taste and need.

Many of these personalities proved to be largely two-dimensional—players assigned specific tasks by the ruling consciousness. In the beginning, the main task was to sequester harmful or upsetting information; as the problems multiplied, so too might the number of alter egos needed to conceal the pain. Once started, the personalities often proliferated, sometimes reaching byzantine complexity. The hypnotic mind would create characters not just to preserve memories but to carry out very specific tasks. This in turn meant these personalities took on a dual aspect; they were more than containers to hold sundry unpleasantness, they became part and parcel of the unpleasantness itself. In effect, their content came to dictate their form, and what resulted was a personality—or group of personalities—too fractious or dangerous to keep confined in the unconscious for any length of time. But some personalities had the power to assume control of the body, to emerge while the victim disappeared.

Most of Dr. Bliss's cases had manifested classic instabilities: hallucinations, many somatic complaints and chronic depressive episodes, besides the more histrionic "mood swings." The profound cases often demonstrated antisocial personalities, some of which, Bliss suspected, were perfectly capable of violent acts like self-mutilation, child abuse, rape, even murder. Indeed some of the most notorious mass murderers he'd read about seemed examples of the multiple personality syndrome. It was, to say the least, a disorder that offered considerable danger, not just to the patient but to the unsuspecting therapist as well.

To say multiple personality syndrome represented an extreme example of self-hypnosis was not to say it was a particularly rare ailment. To the contrary, Dr. Bliss began collecting compelling evidence that the syndrome was anything but rare. The more cases he saw, the more convinced he became that many other disorders masked a case of multiple personality. The more adept he became at using hypnosis, the more of these cases he uncovered. Some were not severe, and after a reasonable time for interrogation he could integrate the disparate personalities, providing occasional "miraculous" recoveries.

It was part archaeology, part magic. Never had he enjoyed such exciting "live theater." It was truly amazing. One case—a rarity, it turned out—took him only two hours to cure with no apparent relapse over two years' time. Several more patients showed remarkable improvements after only a few months of hypnotherapy. He felt like an ancient thaumaturge, using "incantations and spells" to cure the sick.

Dr. Bliss's first fifteen-minute interview with Andrea Biaggi assured him she fit the basic criteria of a multiple very well. There were all kinds of elements that added up to his diagnosis: possible abuse by her father, rejection by her mother, the powerful role of Catholicism in her life (which had produced an abundant sense of sin), incidents of self-mutilation, amnesias, trance episodes, rapid shifts in facial expression and mood, a large number of diagnoses attributed to her over the years, and the striking dichotomy between her work and home life.

All these symptoms he'd come to associate with this peculiar disorder. But there was another and, in his mind, far more conclusive testimony to the fact that Andrea was a multiple: she was a spectacular hypnotic subject, one of the best he'd ever seen. As soon as her eyes had rested on the spot on his wall, as soon as he'd given the suggestion to go under, she'd fallen into a deep hypnotic state. It took thirty seconds or less. And then her eyes had grown large, her cheeks flushed pink, and she'd begun to speak in a disjointed, inarticulate way:

"I . . . where . . . who . . . I don't . . ." It was such an eerie transformation from a genial, articulate woman to this other one. Not just the speech but the tone of the voice: dull, flat, unmodulated. He'd seen this before.

11

The First Session

ON September 7, 1979, Andrea came into the small room, looking uncomfortable. She sat down. Bliss, all smiles and unruly countenance, talked with her for a few moments about other matters: her job, the weather, the advantages and disadvantages of living in Salt Lake City. At last he cleared his throat.

"I'm going to use hypnotherapy on you," Bliss said. "Little more than the technique you've been using on yourself for years."

"Self-hypnosis?"

"Exactly."

"How do you know that's what I've been doing? Couldn't I just be going nuts? Bouncing from one psychotic episode to the next?"

"I don't think so—not in your case. I know there's no clear line, and God knows you've been diagnosed many ways. Tell me something about your trance states."

"Like what?"

"What are they like, and when do you first remember them happening?"

"They began a long time ago. Before the convent even. School I think, the Polish convent school. They began with a sense of fear but then, there would be quiet, darkness, safety, forgetfulness at times . . . timelessness. It helped get over the fear, but it didn't help my grades much."

"So it's always been basically a positive thing, these trances?"

"No," she shook her head emphatically. "No. Not for a long time now. It used to be a way to escape, I guess. But since I entered the convent, they've turned crazy on me, frightening. I can't control them and they happen all the time. Now it's not just fear inside but panic. Voices fighting. Weird hallucinations. Real craziness."

"Okay, let's see what we can do about it," he said. "I'll tell you the way we're going to proceed with your therapy. I believe a lot of your problems come from traumatic memories you've been squirreling away over the years, using self-hypnosis to create sanctuaries for the problems. You've built a support system around these problems. I'll just try to tunnel in the same way you did and see what I can find."

"By all means," Andrea gave her consent. "Tunnel away."

"Great. Now just lean back and relax the way you did the last time and concentrate on that same spot on the wall . . ."

This time he didn't have to go through the initial protocol; she was under instantly.

"Now I want you to tell me about your first memory of this trance state."

Andrea flipped herself around in her chair, shuddered, her pupils grew very small, and her head tilted to one side as if listening to something. "Nothing. I—" More gyrations.

"Andrea? Andrea?" Bliss kept addressing her and each time there was the shuddering and the inarticulate stammering. "Andrea? What's going on?"

After ten minutes of this, Bliss brought her out of hypnosis and abruptly her eyes cleared.

"What happened?" she asked. "I don't—" Suddenly she gazed at Bliss fixedly and her eyes went blank.

"Andrea?"

She was back under again, on her own. He tried to bring her out of it but each time, just as she seemed to be clearing, the head would flip, the body gyrate, and she was right back into it.

Over the next two hours Bliss tried to carry on a coherent conversation with her, but found himself blocked at every turn by a dizzying array of mute faces. Replies, when given to his questions, were stammered, barely audible, inevitably confusing except in some secret vocabulary Andrea had reserved for her own private use. Bliss had seen this before, though not in such a virulent form. In that first session Bliss could ascribe only a few minutes to Andrea herself—the rest of the time was taken up with people and places he knew nothing about. The most savage flurry of activity came when he brought up the subject of Andrea's father.

The twisting and turning increased threefold, her eyes expanding and contracting like pinwheels, her face alternating with flushes and white pallor. Only once did something approaching coherence come from her:

"He hurt. I was very bad, and he hurt me. He hurt us all. . . tried to kill all of us . . ."

"How did he do this, Andrea?"

" . . . he went crazy, just like me. Punishing me for my sins. Trying to kill all of us in here."

"All of you? What do you mean by *all* of you?"

"Mustn't tell. Don't tell anyone . . ."

He could get very little else out of her, but it was enough.

DR. BLISS'S NOTEBOOK
September 11, 1979

She is proving to be a fragile, explosive patient. My attempts to proceed slowly and cautiously, despite all efforts, have agitated her more than I would wish. Today I tried to calm this by giving her a brief description of the nature of self-hypnosis and some of its problems.

She told me her trances began many years ago. They began with a sense of fear but then there would be quiet, darkness, safety, amnesia at times, and timelessness. But for many years they have changed into frightening experiences.

During our session, despite all efforts, she became more

frantic, going in and out of hypnotic states. In desperation I finally asked again whether there was something I was doing, or something about me that might be culpable. She then had another paroxysm, became aphonic, and then finally blurted out, "You look like my father!" It developed that my hair and face favored the resemblance, but it was much intensified "when I went into the twilight—another space. I was scared of you—afraid you would hurt me."

I might briefly review the history that I took at her initial interview. Andrea is 31, unmarried, articulate, obese, and clearly intelligent. She was referred by a psychiatrist who suspected multiple personalities.

She has been studied, treated, and diagnosed by numerous internists, psychiatrists, and neurologists. Dr. Good treated her for three years with no significant gain. For a period of two years she was completely disabled but is now holding a responsible administrative position in a non-profit agency in Ogden. She has been diagnosed in Boston as a patient with temporal lobe seizures, which I can't buy. In fact, her electroencephalograms here don't confirm it.

Her symptoms include grave panics, self-destructive behavior, great fears, sensory problems—the lights too bright, noises too loud, or distortion of distance and touch. There has been a loss of feeling—anesthesias, etc.—happening as long as she can remember.

Interspersed there have been multiple hospitalizations and a ton of drugs, including anticonvulsives. No drug has given meaningful relief. She has severely burned herself on her left hand and also in her vagina. Significantly, when she has burned or cut herself, there has been no pain.

Her father sexually abused her and "tried to kill all of us." He was an alcoholic. Despite this horrible background, she has pushed herself to acquire a college degree and several years of graduate work.

During these episodes of panic, she loses her speech and can't think straight enough to speak—something I have now witnessed in the therapeutic sessions. I can only add she was in a trance when this occurred. Finally, she has periods of amnesia and can't remember much about her childhood.

My diagnosis is certainly one of self-hypnosis, probably with multiple personalities.

The next day, September 12, Bliss tried penetrating Andrea's mind more deeply using hypnosis. Something about the look on her face made Bliss think he had another personality in hand:

"Am I talking to Andrea?"

"Yes," came a sad, tired voice.

"You sound fatigued, Andrea. It's not like you. Anything wrong?"

"So much fighting going on. So much panic. No one is happy."

"Fighting? Are there any others there besides you?"

A long pause followed. Then, reluctantly, "Yes."

This was the first moment of discovery, one of the exhilarating moments Bliss had learned to expect in such cases.

"Who are they?"

"I can't tell you . . ." Andrea began to twist about. "Don't want to."

"Andrea?"

"Sinful . . . not good . . . bad . . ."

Andrea began to hyperventilate as she looked down into her lap. There was such a deep terror inside her, such a loathing to reveal.

"Andrea? Tell me about the other people there."

"There are about four of them."

It was a beginning. Four other personalities besides Andrea.

"Can you tell me about them?" Bliss asked.

"No. Can't. Mustn't." She spun around. "They're strong. Evil. Have no names. Strong and dangerous. Make her feel weak."

She subsided into inarticulate stammerings once again,

interspersed with silences, until at last, near the end of the second hour, she seemed to come out of it slightly, enough to say, "They're choking me. They don't want me to talk to you. I mustn't."

He could get nothing else out of her. She was either too scared or too controlled to be of any further help.

After Dr. Bliss had brought her out of hypnosis, he tried to find out what she could remember.

"Nothing," she told him. "Nothing at all. Why? Did I say anything to you."

It didn't greatly surprise him that she couldn't remember. After all, that was the reason for the self-hypnotic state in the first place—to forget, to place something painful in a safe concealment.

"You'll remember in time," he assured her. "It will come clear."

"But how can I be sure?" Andrea asked.

"Give me some time," Bliss said. "We'll be co-therapists in this enterprise. Think of it as a kind of partnership where both of us have a great deal at stake. You want to get well, and I want to cure you. Now if we can see each other as allies in this fight and struggle toward the same end, then obviously, if we work hard enough at it, we'll get there eventually."

"How soon is eventually?"

"I'm a psychiatrist, not a seer."

"A seer would be more useful," she said, and they both laughed.

She had never received such intensive treatment before, and at first she found the experience exhilarating. Here was someone who really seemed to care. There was so much optimism in the man no matter how unorthodox his methods or ideas. He'd infused her with renewed hope for the quest.

But something was going very wrong. Her mother's death had started it all off on the wrong foot—like beginning a new job on a Sunday. And then there had been the weirdness and the scariness of the hypnosis. Wild things were happening. They were keeping her up at night, pushing her closer to the edge. Every time she left Bliss's office after a session, she had gone crazy. The panic was wild. Uncontrollable. She had barely made it home. And now, with the job becoming more of a hassle every day and the board chairman becoming more and more inquisitive about her strange moods, it was worse.

By the next session it was obvious that Andrea's courage had diminished appreciably.

"They're fighting. It's dangerous. Bad," she told him. "The evil forces are taking control. I can't stop them. They're so angry at me."

She seemed to cringe with the fear of what she saw.

Bliss saw this and decided to try a method he'd used successfully with hypnosis before. "Let's pretend that we're both watching what is happening through a large telescope. The event is miles away . . . light years away. It's merely something happening 'out there.' Something you are going to comment on as you might comment on the behavior of a sparrow or a cloud. Got it?"

"Yes." That seemed to calm her.

"Now then, let's see if we can't see the evil forces."

Abruptly Andrea began to beat her head with her fists. Not soft slaps to the face, but hard, driving blows to her jaw and eyes. "She is stupid, stupid. I hate her!" screamed a low, malignant voice. "She is stupid, bad, won't pay attention. Always getting us in trouble." The explosion of violence continued. Bliss grabbed her hands, sat on her lap to restrain her.

"Why is she bad?" Bliss asked, still tightly holding Andrea's hands.

The voice was low, menacing. "She is bad. Bad. Went into box for confessional. She didn't tell and she knew . . . she knew."

"Knew what?"

"Knew everything . . . everything. It's a sin. A sin. She needs to be punished. Needs to be hurt bad."

"Why is she evil?"

"She knew and didn't tell. Did and wouldn't die. Bad. She should be dead."

Bliss could make little of this telegraphic language. Something had been done, and some personality inside her was now demanding punishment for it. That was as far as he dared go, for now.

"Andrea, come back now. I insist on it."

The aspect of Andrea's face changed. The lines of anger and hatred cleared, becoming more placid. Andrea, or some part of her, was back in control.

"Yes?" The voice was quieter, calmer.

"What is all this about punishment and sin, Andrea? The evil force tells me it is very angry at you and wants to hurt you."

"Yes. It is like wanting to die. They want her dead. She is scared." A sudden change took place, and the face became more turbulent. ". . . is scared will work on the burn, tear at it . . ."

She had recently burned herself on her arm with oven cleaner, another in a long series of self-mutilations. But even with so serious an injury, she wouldn't leave the wound alone. She kept burning it, trying to prevent the wound from healing. One of Bliss's immediate tasks, it seemed, was to somehow keep her from worrying the injury any more than she already had.

When finally he brought her out of hypnosis, she remembered a portion of what had gone on.

"I've got to have treatment immediately."

"Why?"

"Because once before when I burned myself there, they took care of it right away, and afterward I didn't try to hurt the wound."

"But why are these Evil forces trying to hurt you? Why do they believe you are so sinful?"

Andrea couldn't answer this. She stared out into some indeterminate space and was lost for a short time until Bliss retrieved her. There were many, many questions— perhaps the majority of the important questions—that she could not, or would not, answer. Exactly why this was,

Bliss wasn't sure. Perhaps it was the proximity of those questions to the central issues. He could already see that almost everything scared her primary personality, sending her into hypnosis, and it was always difficult to bring her back.

And now there was another strange thing. Several times he'd summoned Andrea to talk under hypnosis and instead he'd heard a calmer, sweeter voice referring to Andrea in the third-person and always in a sympathetic tone. Now who was this? He had not yet asked, and he promised himself that the next time he must ferret this personality out.

The next session the sympathetic personality reappeared—a personality who would prove pivotal.

"Little Andrea-Ellen is scared, she's afraid to talk to people."

"But can't I talk to her?"

"She can't. She won't come out of the closet. She is too small, too hurt . . ."

"Hurt? How?"

"She is very young. Just a sad little child. Her dress is covered with blood."

"How many others are there in the closet?"

"Lots."

"How do they feel?"

"Right now, there is no fighting. Just sadness and quiet. But last night, there was lots of fighting. A feeling like jumping out the window yesterday."

"How did she resist the impulse?"

"There are some parts that still want to live. Not all are wanting to die. But the other parts, the evil ones, they try to get it done. They send messages in blood."

"Well then, let's see if we can't talk a little bit about it. What is the child's name?"

"Call her what she is," the voice said. "Call her Little Andrea-Ellen. That's her name."

"Good enough. Now what do you think is in her mind?"

"She . . . she has a secret world in there . . . no one

knows about it. She is afraid to talk about them. Lots of danger.'' The eyes rapidly focused and unfocused. The ploy was a delicate one.

"Now don't you worry about Little Andrea-Ellen. I'll be very kind, very cautious with her. Like a good teacher.''

"But she can't go alone,'' the voice was pleading. "Afraid they will leave her. People, when they see what is inside, leave her.''

"Once they understand, no one will leave her. People are more decent than that. And besides, once she understands herself better, she'll be able to stop the fighting and the illness.''

"But how can she?'' asked the voice. "Every time the fighting begins, part chokes her . . . makes everything go black. There's no way for her to help herself.''

"What do you mean by choking?''

"One wants to tell what the others can't say. Tell the others when things are dangerous outside.'' Her tone was almost patronizing, as if explaining an obvious fact to a dull-witted pupil.

"But don't you think,'' Bliss asked, "Little Andrea-Ellen is too sensitive? That it really isn't as dangerous out of the closet as she says it is?''

There was no answer to this, merely a few gyrations. Andrea stared straight ahead, unseeing.

Finally Bliss asked: "How does this person enforce the silence?''

"Has a knife. Uses it when the others have been bad. Little Andrea-Ellen is often bad.''

It was a circular argument. The more Bliss tried to defuse the situation the more dead ends he discovered. Like someone in a great maze. There were few ways to penetrate the system Andrea Biaggi had devised for her private world—very few. For the moment Bliss could do little except try to calm Andrea down, try to keep her from getting so frightened that she would do something very self-destructive. He let her go that day with qualms. There was something brewing, but he didn't know quite what. It would do no good to put her in the hospital as he half wished he could. That was no way to build up her confidence in him, particularly after her history of commitment. Best to let her go and see what happened.

The next day Andrea spent twelve hours at work, making seventy-eight hours for the week. During the whole week she had followed her usual pattern. A bright, unemotional problem-solving day filled with accomplishment and smiles for everyone; but then at home, at night alone, reduced to her basic essentials, facing a small room and the prospect of another weekend, she became something else. Something smaller, wilder—something that cringed in corners and curled up under bedsheets as the parade of visions bore down upon her. The emotional pain and her exhaustion were unbearable to her now. It was much, much worse than she could remember it being for many years. There was her mother's death, her isolation from home and family, her loneliness in a city she did not understand, her distrust of a new psychiatrist. What was all this about multiple personalities? What was this thing about hypnosis and buried traumas? It was all foolishness and lies. The truth of the matter was much clearer than that. She was simply, irrevocably crazy, just like her father had been, just like her sister was becoming. A hard genetic insanity that slowly ate away at reason leaving behind it a screaming, blaspheming, crippled creature. What was there for her to do? There was panic in the air. She felt herself giving way to it. She fought against the invasion, but within moments it had overwhelmed her.

Two days later some of her friends at work missed her at a party Andrea was supposed to attend. They tried calling her home but there was no answer. Several more times they tried, with no result. Finally, becoming apprehensive, they drove over to her house. The front door was unlocked and fearing that something had happened to her, they entered.

Something *had* happened. They found her curled up in a corner next to her bed, staring out into space. A shawl was wrapped around her. The oven cleaner had eaten away the skin on her left leg. Where the shawl had covered her leg, it had melted into the flesh. The damage was very severe, that was perfectly obvious. They didn't waste time, but carried her to the car and raced for the hospital. Andrea seemed unaware of where she was or who was with her. She kept repeating over and over: "Please, don't let it hurt. Please, don't let it hurt." And to every appearance it did not hurt. That was the most astonishing thing of all to her friends. That she could have lain in that corner perhaps for days and never felt the excruciating pain.

The nurse who first examined her at the emergency room was no less surprised. Her astonishment took the form of anger at Andrea for having done this thing to herself.

"You should have come in earlier! What was wrong with you! Didn't you know how seriously you were hurt?"

There was no way that Andrea could know, for she felt nothing, hardly even that she had injured herself. Later, when her leg was swaddled in bandages, and she was put into bed, the attending physician tried to urge on her a large dose of a painkiller, believing, as was normal to believe, that her pain must be exceedingly great. Andrea declined the shot, saying she felt nothing.

To suffer an extensive third-degree burn on the leg and never feel the pain! It was impossible for either the physician or his assistants to understand such a thing. But for Andrea there was no trick to it. She had rarely been aware of physical pain in her life, no matter what its origin, and now was no exception. The burn required several grafts and some plastic surgery to repair it. Even then, the injury left a large, livid scar that would fade only gradually.

As soon as Dr. Bliss found out about the newest mutilation attempt, he saw Andrea. They talked for several hours, and Andrea seemed remarkably calm, as if in some way the injury had cleared her. When Bliss inquired about this, Andrea told him that this often happened after an attack—that hurting herself helped "relieve pressures inside," like pulling the cork on a wine bottle or lancing a boil.

"Why didn't you tell me you were so close to an incident like this?" he asked her.

"I didn't know it myself, Dr. Bliss. When the fighting began I couldn't tell how frightened I was. I wasn't getting the right signals. Everything was blocked off. I never knew I was so close to losing control. Really."

"Okay. But just to give me some peace of mind, would you agree to stay in the hospital until we're safe."

Andrea thought about this for a moment. "All right. I don't like hospitals, but I see your point. You've got to let me out when I ask though . . ."

"Agreed without condition."

It was something he'd seen so many times before but was nonetheless impressed each time it occurred anew. Andrea Biaggi was so lucid now, so obviously in her "right mind" (whatever *that* was); it seemed irreconcilable with the state of mind that had brought her to such a brutal attack on herself.

Andrea Biaggi would be a very tough case to unravel.

DR. BLISS'S NOTEBOOK
September 21, 1979

During Andrea's last few days on the ward I have been trying to strengthen her, so there might be some protection against further devastating self-mutilation. She insisted on going back to her apartment and job, in fact, cogently pointed out that being on a ward is meager protection. One of her most serious suicide attempts apparently occurred in a hospital, and she fights self-mutilation just as ferociously in the hospital as out of it.

In hypnosis she presents a delicate problem, for any approach to critical processes sends her deeply into self-hypnosis, out of control. She keeps reiterating the danger and the fighting. There is a grim, powerful force that threatens to destroy her. I have attempted to enlist Berna-dette, Mother Mary, Christ, even God, but they bring only temporary surcease. I have suggested, even had these divinities *tell* her, that God is forgiving, a being of love not hate, but the intensity of the central core soon overwhelms even this assistance.

I have urged the male, who is a malevolent spirit, to speak with me while Andrea is absent, but have insisted that the discussion be calm and peaceful. I have repeated my offers, but Andrea is fearful, and he is unwilling to appear. I could force the issue but this would create chaos and unhinge Andrea, so I must be patient. However, I am subtly building the case, I hope, that this reluctance is a sign of his weakness and uncertainty—else he would meet me for an open discussion.

Andrea keeps speaking in hypnosis about "a great fight inside." In her case and many others, it is obvious that the adult takes a powder, leaving the unprotected child in the traumatic world of those earlier years. Furthermore, adult reason doesn't easily penetrate into that crazy hypnotic world, and her panics make it impossible to proceed.

In a session where I invoked Jesus and Mother Mary, Andrea cried out as she wept, "I feel unworthy—what Jesus and Mary say—I'm not all bad—punishment too much—try to love self more—I'm worthy but don't feel it. The others inside fight so much."

As a trial, I attempted an intellectual reconstruction with Andrea of the processes at work. I recognize full well that this may have little therapeutic benefit, but the hope is that my intellectual efforts may prepare her a bit for later hypnotic experiences.

I was also curious to see how much she might reconstruct since this unconscious material is so close to the surface. These people have total amnesia for so many early memories although many seem so obvious. This seems to be a cardinal rule in all of these cases.

We began by examining in the conscious state the possible meanings of fire and burning. She said, "Impure thoughts. My father tricked me. At times he was affectionate, hugged, kissed, and touched me"—the last being some digital sexual play.

From our hypnotic sessions I have reconstructed that he also blew in her ear, which was apparently erotic. At first all of these activities on the part of her father, including masturbating her, were perceived as signs of affection. But a cruel awakening occurred when her mother and the nuns educated her to the "evil" of sexuality. She came to feel herself an evil sinner, necessitating punishment. At nine or ten she decided to expiate her sins by entering a convent and becoming a nun—something she did later. And when her father was committed to a psychiatric hospital, she perceived it as her fault. The Catholic ethic was doing its work. In the convent the self-burning began.

There was also another thread to this story. Andrea was afraid for her family—fearful that her father was so dangerous he might kill them. Before entering the convent, she felt "sexual as a person." But the nuns preached "perfection," and the garb was designed to give "no shape to the body." She curbed all sexual feelings when she became a nun as that was part of the path to perfection. However, the potent preachings against sexuality, mingled with guilt and early sexual experiences with her father, were obviously fermenting to produce a monumental guilt.

12

Sister Jeanine

BLISS pressed on with greater speed now that he had seen firsthand what the Evil Force could do to Andrea. There was need to isolate that malevolence and, if possible, force it out in the open where Andrea could understand it and, he hoped, extirpate it. But how to do it was the problem. The principles might be simple, but the process could be difficult. Integration seemed the most logical means of effecting a cure, but sometimes Bliss wondered if such a process was not superficial. He had treated a few cases of women and men who could reintegrate personalities at high speed, but these were the gratifying exceptions.

From Andrea's point of view, the process was no less difficult and certainly a good deal more traumatic. Dr. Bliss called himself a psychiatrist, but he quite obviously practiced an occult form of the discipline. His zeal revealed the soul of a guru more than the plodding spirit of a physician. It was hard to trust him completely, or at least trust him the way one was supposed to trust a doctor. It was easier to have *faith* in him, as one would have in a priest. Perhaps that was what kept the relationship going.

Something about it felt right. There were certainly people in there—in Andrea's closet. She had known of them—or at least had recognized them in certain states of mind. But she had never identified them by name. The naming was a new experience. Now, as the characters were forced from the closet to speak, she became involved in a rite of baptism—giving names to the voices she had housed all these years.

The first definite personality to emerge was on September 27, 1979. It was a voice and a look that Bliss had seen before but had not yet identified conclusively. From the outset, he recognized the personality for what it was—a very important ally in the struggle for Andrea's sanity.

"What is your name?" he asked after summoning her.

"I am Sister Jeanine." Andrea's face had become expressionless, and the voice he heard reflected that lack of expression. There was no emotion here—nothing to obscure or subjectify observation. She was only intellect—a thinking machine.

"What do you do, Sister Jeanine?"

"Andrea is torn in many ways, Dr. Bliss. Some of the ways are very dangerous." Her sentences were clipped, concise, unblurred. "I help her keep order and discipline— things kept clean, so she goes to work and does things she is supposed to do. I drive her hard. When she was eight and decided to become a nun, I came."

"Why was that?"

"It was before her father came back from the hospital. She had scarlet fever and a bad kidney infection and was in the hospital for a long time. Her mother was busy with the other children, and the nuns in the hospital were the only ones who gave her comfort. I became part of her from that time. I came the night she couldn't breathe in the hospital. She was really sick and could hardly breathe and she became very scared. A nun came in and helped her. She could breathe again and felt safe. The nun's name was Sister Jeanine."

"And that was you?"

"Yes. Before that time the nuns and schoolteachers were very harsh to her. After she left the hospital and was sick, her mother couldn't come, so Andrea had me come instead. Later things changed, and I helped her with self-discipline."

"Who else is there, Sister Jeanine?"

The answer was prompt, even matter-of-fact. "There is

a young little girl, Andrea-Ellen. She is just there. She is frozen—like in a cage. She can't get out and has been there for many years.''

"Yes?"

"There are lots of other voices. The worst is the one trying to make her die and that is the older one—very strong now. He was there the other night when she hurt herself so badly. Then there is one who laughs at her all the time. That one is a teenage girl who says Andrea is ugly. She is very cruel. And there are others, but they are hard to separate because they come together and live in the same space.''

"Try to separate them."

"There is another helper who tries to calm her down and tell her everything will be all right. She is an older woman.''

"Do you think this older woman will help now that Andrea is so sick?"

Another voice appeared suddenly, replacing Sister Jeanine's. It was softer, more mature—for all the world like an older woman. "I haven't helped her before except to work, but I think I could help now." The look on Andrea's face changed abruptly, and Bliss knew that Sister Jeanine was back.

"Andrea felt more secure to come here today. She had a psychiatrist who was a Gestalt therapist, and sometimes it was like hypnosis. He would have her close her eyes and picture things.''

"I see." Things were beginning to clarify. "Are you hard on her at times, Sister Jeanine?"

"I always say she can do things even when she says no. When she is tired at work and says she needs rest, I say she must work. When she was little she was very lazy. I have a hard time knowing when she is lazy, but she has pain now. I won't push her. She wants to stay in bed. Most of the time I wouldn't let her. It brings on panics. The more she feels like panicking, the more I make her work. I keep the panics away.''

"But maybe it would be better to let up a bit."

"You think so?" It was a sincere question, like one specialist consulting with another.

"Yes. But you know her better. I'll leave it up to you."

"Then I say, she must work. We must work together on her, Dr. Bliss. I don't know what else to do except make her work harder. Perhaps you can come up with another cure."

"Well, the first thing I think we should do is work on her guilt. Can you help me with that?"

"I'll try," Sister Jeanine said. "I like you. I've come out because you want to help her. Not like those others. It is important that you think she can be forgiven. She doesn't know that, you know. She thinks she is damned. She pictures herself as an adulteress, with people spitting on her, hitting her, calling her names. When you said it didn't have to be that way, it was the first time she considered it. Before she would always stand there and take it because she thought she deserved all their abuse."

"That guilt isn't deserved," Bliss said. "If what I think is correct, Andrea isn't responsible for any of the things that happened to her."

"We will work together then," Sister Jeanine said. "It is very hard to tell you about the inside. It is so fragile, you see. She is still in grave danger. Some of us are getting stronger but we aren't near as strong as the evil ones. And she is losing the part of her that thinks well. She needs to get that part back if she is to understand. Once that happens she can be very good. You need to help her get stronger."

"Any suggestions?" Dr. Bliss asked.

"Yes. She needs more support for awhile. She thought her friends would visit her in the hospital more. But no one has. She is reluctant to ask them to come. It was difficult for her to ask to see you, even. She needs more from you for a little while, Dr. Bliss. When she is stronger she won't demand so much."

"The big thing, I think," Bliss said, "is to convince her she isn't wicked."

"That will be very difficult. She believes that she is very bad and that her punishment is perfectly deserved. She thinks she will be stoned to death. That is the picture. She still feels very bad. She doesn't know whether life is worth living. You can't imagine the fight inside of her. It goes on all the time now.''

At the conclusion of the interview, when Andrea returned, she remembered nothing of the conversations, denying that she had ever heard of Sister Jeanine. Bliss had a feeling that Sister Jeanine would prove to be a valuable ally, denied or not.

ANDREA'S JOURNAL
September 23, 1979

I woke up around 4 a.m. yelling and crying—half in a state between nightmare and waking. I was very confused as to where I was and what time it was and what had actually happened. I finally got out of bed to go into the living room to sit and calm down. Instead of being able to calm down though, I became more frightened and after about one hour was very out of control—feeling like another person. For some reason I turned on the fireplace, and went over to sit in front of it. I stared at the flames for a while, which then started changing colors, becoming part of me. Before I knew it, I was putting my hand nearer and nearer, finally into the fire. This time I could feel the pain and tried to pull back. I brought my hand out before any real damage could be done. Then I remember feeling angry that I could still feel—tried putting my hand in again—this time more intentionally. The intensity of the heat prevented me from being able to keep it in long enough. I was fighting with myself inside. Many voices inside yelling at each other. Then, it all just calmed down, and I closed the curtains to the fireplace and turned it off. I then lay down on the couch to try and sleep while still feeling very depressed, but, luckily, no longer panicked . . .

Sister Jeanine continued to be a pivotal figure in deciphering the thicket of emotions and motivations that had reduced Andrea Biaggi to such madness. Had there not been so many components to that tapestry, there would not have been so much craziness. First and foremost, there was the madness of her father, Joseph, who had done many things both to endear and repel his oldest daughter. Exactly how many incidents of abuse there had been between the two, Dr. Bliss still couldn't tell, but he had a feeling the number would prove to be substantial. Next, there was the apparent indifference of her mother. It was all well and good for Andrea to remember how frightened her mother had been, how incapable of stopping the abuse, but this only ameliorated the situation now on a rational and conscious level. The main dilemmas were still decades deep and dwelt on an irrational and unconscious level, having nothing to do with later "deathbed confessions" and last-moment friendship between mother and daughter.

Next there was the question of the family's extreme poverty. Many agonies are saved the well-to-do or even moderately well-off family; poverty invokes many strictures not only on family economies but on family relationships, proving a corrosive influence. Add to this the nature of the family—the Italian and Corsican priorities stressing an almost martial obedience to father and husband and a mindless fidelity to family and kin that strips away both reason and humanity. Under such a system, few people prosper.

Finally there was the intensity and nature of the Catholic influence. Andrea's early life had been wrapped up in the many cultural and religious activities of the church. They had effectively created a mythology that further rigidified an already overstructured moral system for Andrea. There were few shades of gray in such a world—only blacks and whites, with borders and margins and stop signs, leading down a very narrow path. On either side were saints and priests adjuring faith, asseverating obedience without question. There was no room for questioning or, at least, very little—and that given over to catechism. Religion and rigid doctrine at its most fundamental, at least for the child, is a take-it-or-leave-it proposition with dire consequences for leaving.

Added to all these other factors, Dr. Bliss hypothesized, was a genetic predisposition to hypnosis that needed only to be actuated to start the whole self-hypnotic process. Whether, of course, he was correct in his assumption still required investigation.

Andrea Biaggi was more than just another patient. She was a test of Dr. Bliss's theory and the therapeutic process. She was as sick as any patient he had seen with this self-hypnotic pathology. If she could be helped, perhaps cured, it would mean that it was, in principle, possible to heal even extreme cases of the disorder. His tactics were obviously crude, but the important thing was to find out whether her pernicious illness could be affected at all.

In their very next session Bliss found himself involved in a three-way conversation, in which his role was largely that of a moderator while the other two parts were played by Andrea and Sister Jeanine. The curtain went up as soon as Bliss told Andrea to go into hypnosis. She was under as soon as he said, "Let me speak to Sister Jeanine, Andrea."

Bliss began by asking Sister Jeanine a question that had been gnawing at him since their last session—one he felt was basic to an understanding of Andrea's self-destructive impulses:

"Why do you think Andrea feels so evil, so sinful?"

"Part of the reason," came the calm reply, so characteristic of Sister Jeanine, "was that Andrea felt so responsible for her father's hospitalization."

"Yes?"

"That is why she decided to become a nun. As a penance for her part in his commitment."

"Is there anything we can do to correct that misconception?"

"I don't know. She was so young. The lesson was learned so deeply. Her father was such a big person in her life, and her mother made Andrea believe that she was responsible."

"How?"

"That isn't clear, Dr. Bliss, but there was a lot of yelling between them—and her mother punished her. Her mother thought she should have resisted. But there were many times when she couldn't get away. She would never know when he would come after her. Sometimes he would give her candy bars, but other times he would hurt her. Sometimes she would hide in the closet, but other times her mother would be away and he would catch her. He would do it when he was drunk but also when he was sober. It was hard to tell. It went on for many years at frequent intervals. Andrea didn't ever tell her mother because he threatened to use a knife on her if she did—that he would really hurt her. She tried to hide when she thought it would be bad, but she was confused by him a lot of the time. He would change his moods so quickly."

"What kind of things would he do to her?" Bliss asked.

The reaction was immediate. Andrea's face became contorted, the eyes fluttering, her whole body tossing about in the chair. "I . . . can't . . . must not . . . Hurt . . . Hurt. Bad, bad, bad!"

A storm of fists buffeted her head, and it took all Bliss's strength to restrain her.

"Let me talk to Sister Jeanine," he demanded.

The turmoil subsided; Andrea's arms dropped to her side, and the face returned to a passive attentiveness.

"Yes, Dr. Bliss?"

"What just happened?"

"You asked . . . a difficult question. The others will not let me answer."

"All right." Bliss struggled with a stratagem for circumventing this obstacle.

"Why aren't you free to tell me these things?"

"You need to know, Dr. Bliss, that I'm being pulled away. I am not in full control here. There are others."

"Does Andrea know any of these things?"

"Only what little she learned with Dr. Holt in the one Gestalt session, and she doesn't believe it. She suspects, but most of her doesn't want to know, and the others protect her from the truth."

"So she really doesn't believe that her father hurt her?"

"No. She would not want to believe. Her memory is very selective," Sister Jeanine said. "She only remembers that her mother blamed her for destroying the family. That is part of the fighting inside—her mother yelling at her . . . I can hear her voice saying that even now. I can hear her say she was the one who destroyed the family and made him go away."

"You mean Andrea's mother, Dara Biaggi, is inside of Andrea?"

"Of course." It was another matter-of-fact statement implying surprise that such a situation was not perfectly obvious to Bliss. "Her mother was scared, you see. There were so many children and so little money—sometimes none at all. She never wanted to break up the family, but it made life very hard for her. It was only when Andrea was caught that the breaking became necessary."

"But it wasn't really Andrea's fault. It was her father's and her mother's fault. How can we get Andrea to realize this fact?"

There was a pause of several minutes while Sister Jeanine and several other shadows passed across Andrea's face. Finally, "There is a lot of fighting, too much fighting, they are trying to choke everything off . . ."

"Can I help?" Bliss realized that Sister Jeanine's voice was growing fainter, as if she were being dragged away.

"It is hard now. I feel I'm losing control. I feel like I'm drowning . . ."

Had that been Sister Jeanine's voice or Andrea's? There was a quality that partook of both. It was a transition voice, as the one character rose reluctantly to the surface and the other was submerged by characters and opposition about which Bliss knew nothing yet.

"I feel like . . . like I'm drowning. There . . . there is . . . fighting. Lots of fighting. A feeling like . . . like wanting to hurt. Sin. Badness. Evil . . ." The eyes fluttered open and shut as Andrea went through several contortions, careening wildly from mood to mood. Or was it from character to character?

Suddenly Sister Jeanine reasserted herself: "Her mother was dying. She wanted her mother to say it was all forgiven. But she died before she could talk to her—that made it harder. She is still dying, you know. Always dying—the same present in the past and past in the present."

"If I were to talk to her mother now, Sister Jeanine, would that help?"

"Her mother is dead," exclaimed Jeanine in surprise. "It is impossible to talk to the dead . . ."

Suddenly Andrea appeared again. "You must know I am drowning. Please. I . . . am . . . drowning . . ."

Then, just as suddenly, Sister Jeanine reappeared, and the look of turmoil on Andrea's face cleared.

"How does Andrea feel now?" asked Bliss.

"Almost as if she'd been in a physical battle and someone had beat her up. The dangerous part is the fighting. When that stops things are a lot quieter."

"But can Andrea hear what is being said? Does she understand that she is not guilty?"

"She is a little girl, and she is very scared and mixed up. She is pure fear—afraid of her mother and father. They yell at her, and she is afraid of being physically hurt. She was told never to say anything to anyone about it."

"Have you tried to comfort the little girl yourself, Sister Jeanine?"

"Last night when she was scared I was able to rock and comfort the child so she could sleep. She needs her mother to tell her. That is what she has wanted for years. It has to come from her mother." Andrea's eyes seemed to look beside her as if someone was whispering into her ears. "She has been calling for her mother a lot, but I have told her to let her mother's spirit rest. She isn't sure at times that her mother is really dead."

After a little more conversation Andrea reappeared, looking pale and shaken. Once again, when asked if she had heard or understood any of Sister Jeanine's revelations, Andrea could only shrug. Yes, some of it had been heard, as if in a dream, but most of it was still too vague.

ANDREA'S JOURNAL
September 28, 1979

Despite these revelations in therapy, my day-to-day life continues in a state of one crisis after another. I returned to work after the skin graft surgery for the burn. I am still quite physically ill, and the graft site on my leg became very infected so that I can walk only with great pain. Most people around me are very considerate and concerned. They all keep asking how it happened, and I have to tell lie after lie, only making myself feel more alien from all of them and less able to reach out for any help from even my closest friends.

It is so very critical that there be no knowledge of what really happened. I fear losing my job if any revelation of psychiatric problems emerges—it is a fear well-grounded in reality. I also have to try to work even harder and longer hours again. This time to prove to myself that I can still attend to "normal" things despite the insanity surrounding my life. Being at work and being an administrator are both vitally important symbols to me. They are my total identity outside my crazy world, and the loss of that job would mean the loss of my life, or certainly another attempt at suicide.

It is important to note that I did not merely maintain the "appearance" of a normal working person during these crazy times—I was actually a highly capable and productive worker at whatever I attempted. I could also perform a variety of complex tasks, for example, supervising a staff, administering a budget, meeting with various agencies, and designing new programs. I could do all these things and do them all quite well. That ability was there just as long, and often as strong, as the crazy times. That is why I had so often thought of myself as Dr. Jekyll and Mr. Hyde. In the nine to five working world I was very successful, with professional acknowledgments from national organizations and many peers. But in the evenings and on weekends at home, I was often unable to make even the simplest decision (what clothes to wear, what to eat, what to do) and frequently my behavior would become dangerous, self-destructive, completely out-of-control.

13

Andrea-Ellen

DR. BLISS'S NOTEBOOK
September 29, 1979

ANDREA was in a light trance when I saw her. She told me that self-punishment stops her from seeking help. She needs friends now and medical care for infection in her leg, but a "force" prevents her from seeking it.

"I must get myself together, but I'm so out of touch with my body that I don't know what is right." I tried hypnosis to calm her, but she became frightened. "Voice saying I have control, and you will stay here forever."

But after a little more talking I managed to calm her fears sufficiently for her to talk more rationally.

"I feel calmer now. Part inside says it's okay and no one will hurt you—and I concentrate real hard. I feel drained after all this."

I asked her to go into hypnosis and, as usual, she was immediately under. Then I asked to talk to Sister Jeanine, who appeared.

"I got lost again yesterday. This morning, I tried to get her going. I had her take aspirin and do some work. Maybe I'm pushing her too much. She needs more help. I had her drive here, but it was dangerous driving. She can't concentrate enough yet."

I asked her if there was anyone else there who could help. Sister Jeanine answered, "She was calling for Jesus and Mother Mary, but they didn't come and she felt abandoned. Others are so strong now.''

"But Jesus and Mother Mary help the weak and the sick,'' I suggested.

"But she has to be able to hear and feel them. The others yell so loud—almost as if her mind and senses are possessed.''

"Don't Jesus and Mother Mary have greater power?''

"I think there is something else blocking. She can't even ask for simple help, like taking out the garbage.''

I asked, "Please take a look and see what the block is.''

There was a pause while Sister Jeanine looked, and then, "It goes deeper than voices. She thinks she doesn't deserve help—just punishment.''

"Can we open her mind to the possibility that punishment is not correct?'' It was the same tactic I had used on the last few sessions, but so far with little or no success.

"There are times,'' said Sister Jeanine, "when she sees it. But then the voices come back.''

I was stumped for a second or two. Then another strategy occurred to me, and I immediately tried to implement it.

"Would it be helpful if I spoke to the little girl?''

Another transformation took place. Sister Jeanine abruptly disappeared. Andrea seemed to shrink in front of me. She curled up on the chair. Her whole manner suggested fear of me and suspicion.

"I'm Dr. Bliss,'' I said, "and I'm here to help you. You don't have to be afraid. How old are you?''

"I'm seven.'' It was a small, childlike voice and, if I had merely heard the voice without seeing the face, I would easily have assumed it came from a seven-year-old or someone even younger.

I then spoke at some length about her unreasonable guilts—the torment of a little girl who misunderstands. At the end of my talk, she said, "Confusing,'' and that was all.

"Let me say just one more thing,'' I offered, feeling that she was slipping away. "You are a little child and you don't understand. If you did, you'd know that you weren't responsible for your father's problems or your mother's anger.'' But the child wasn't there anymore. Sister Jeanine was back, sitting straight in the chair.

"She wanted to run away. I kept her from running, but she was very scared. She is very mixed up. She is Little Andrea-Ellen. She is pure fear.''

"She needs psychiatric help,'' I told her.

"I can hold her more and make her feel warm, not so scared,'' suggested Sister Jeanine.

"Do you think Andrea is less blocked now?''

"Yes.''

But despite Sister Jeanine's assurances, when Andrea re-emerged she seemed completely out of it.

"The time doesn't feel right yet—I feel like I'm drowning again.''

I then gave another long recital about guilts, telling her how sure I was that she would be better. And, in truth, when she left the office, I felt as though there had been some improvement in her condition.

ANDREA'S JOURNAL
September 30, 1979

This incident happened about a month ago. I was feeling very tense and anxious for several days. I would go to work and could fairly handle my job, but would totally fall apart when I went home. Then I would get frightened of noises—lights were too bright—and I kept feeling like I wanted to burst through a window or something. Whenever I closed my eyes, I would see a gun pointed at my head. Then the gun would go off, and there would be an explosion of blood. This went on for several days, and I was feeling desperate. One night late, I took a walk to try and calm down some. I wasn't able to walk far as I became frightened of everything outside. I had nearly gotten back to the apartment when I spotted a cat at the entrance way. I took the cat in, I remember, and I felt very calm. I could tell it was an alley cat—it had that look about it.

I got out some milk and cheese and started feeding it. I walked to the linen closet and got a towel out while the cat was still eating. I then grabbed the cat with the towel and started to strangle it. It was a large cat so there was a lot of struggle. It then became like a fight for the cat's life or mine, and I used all my energy to kill it. In between, a voice inside me would say no, no, no, but I coldly kept doing it.

When the cat finally died, I got some heavy string and a bag from the kitchen. I tied the string around the cat's neck tight in case it wasn't really dead, and put it in the bag. I don't remember the rest of the evening. The next morning, the cat smell was very strong and repulsive. I put it in my car to take it somewhere—I finally brought it to a garbage dump. I left it there and went to work. No one knew anything. I tried to work like nothing happened. But the cat smell would come back to me whenever I was panicky that entire next week.

For the first thirty minutes of their session on October 1, 1979, Bliss discussed his theory about self-hypnotic states, and Andrea seemed fascinated. Until quite recently, it had never occurred to her that such an explanation for her condition existed.

"If I'm right," Bliss said, "you've been going in and out of hypnotic states most of your life, actually spending a very small percentage of your time as Andrea Biaggi."

"But how?"

"Simple. At least simple for you. Because of both upbringing and heredity, you've developed this ability—as many as 20 percent of all people may have it—of hypnotizing themselves at will, without knowing it. Only in your case, like some others, the mechanism has gotten out of hand. You can do it anytime when something unpleasant comes up, transporting yourself into another place."

"Not literally into another place—not like, what is it, teleportation or something."

"Of course not. But the hypnotized person sometimes doesn't know that. There's no objectivity there, no way for them to say, 'This is only imaginary,' or 'I'm just dreaming,' or something like that. For them, it's perfectly real. I'll give you an example. As an experiment I've sent a subject to the moon.''

"Oh, really?" Andrea looked at him strangely.

"Again, not literally. But in a trance state. I just hypnotized him and then told him he was on the moon, and damned if he wasn't on the moon, at least as far as he was concerned—surrounded by craters and moon dust. For him, it was perfectly real while he was in hypnosis. That's the fascinating thing about hypnosis. You're not only seeing a hallucination, you're hearing it and smelling it and touching it. It defies detection by all of the senses, like some kind of complete, sensory theater inside your head.''

"I wish it were as pleasant as going to a movie. But for the most part, whatever happens, it sure doesn't seem to be.''

"That's because of the forces that cause you to go into self-hypnosis to begin with. You're reacting to pain, to experiences in your past too painful to deal with.''

Bliss asked her to go into hypnosis. As usual, she was immediately under.

"Now I want you to remember what goes on there, Andrea," Bliss said.

As if from some deep cavern, Andrea's voice came querulously. "I'm listening. I'll try."

"Good." It was the best he could expect right now. "Well, then, let me talk to Sister Jeanine."

Andrea seemed to sit up straighter in her chair, and her face lost any vestige of anxiety or fear.

"Yes, Dr. Bliss." The voice was soft and emotionless.

"How is Andrea doing today?"

"Better. Going back to work helped her. Her friend was also helpful. The house is back in order. She was surprised how much the friend knew already—realized what had gone on when she was alone.''

"Would Little Andrea-Ellen remember?" Bliss asked.

"I don't know. If you talk with her, my instinct is to stay away from those feelings."

"What would you do?"

"There is less danger today, so it might be all right." But Sister Jeanine didn't sound sure.

Bliss went ahead. "Well, let's hear from Little Andrea-Ellen then."

Andrea curled up in the chair. Suddenly she was a fat little girl, looking at Bliss from between her fingers.

"Are you afraid?" Bliss asked gently.

"Because you will hurt me," came the piping, muted answer.

"But I won't hurt you. I'm a doctor, and I promise not to hurt you."

"I'm—I—I'm n-n-not sup-posed to talk . . . 'bout th-th-things." It was an elemental torment to speak. The tongue and palate wavered and rippled, cleaving to each other. Whole areas of her brain seemed simply to have closed down.

"Sometimes it's helpful to talk about these things."

"I don't know . . . what to tell you. Keep . . . keep feeling like . . . like someone is going . . . going to hit me. Hit me if I say something."

"Would it be helpful if I tell you what I know?" Bliss asked.

Little Andrea-Ellen nodded her head.

Bliss took a stab at what he hoped was the root of her problems. "I know you love your father, but he is unpredictable. Sometimes he is very good, but sometimes he does terrible things. At first you enjoyed it, but later you became guilty."

"It . . . it hurt me more later," Little Andrea-Ellen whimpered and began to strike herself forcefully on the head and face.

Bliss had to restrain her again. "You're afraid that you'll be hit by him?"

The little girl nodded her head.

Flushed and distressed, Andrea reappeared. She had obviously been listening and was terribly upset. "She is so scared. So scared. You don't know how scared. She was hurt physically—real bad. You make her remember in the room.''

"The room? What's the room, Andrea? Tell me about it.''

"Please, I can't. I . . . I . . . when the fighting starts . . . *please*, stop!''

The eyes went quickly blank, and for a moment longer Andrea seemed completely torpid. After a few seconds, however, light returned to her eyes. She shook her head very hard.

"Can you remember anything, Andrea?'' Dr. Bliss asked at last.

"No. I don't.''

Warily, he asked the most important question: "Do you wish to remember?''

"No,'' came the answer.

ANDREA'S JOURNAL
October 3, 1979—1 A.M.

I have been reluctant to write since the session the day before yesterday. My memories of the content of the session are not clear, but there is a constant sense of ''dread'' when I approach that time with my mind.

I am more conscious of the dynamics that occurred as a result of the session. When I came out of hypnosis something was wrong—I guess I really wasn't all the way "out,'' since I remember having slight sensory and balance problems for about an hour afterward.

The next thing I remember was wanting to run from some unknown—something trying to hurt me, kill me. The result was that I returned to work and pushed myself to perform even harder than normal.

After work, this ''driving'' force continued as I sat and wrote many letters, yet not daring to write about the session that night.

By bedtime, I was exhausted and in a great deal of physical pain from the graft taken from my leg. Yet I stayed up writing quite late (2 or 3 A.M.) fearful to actually go to bed. I gave little thought to all these feelings, and passed them off quite lightly.

When I finally went to bed, I started to get very restless, then panicky, and cried in an almost childlike way. There were no thoughts that I remember, just an overwhelming flowing of emotions. I slept through the rest of the night.

Today has been filled with much the same pattern and sense. I have pushed and worked even harder—a twelve-hour day with every moment needing to be filled. I have been more-physically ill earlier this evening, running another temperature. I have avoided writing this note until the last moment. It is 1 A.M. now and I can sense my exhaustion, but also a vague mist of fear at having to cease activity. There is no panic, but neither is there peace.

I am also acutely aware of my ambivalence about returning for another session tomorrow. I need and want help—this part which is writing and completing this task. But there is another "fragile other" that wants to tear the papers up and not go tomorrow.

Flashes of the last session return—of being in my parents' bedroom—of grave danger. I want to be numb now and not remember.

DR. BLISS'S NOTEBOOK
October 4, 1979—1 P.M.

I had a very difficult time getting Andrea under today. She seemed to be fighting it with every fiber in her body. When finally I was able to contact Sister Jeanine, she seemed dazed.

"I haven't been there at all—I've been blocked out completely."

"Who is doing it?" I asked.

"She's been working so hard, her director side has been driving her very hard. When she is working, no one else can get through."

"Is there anyone else who helps block?"

"Everything seems blank a lot. I can't think right—when you called me there was a fight going on inside, one part wanted to keep me down . . ."

"Who?"

"I don't know. Only seeing black." Sister Jeanine seemed to struggle even with these words.

Abruptly Andrea came out of hypnosis, still agitated and dazed. After a minute of struggle she managed to say, "There was a lot of fighting. Part wanted to hurt you and hurt myself. I keep seeing myself with a gun. Sometimes I have it to my head. Sometimes . . . there is blood on your white medical jacket. Why would I want to hurt you?"

"Maybe because you confuse me with someone else," I answered. It was an easy enough question to answer because another part of Andrea had already given me the answer about a week before. But with this tricky, overlapping memory of hers, it is often difficult, sometimes even impossible, to determine which part or personality holds which memories. This could prove a severe problem later on in therapy.

"Everything is so vivid and clear, as if it is really happening," she told me. "And it almost always involves my mother, father, and Dalia. My mother was upset with me. I was so confused. Something about being crazy, and I was in the hospital and she was yelling that I did something and I kept telling her I didn't do it."

What followed was very confusing. Andrea seemed trapped and kept stammering—actually babbling—without speaking more than a few real words. She gyrated and gesticulated wildly but without apparent meaning. At last after fifteen or twenty minutes, while I tried to bring her back to some kind of coherence, she gasped out this:

"There is something wrong. Blood—I keep going in and out—want to react and hurt self."

Fearing that she might try to hurt herself, I left the office for a moment to get a tranquilizer for her. It was the wrong thing to do. When I returned, there was a bloody fingerprint on my notes.

I was finally able to get Sister Jeanine. I asked her if she had any suggestions.

"I don't know," she said, "except something very wrong underneath. The fighting is so strong or just blank spaces—can't get in touch with her at all. I have become isolated from what's going on there. She left blood so you would know how awful it is. When there's a lot of fighting going on inside, nothing seems to help except hurting herself. There is a big part of her very angry and something else—very strong feelings. The part that makes her work is still pushing her very hard. But that is the only time when she isn't afraid, when she is at work and never stopping. Inside, though, she feels unworthy all the time. She wants to die.''

She paused for a moment and then went on. "There's a lot of blood. One part sees an image of herself shooting herself in the head. Her father had a gun, you know, and sometimes he would scare her with that gun.''

I asked, "Were there any other old experiences with blood, Sister Jeanine?''

Andrea gave a start in her chair, as if she'd just been shocked by a jolt of electricity. "Something is very wrong when you say that.'' For the first time even Sister Jeanine seemed scared. "I sense great danger to go near there.''

"Near where?''

"The old blood. You mustn't go too close to the old blood.''

"What can we do to help her see that?'' I asked.

There was a sustained silence this time, while Andrea flipped around in her seat. Then, "She needs more safety. She is alone too much. I can't help when there is fighting . . .'' The voice was not Sister Jeanine's. I recognized it as Andrea's matronly voice—compassionate and protective of Andrea's childhood. She was nicknamed Mother Mary.

"It is all mixed up inside her. She was hurt very badly many times. Today she saw the picture—being stoned as an evil woman. She is sitting, tearing at her arm. The blood is coming from her while she is seeing the picture.''

"Do you know about this blood, Mother Mary?''

Several gyrations. "I just saw a picture of a meat hook. In the barn at her grandmother's house. Something is very, very bad. She—she is blocked now.''

Shortly after this I ended the session, without getting

any closer to the source of Andrea's terror, but the suggestions of it are enough to send chills down my back. Whatever happened to Andrea Biaggi, it was about as far from pleasant as the human mind can imagine.

NOTE WRITTEN BY ANDREA
October 5, 1979

Scared, isolated, defeated. Great void, no comfort, want to go home—hide—sleep and sleep and sleep. Feel like personal failure—can be big success at work yet tear myself literally. See gun, see blood—HATE that. Want to be back in closet. Am so cold inside—so empty. Can I ever get better? Such a fragile grasp on life. Where is hope, faith, strength—none left inside. People want to help— can't feel them—a prisoner of cold right now. Want to cry but no tears come. Want to run but no energy. "Despair— the sickness unto death." Beyond despair—too much anger, too many tears—Super Andrea can't help inside. Fantasy, be a baby and held and rocked and taken care of. Reality too much now—what to do, don't know what to do. A terrified child in a woman's body . . .

The dike had broken. That was what it felt like. She was overwhelmed by terror, loneliness, episodes of ungovernable panic. And it never seemed to lessen. The first month of therapy with Dr. Bliss had been too upsetting. The anger and terror were, quite literally, out of the closet. She could deny it all she wanted to—and often did—but something horrendous and terrifying was happening to her. Not that she could remember that much about it. So many of the sessions were blanks to her. Who could believe all that mumbo-jumbo, anyway? Self-hypnosis and altered states and other personalities. Who could believe all that? And yet at other times she was less certain. The snarling, violent cynicism disappeared, to be replaced by doubt and, peculiarly, belief. The "other side" believed while not completely accepting. There was a difference after all; no one could have appreciated the paradox more than a Catholic. Faith and acceptance. But there was no denying the crazy scenes that darted through her head—scenes of her father putting a gun to her head, and blood running down her legs. What was all that about? It seemed to feed upon and fuel her self-destructive actions. She was picking at the scab on her leg, making it bleed, glorying in the drops of red streaming down her leg.

Work continued to be both an economic and emotional necessity. Despite the compulsions to self-injury and the wildness that overtook her at night, she was able to function in her job with a high degree of success. None of her employees, including her secretary, were aware of her complex double life, and Andrea gave them no incident to mull over. In everything having to do with her professional life, she was alert, intelligent, involved. She chaired a good many meetings, and was called upon to deliver lectures at regional meetings and even national functions. Under the guise of a compelling and outgoing alter ego, Super Andrea, she prospered. But sometimes in the midst of a meeting, or in midsentence on the podium at some lecture, she would feel the panic advance on her, crawling over the horizon and coming at her, and she wanted to scream and cry.

It wasn't for several weeks that she was able to understand, even superficially, the relationship of this supercharged version of her to the fearful, lonely creature who emerged after the working day was over. That break came in the second month of therapy, during one of Andrea's calmer moments.

Dr. Bliss had been trying to uncover the names and attributes of other personalities but had met strong resistance. She was refusing to go into hypnosis, refusing to cooperate. When occasionally she had submerged, there were only flashes of scenes from her past to terrify her— gruesome, unbelievable scenes, like shots glimpsed in one of those slasher movies. How could anyone believe that?

But now during moments of restraint, of truce, Sister Jeanine came easily and answered questions directly as long as they did not involve quarrying too deeply. Bliss stayed as close to the surface as he could, trying, for sake of a metaphor, to find some other shaft down.

"How can you work so hard," he asked her, "even while you're in the most pain?"

He knew more than half of what the answer might be, but he wanted to see where the answer might lead.

He did not expect what he got.

The face became animated, the eyes sparkling, and the tone of voice conversational.

"I came in high school. Andrea calls me Super Andrea occasionally. You see, Dr. Bliss, she was failing in school before and was considered stupid. In high school she began to study and got good grades." The person Bliss faced now was contagiously friendly. "The teachers and students liked her, so I helped her to become an A student. I'm thirty-one now, just like she is. We've grown up together. In a way, sometimes I'm a lot younger than she is. I can still get excited like I used to in high school when things go well."

"What about Andrea," Bliss asked, "doesn't she get excited too?"

Super Andrea smiled in a friendly way that was infectious. "Andrea herself never believes in the successes. She believes it is more luck than skill, but I know it is skill. She doesn't trust it as much as I do. I know about her school time—I was there."

"And where was Andrea?"

"Hiding. Trying to survive mostly. There were so many problems at home, and she felt so guilty most of the time. She couldn't take much exposure so I buffered her against the outside."

"What specifically brought you?"

"In high school she was failing French, and that scared her. She had a nice teacher who took her aside and said she would help her if she would work harder. She wanted to show the teacher that she could be a real superwoman— and that's when she created me to play that role. Her grades went up, of course, and the teacher liked her more.

That was very important. She was the first teacher—the first woman really—who showed her compassion.''

"Do you remember your first moments in the world?"

"Of course," Super Andrea smiled brightly. "The hallway was dark—she was scared that the teacher was going to fail her—and so things were darker. The teacher was different. It was like other times, when things didn't look right or sound right. And suddenly there I was, fresh from the womb, so to speak, helping her to manage the world, keeping back the fear and building up her confidence."

During the next few sessions Bliss pecked away at the peripheries of Andrea's problem. The most accessible area of her dilemma was the fact and frequency of her self-hypnotic episodes. When he asked Andrea—or some portion of her—about this, she answered straightforwardly that she thought she spent quite a lot of time in some other "place."

"When things upset me—two or three times a week. When they are more calm—about twice a month. They started before grade school."

About the frequency of the episodes, Bliss suspected Andrea was fooling herself. From the brief observation he'd had in the office, it seemed more likely that she spent *most* of her time under, usually as someone else. But then, he had to consider the source of the information, and in this case it appeared to be Super Andrea, who had become the dominant workday character over the last few years. From Super Andrea's point of view, there would only be two or three occurrences a week when she wasn't in charge. From Andrea's perspective, it was probably much more. But that was only the most rudimentary lesson in the relativity of this problem; the real interest came from Super Andrea's statement that the episodes had "started before grade school." That offered an interesting jumping-off point. He asked for Andrea herself.

"What did you think of these self-hypnotic states at the time?" he asked.

"First off, I didn't think of them as being self-hypnotic," she corrected, but then went on. "I wasn't scared by them then as I am now—I just thought all people had them. How else was I to judge? There I was in this crazy family with all of us trying to survive. It never occurred to me that other people might not have a place they could go and hide when it became too much.''

Bliss watched carefully as her face suddenly changed contour. For some reason, the question had tripped a few too many switches, and her eyes grew large with terror. She began to pant, and sweat ran down her brow. The panic had set in. By now he recognized all the symptoms of one of Andrea's frequent panics. It took so little to scare her, particularly when she was in her Andrea mode.

Before she slipped into some character, Bliss asked for Sister Jeanine, and instantly the terror disappeared. With a calm voice utterly devoid of the emotion he had witnessed just seconds before, Sister Jeanine said, ''The fighting is starting again. After you asked her to go into hypnosis, she saw pictures of fire.''

Instantly, Super Andrea was back, a bright, sunny smile on her face.

''I have been very busy this morning. People in the office have been complimenting me—''

Spontaneously, Andrea came out of hypnosis and sat there looking dazed. ''I'm . . . I'm a little spacey.'' She shook her head. ''I'm back now.''

Bliss asked her the same questions about her weekend and received completely different answers from those Super Andrea had given him. For Super Andrea life was great, wonderful, fabulous, couldn't be better. Weekends were no big deal because she wasn't there.

But for Andrea, the weekend was a horror spent in trying to avoid suicide. The recollections of the two characters were so antipodal that it was hard to reconcile them until one considered the nature of Super Andrea's bias. She had been created to protect Andrea—to be the working, potent achiever, the public face that everyone would see and admire for her intelligence and energy. The other Andrea—the tentative one who seemed the original personality—was no more in contact with her real feelings than Sister Jeanine, who had a sometimes clearer image of the way things really were. But it was hard to push Andrea—she teetered on the brink, and seemed utterly incapable of supporting even the slightest shock. Almost anything seemed to launch her into another realm, another personality. But sometimes, like now, it was possible to explore with her certain aspects of the problem, as long as the investigation did not frighten her and cause her to bolt back into some kind of hypnotic hyperspace.

"I got drunk last weekend," she told Bliss, "shortly after I got to this party I was supposed to attend. It wasn't getting drunk like I ever remember happening before. I felt—like two people. The people at the table asked me about the programs—but it was another person who spoke for me—the inside person, the part that was me—was in panic. And I didn't have that much to drink, but somehow. . . . Anyway, I went to my room that night and panicked completely. I was thinking about dying again and about religion. Usually there isn't such a radical separation inside of me, but this time it was phenomenal—a *real* split."

"You've been doing that most of your life," Bliss said. "The only difference now is that you're more aware of the fact."

This seemed to jibe with some understanding she had gleaned from the experience, and she nodded, perhaps not comprehending the situation completely but at least beginning to sense the true nature of it. After that they talked for awhile about her days in the convent, a period that shed considerable light on the sensations she experienced whenever she "split."

"During meditation time, on occasion I would totally lose contact with the environment. Sometimes I would not even be conscious of my body—space, time, the whole thing. There would be a yellow or white light, comfort, warm sensations. It would happen a lot when I was feeling very intense."

"And, of course, you believed you were undergoing a religious experience of some sort," Bliss said.

"No, strangely enough, I didn't have any illusions about that," Andrea said ruefully. "I never kidded myself that it was anything like God calling me. I kept thinking the whole time, there's a frightened child inside this woman's body, trying to get out—not God trying to get in."

The problem was not resolving itself as readily as Bliss might have hoped. He had long since given up on the idea that Andrea Biaggi would be an easy case to solve. There were still characters that were fundamental to her problems but which, for many reasons, had no intention of showing themselves. So far, Bliss had had no success at finding a loophole in Andrea's psychic armor. The main sticking point—at least for now—was Andrea's child self, Little Andrea, who provided the sadness and the guilt for the component parts that made up Andrea. But Little Andrea refused to talk to Bliss—for some reason he reminded the child-self of her father, and even a glimpse of him would usually send her scuttling back into obscurity without so much as a word.

"She is sad and angry," Sister Jeanine would tell him, "and very scared. Especially by men."

"I think it's time we gave Little Andrea an education," Bliss suggested.

Jeanine shook her head. "Super Andrea has studied for all of them, learned psychology, all about mothers and daughters, and read all sorts of things on a lot of subjects. But it doesn't free Little Andrea-Ellen."

"I think I understand," Bliss said. "If you learn these things outside of hypnosis, then there is a block, and it doesn't get inside to the little girl."

"Yes. The only one who came close to her was her father—but then people said that was evil. She could never get close to her mother. When she brought her mother wildflowers—dandelions—her mother would yell at her and throw them away. She has wanted to be close to her mother, but she wouldn't allow it. Now she is screaming for help, but no one will give it to her."

Bliss tried repeatedly to coax the child-self out into the open, but without success. Always the meetings ended with Bliss trying to grasp something that was elusive as air. Despite repeated assurances from him that everything would be all right, that he wouldn't hurt the girl, Sister Jeanine or one of the other personalities would have to interpose, informing him that Little Andrea-Ellen had gone back to her closet and was hiding from him, refusing to come out.

And then there was the fighting, incessant and bitter arguments that often ended in some bloody act of self-injury. Atop it all was the spectacle of Andrea herself, constantly disoriented, forever finding herself in precarious circumstances, forever running from forces she could only dimly understand. She could remember nothing about most of her life, particularly that period before she entered the convent, and certainly could recall nothing of the stories her alter selves were telling Dr. Bliss. It was like dealing with disappearing ink—the writing would appear, spelling out a story from Andrea's past, and then quickly vanish as Andrea came to. There was a conspiracy afoot inside her mind to keep her from understanding the motives behind her actions.

"I felt funny," she told Bliss three weeks into the therapy, "because I didn't remember anything. The next day I concentrated and remembered some of it, then something blocked it off and I forgot it again. I sort of remember—sometimes—but then . . . I keep wanting to tell you something and then suddenly it's no longer in my head, like trying to remember a song you've heard before."

Often, talking to Andrea was like talking to a senile woman. Had it not been for the presence of Super Andrea, Sister Jeanine, and certain lucid moments from Andrea herself, Bliss could just as easily have diagnosed her as a young case of Alzheimer's Disease or dementia praecox.

14

Cats

THROUGHOUT October and into November, Bliss waged a tactical war with the forces inside Andrea Biaggi. Through Sister Jeanine, Mother Mary, and Super Andrea, he was able to glimpse a hazy image of that interior landscape; but there were no road maps there, no names or descriptions—above all, no familiarity. The only other personality that Bliss had so far uncovered, Little Andrea-Ellen, obdurately refused to come out and talk. Everything and everyone in the world seemed to scare her, and Andrea herself was little better. Every session was a roller coaster ride—in and out of hypnosis at breakneck speeds, with sudden, unexpected shifts from one character to another, from the pleasant smile of Super Andrea to the malevolent threats of some as-yet-unidentified character still hiding behind the terror and panic of Andrea herself.

But with all the dead ends and false starts, some progress was still made. Tentative contacts were set up with Little Andrea-Ellen and, though she continued to cower and never felt safe when revealed, she would come to stay for longer and longer periods of time. Occasionally, Bliss would have her long enough to talk to her—but it was really no more than a lecture. Little Andrea-Ellen would just sit there, looking at Bliss with big, frightened eyes.

It was usually left to Sister Jeanine to explain the problems inside. "You see, Little Andrea-Ellen is screaming for her mother and is back in the blue room, her parents' bedroom. She wants to be with her mother. She needs help because that world is too frightening.

"Big Andrea is in trouble. There was a family with whom she lived in Boston. They understood. The woman would hold her when she cried. The woman knew why she was having trouble, and Andrea would be comfortable there.

"It would help most if Big Andrea would be comfortable there. Little Andrea-Ellen can't speak to you yet. She has been trying to tell you—the angry part is mixed up. It isn't clear. She was thinking about killing a cat and bringing it to the hospital and have it hang somewhere. She would do it, but no one would see it. Some strong part can't talk to you. Like the day she put her bloody fingerprint on your notes. She is trying to tell you something. She is very little and very confused."

"When did this cat-killing begin?" Bliss asked.

"She . . . she was living with a family in Boston. She killed one of their cats—"

Abruptly Sister Jeanine was gone, replaced by a frenzied Andrea, her eyes wide with terror.

"No! It's not true. Don't . . . don't listen!"

The roller coaster was off again at top speed, and for the next twenty minutes Bliss could do nothing to calm the series of attitudes and voices that played across Andrea's face. When Bliss tried to bring some measure of order to the chaos, he was shouted down by a whole chorus of Andrea's internal characters. She would not go into hypnosis. She would not! She was wicked, she was stupid, she should be dead. Just let her die—let her die.

The riot was finally quelled as Bliss restrained Andrea from hitting herself. Abruptly, the cool, emotionless voice of Sister Jeanine was back.

"It's the cat. Last night she was thinking about killing another one."

Bliss asked her again about the cat-killing.

"When did it begin?"

The matronly Mother Mary was suddenly there—her

brow furrowed, her voice deep and compassionate. "She has had a cat problem for a long time."

"She must be told about it," Bliss suggested.

"I remember when she started being mean to cats," Mother Mary said. "She always loved dogs. But cats—there is something there."

"What happened?" Bliss asked.

"I don't know. But Little Andrea-Ellen would know. She was there."

Another cul-de-sac, Bliss thought. Go ask Little Andrea-Ellen—but how to make her answer? There was no help in that direction.

Or was there? A new strategy occurred to Bliss. It was perfectly true that Little Andrea-Ellen would not talk for herself, but what if—

"Mother Mary, could you look in Little Andrea-Ellen's mind and tell me if you can read anything there?"

"I could try," came the answer, and Bliss waited tensely to see whether his ploy would work.

A pause, and then Mother Mary returned. "It isn't very clear, but she got very scared. There is a picture in her mind . . ."

"Could you describe the picture?"

"There is her father in the hospital, down in the furnace room, working. He had a repair shop down there."

"Yes? Go on."

"He is opening the door of the furnace—there is a lot of heat and light."

Without warning, Andrea reappeared, shaking her head, sweat breaking out on her brow. "It is not right. You know, it is probably all lies. He was mad at me, you know. I had been bad again. He wanted me to do something, and I didn't want to, and—" She began to pant and gasp, her hands trembling and clawing at the arms of the chair. "That room always scared me—The . . . cat was there. He grabbed it and threw the cat into the furnace. I . . . I was only five or six. I cried and cried. No, it isn't real. How can it be real?" She looked up at Bliss imploringly.

"I think it did happen, Andrea," Bliss said. "I think you must come to terms with that fact and learn how to cope with it if you want to recover."

"Then he really was crazy? He really was a very sick man?"

"Yes, Andrea, I think he was," Bliss said. "A *very* sick man."

"He threw the cat in the furnace?" She was crying now. "Threw that poor cat into the furnace."

"Do you have any idea why he did it?"

"I . . . I think—that is—what he wanted was some sexual stuff, and if I did it he promised he'd take the cat out of the furnace. So I did it. I let him do it—and then he laughed at me—laughed and said the cat was dead and no one could save it. He told me he'd throw me into the furnace if I ever told anyone." She was crying very hard. "But it can't be true. It's all something being made up. Just lies—"

On that note, Bliss had to close the session, knowing full well that the weekend would be hell for Andrea. The unresolved material was sure to fester, undigested, and cause her anguish, but what could he do? He sensed that putting her in the psychiatric ward would do nothing to safeguard her against herself. He would hope that nothing too untoward occurred between Friday and the following Tuesday.

As it turned out, Andrea did have a wild, chaotic weekend, with lots of crying and depression. But something unexpected had occurred to hold the panic in check. She had received several phone calls from her family inviting her for Thanksgiving and, at the same time, she had received a letter asking her to speak at a national conference the following week. There was still conflict, but the professional part of her—Super Andrea in particular—was sky-high about the recognition by such a prestigious national organization. It helped calm her, and, though she had tried to hurt herself several times, the incidents had been minor. At the next session she seemed calmer, more able to talk, and after a few minutes came to the point.

"I was very angry at you when I left and became more so at home. I kept telling myself that what I remembered really hadn't happened. But then when I thought back over it, I decided I wouldn't have gotten so angry if it hadn't really happened. Does that make any sense?"

"Plenty."

"I cried a lot about it, but it was hard to deny. I remembered the first time I tried to hurt a cat. I did the same thing my father had done, except I put it into the refrigerator. That's when I was ten, I think."

"Why cats?"

"They're the only animals I've disliked. It has a lot to do with that day in the furnace room, I guess. And it makes sense in my head when I think about it. You see, it's a struggle between the cat's life and mine. I only do it when things get totally, radically out of control. Part of this weekend, I kept believing none of it had happened. A part of me hid under the covers this weekend. Isn't that strange? A part of me hides under the covers, and another part gives speeches to a hundred people."

"What happens after the speech is over, though?" Bliss asked.

"I feel high for a while and then crash. I was angry because it was too hard to be alone. I was yelling at you, inside, and saying I couldn't do this alone."

Sister Jeanine then appeared and reported, "There have been extreme feelings—some hurting of herself again but not bad—some thinking of dying. Recalling memories is good, but it is hard. She doesn't know how to handle them yet. She has a lot of bad memories. But she needs more safety first before she can really afford to remember."

"I understand. How is Little Andrea-Ellen doing?"

"Right now she is quiet but she trusts you a little more, I think, though she is still very scared."

"Do you know any of the other people with Little Andrea-Ellen?" Bliss asked.

Andrea was abruptly out of hypnosis, and babbling. "There was something angry. It was . . . was laughing at

me. It slit throat with knife and I saw blood. Awful.
Bad—''

Bliss's tactics could not, at this stage, have been compared to a traditional psychotherapeutic approach. Andrea
Biaggi's problem did not reduce itself to the usual forms of
investigation. The group of ''people'' who made up Andrea's secret ''family'' were bent on preventing both their
own exposure and Andrea's recovery. It hadn't promised
to be easy to outwit them, and it hadn't proved to be. Most
of the more straightforward approaches had failed misera-
bly. What was left to Bliss were the hit-and-run methods
of the guerrilla: trying to keep the opposition off balance
with a string of unanticipated questions; using sneak attacks and camouflaged questions to undermine their strength;
backtracking and faking attacks to disorient them. Sometimes it was he who felt punchy, used up, ambushed, and
only occasionally would he slip through the defenses and
open up a new area of inquiry.

One of the ploys that worked was having Big Andrea act
as a co-therapist, deputizing her to look into the workings
of the forces that ruled her inner world. One of the first
things uncovered was a peculiar incident involving Andrea's mother.

''Fire was with both mother and father,'' Big Andrea
said, talking of herself in the third person. ''There was a
very bad time with her mother. It was after her father left.
Her mother was always upset and yelling at her. She was
always bringing her mother flowers. And she went to work
to make money to buy her mother a dress and help support
the family. She came home one day and brought the dress
in a box. Her mother was out in the back, burning leaves.
She handed the box to her mother, and her mother started
to scream at her. She was very angry because Andrea
wasn't home to help her, so she threw the box into the fire
and kept yelling at her. She became very upset then, and
stopped feeling. It was like being in the closet—she just
stopped feeling.''

''What was the problem with her mother?'' Bliss asked.

''She had many problems with money, but she also was angry at Andrea. She blamed her, said it was her fault that her father was gone.''

Andrea tried to remember this episode outside of hypnosis, but it was difficult for her. The recollection of her mother's anger and blame went counter to the way she wished to remember her. Every time she tried to recall the details, she would get dizzy and the walls would begin to reel and waver, becoming insubstantial. She would flush and begin to sweat copiously. For awhile, she felt like she was coming down with the flu, but Bliss managed to convince her that the symptoms were probably psychosomatic, arising from her internal conflict over the nature and veracity of the story. Such a mild story too, Bliss suspected, in comparison to the ones that still remained undiscovered. If such radical symptoms could be evoked with a tale about her mother's petty cruelties and misguided accusations, what more dangerous reactions awaited the disinterment of more pivotal horrors?

He didn't have long to wait, and when it came it was like a catalyst, unlocking a whole chamber of horrors.

She had been working very hard, while grieving almost constantly over the remembrance of her mother's rejection. This, in turn, had flooded her with panic, and it had taken all of her willpower to maintain her pose of quiet, efficient sanity at work. She had been experiencing a constant barrage of physical sensations throughout this period—she might be walking down the hall when, suddenly, dizziness would overwhelm her and she would start shaking uncontrollably, losing her balance. Then she would begin to *separate*—that term that had become over the last two months a permanent part of her vocabulary. Her depression increased as her physical symptoms persisted, and the separations grew more radical (another term in her new lexicon). The hallucinations, especially when she was inside with the walls closing in on her, would generally throw her into panic. Often everything would go blank. What was going on?

It wasn't until after Thanksgiving that they began to dig

down to the root of the problems. As so often happened, it began to emerge near the end of a long session and carried over to the next one. They had been working for two hours, trying to coax Little Andrea-Ellen out of her closet, but without success. Little Andrea-Ellen had just sat there, no more communicative than a mushroom, staring, or actually glaring, at Bliss, when suddenly Andrea seemed to dive out of hypnosis and appeared, panting.

"Something . . . something remembered last night—oh! Came back—then split—when try to think, get scared—afraid to remember. Oh!"

This shattered statement was followed by ten minutes of wild gyrations and flailing of arms. Bliss stood by, ready to prevent her from hurting herself, but also willing to let the paroxysm continue if it led to the discovery of some new fact.

Suddenly Sister Jeanine appeared.

"Let me calm her, okay?" And within another minute the flailing and crying had stopped. Andrea's tortured face relaxed.

"What's going on?" Bliss asked.

"It had to do with her father. He was angry and physically hurt her and did things to her. Not clear, but it terrified her, the memory of it. Whatever it was, it brought back danger. Something about blood. She was . . . she was hit in the face, and there was a lot of blood—that is the picture that came to her. She never remembered how that scar got there until now—" Andrea pointed to a long scar over her left eyebrow. "There are just pieces and pictures of blood."

Andrea came out of hypnosis, gasping. Then she was under again.

"What's going on?"

Andrea came out again. The words came in gasps. "Little Andrea—still scared—keeps wanting—to hide. When you said father—hit me—caused a scar—something . . . something inside—a lot of fighting. She . . . she has scars on her face and arms, too. One part says it happened.

Another, no it didn't. A part is yelling at you—wants to hurt you."

Before matters got too out-of-control, Bliss brought Andrea out of hypnosis and tried to calm her. That took some doing; by the time she left, more than four hours had passed—a long session even by the standards they had established for their meetings.

Not surprisingly, Andrea was in terrible shape the next day. She had been losing control in her car—going crazy while she was driving—and getting home by pure instinct alone. So crazy had things become that she hadn't even gone to work the next day. She stayed home, weathering the tempest that swept over her. She had calmed somewhat in the hours that followed and, by the time she arrived at Bliss's office, felt somewhat better. Of course she had forgotten everything that had happened the session before, and had to be reminded. But once reminded, the story continued to unfold, once again under the guidance of Sister Jeanine.

"It was part of a very bad time that came out last time, and she felt better. Then she went to bed and became terrified that a man was going to attack her. She was afraid for her life."

"Why?" Bliss asked. "Can you reconstruct the source of her fear?"

"I can feel it from another part—but that part doesn't want you to know. It's trying to make it all black."

Bliss struggled for some new method by which to approach the problem. He had to objectify the episode for Andrea and her other parts; he had to impose some measure of fiction on the scene so as to make it less violent, less threatening.

"Tell the other part you are just looking around," Bliss said to Sister Jeanine. "It is not Andrea we are looking at but another person. Call her Lois. We are interested in the story of Lois."

"Yes. That might work." Sister Jeanine was quiet for a moment and then continued. "Lois is in a big house. It is evening, and she is alone with a man there. She is very little and taking a nap—she is sick. Her mother is out with the other children. She wakes up and something is wrong. Her father is very angry with her mother—'' There was a pause while emotion creased Andrea's face. ''This . . . this is hard. Little Andrea-Ellen feels mixed up with Lois somehow. I keep seeing her house—no lights are on—and he was trying to make Lois do things—he was so angry—then he tried to—oh! He threw the glass and broke it on the floor—then he grabbed her and tried to kiss her, and she got very scared and tried to run, but she was weak and couldn't fight him—Oh, no! No!''

Sister Jeanine started to shudder and couldn't go on until Bliss had calmed her sufficiently. Despite the fact that there were only two physical bodies in his small office, the place suddenly seemed crowded with people, clamoring and screaming all around them.

''Let's look at it from a distance, Sister Jeanine. Like in a movie. It's up there—just two-dimensional, with two actors you don't even know playing the parts. Got it?''

''Yes.'' The look of confusion faded from her countenance. ''The man took off her clothes—Lois was sick and naked. He hurt her—sexually first—then he had her do it with her mouth. She was crying, trying to get away. But he held her. Then she bit him. He got really crazy then and hit her hard—with broken glass. He went wild. Then just her body was there. He did things with the glass, but she didn't feel anything anymore. He hit her over the eye and cut her wrist—blood made him wild. Then he cut her in the vagina, but she didn't feel that anymore . . .

''She was thrown on the floor—where more cutting happened. Then he started to cry. He picked her up and said he was sorry. She was like a dead thing in his arms. He kept saying he was sorry and told her how much he loved her—then he washed off the blood and put on bandages and got her a clean nightgown.

''She heard him clean up the glass, then leave the house. The other times—he would be very angry. But this time, he was wilder and hurt her a lot more all over than ever before . . .''

Incest and child abuse were all too common, but this was a level of savagery Bliss hadn't expected to find. And the worst part was that there was more—Sister Jeanine had said as much. There had been "other times," probably many other times, and perhaps all of them had involved more than rape; there was a level of cruelty and madness here that Bliss was just beginning to plumb now. How had the child survived? By going into self-hypnosis—her only escape from the gruesome reality of her predicament.

"Andrea?"

Andrea came out of hypnosis, looking very frightened. "Yes?"

"Can you remember what Sister Jeanine said?"

"She said it was a movie. It didn't really happen. It was a movie—" Then Andrea was under again. But after five minutes she came out, tears running down her cheeks. "It was real? Not a movie?"

"Yes, Andrea," Bliss assured her. "It was real, all right. Lois was you and your father did all those things to you."

"Some part is very angry at you," she said, skirting the issue.

"Yes, but do you believe what Sister Jeanine said?"

"Couldn't I have just imagined it?" It was a plea more than a question. "There is a lot of anger—they say 'no.' No."

"Your mind just doesn't make those kinds of things up, Andrea."

"They are very angry at you for making them remember," Andrea looked at Bliss accusingly. "You shouldn't have made them remember."

"But you had to see the truth. It is the only way you'll ever be able to understand why you separate, why you go through such craziness and hurt yourself. Don't you think that's worth remembering?"

Andrea looked undecided, frightened, chewing on her upper lip as she considered this. "Do you think that was why I was scared Monday night? Being sexually hurt and then beat up?"

"Probably the event was in the back of your mind then."

"Yes. My mother must have known something about it. You think?"

"How could she avoid it?"

"I . . . I was feeling sick today—before coming here—the same as I was that day. It wasn't the tension at work, was it? The little girl is still crying. She still thinks it was her fault, but it wasn't."

"Do you know why she didn't feel anything when her father hurt her?"

"She'd left her body." Andrea went automatically back into hypnosis. "She didn't cry. Nothing. She was awake but didn't feel. I don't want to feel any of it now." Suddenly Andrea started out of hypnosis again. 'You're sure those memories are real?"

"Absolutely," Bliss said and meant it.

Andrea left feeling calmer and more at peace with herself than she had for a long, long time. Dr. Bliss also felt better, even a little jubilant. And the next day, he still had reason for his optimism. Sister Jeanine reported that Andrea was feeling better and that she wasn't so afraid anymore. Sleeping was easier, and Little Andrea-Ellen was quieter, less angry. Even out of hypnosis, Andrea was now able to admit to herself that her father had done many bad things to her—there had been a lot of incidents with her father as Bliss suspected. Not that the nightmares had stopped completely; in many ways they were more vivid than ever, now that some of the episodes had been revealed. In general they finished the week feeling better, now that one of the most painful episodes had been uncovered.

But by the next week, Andrea had forgotten everything that had happened. She refused to go into hypnosis, complaining that she couldn't concentrate. When Bliss asked her if she recalled any of the incidents with her father, Andrea snapped back a quick "No."

"All I can remember is my Christmas tree and how good he was to me," she said.

"What about little Andrea-Ellen?" Bliss asked. The smaller self surely would feel the duplicity of Andrea's memory.

"She's fine," Andrea said.

Bliss could get nothing more from her. The world was in order, everything was back in its correct box and closet. All the voices were silent—or so Andrea said—and the memory of her father's attack had been completely and efficiently erased.

Bliss recorded in his notes: "Something strange is going on because Little Andrea-Ellen is calm, but damned if I know what it is."

Things did not stay calm very long, as Bliss could foretell. Nothing concocted by Andrea or her fellow personalities could keep the terror and the panic from returning. By the next day she was in terrible shape, hurting herself, "separating radically," dreaming of black shadows with long knives that followed her around her house.

DR. BLISS'S NOTEBOOK
December 14, 1979

Andrea reported that things "have been pretty crazy," and she gave me a paper with blood on it to prove her point. It is no less than I expected. These gross traumas could not be concealed forever. They must inevitably surface.

I talked to Sister Jeanine, trying to find out what the last few days have been like for her, and she told me what she usually tells me these days—"There is a lot of fighting going on." It has become a stock phrase, and because I have yet to learn the identities of the others, it is still a phrase without full significance.

"A big part wants to run," Sister Jeanine went on. "She has been going in and out of remembering last session when the memory came back. It is part of it."

"Shall we look at a movie?" I suggested.

Sister Jeanine shook her head, looking unaccustomedly upset by my suggestion. "I'm scared," she said, and suddenly there was Andrea, looking really startled, staring at me, obviously completely out of hypnosis. It took me a long time to get her back under, most of that time spent calming her fears.

Later Sister Jeanine explained to me: "She goes back into time and sees scary things and doesn't know what is real. The Christmas tree. There were times when it wasn't real and she saw fire. She is hurting herself again. She hurts herself. What came out the last time—the bad time—angry—'her monster.' She called it her black shadow—but she saw it—evil and scary with a knife. There is a part still missing—where she went. She was blank. But it isn't real."

"Well, let's try a little harder," I suggested. "We'll watch it all through a telescope and see what happens to Lois, shall we?"

Andrea jumped out of hypnosis then, panting.

"I can't see anything," she reported, but it sounded to me more like a denial than a statement of fact. I pushed on.

"Look harder."

She held up her right hand above her head, as if she were grasping a knife. Then in a deeper voice she said, "In a room, got scared, blood, and she could feel the blood coming down, couldn't feel anything else. Monster came out, angry, full of anger, ugly, dark—big shadow—small light was on—mother gave her night light because she scared. Monster came out from shadow. Monster had knife. It is mixed up. Monster hurt you."

"We are watching a movie," I reminded her, "don't be afraid."

"Can't see what happened."

"But if you see what happened, Andrea, the danger will go away."

This apparently did little to mollify Andrea. She quickly disappeared, leaving me to Sister Jeanine's calmer narration.

"Things would start coming and then she would be scared," she apologized. "Part of her is just a frightened little girl."

"But who can give her the courage to see this stuff?" I asked.

Sister Jeanine just sat there, staring over my shoulder. After a few minutes, I decided to call on yet another personality.

"Mother Mary? Are you there?"

But instead of Mother Mary coming out, suddenly I was regarding a very angry face, contorted with rage, and a gruff, gravelly voice.

"It doesn't matter," the voice said. "She is bad and has sinned. She must be punished. She is bad. Her mother told her so. Now I have the knife and I will stab her."

Andrea made several jabbing motions, or the violent personality who had taken control at the moment did. Andrea herself then emerged, shaking uncontrollably, gasping for breath.

"I . . . I can't see right. The movie from last time did it. After she went to bed and could feel the blood—no pain at all—she was first aware of the blood. Then she got scared but everything was so quiet and no one was there but he wasn't gone—he turned and came to her room with a hunting knife and . . . I can't see anymore! He was angry, real angry! She said, 'No, go away!' She fought. But he put his arm out and held her and with the knife said 'If you fight me anymore, you get this knife inside you. Stop it!' And then she stopped fighting and lay there, and she was all mixed up then. He took covers off, and he had sex with her. He didn't hurt her with the knife, but with his body—"

Andrea paused for breath and then rushed on. "Then she heard the door open, and she yelled 'Mommy!' and kept on crying for her. Yes, Mother came. She fought him, and he put the knife in his pocket quickly. They fought then and he walked out, and Ma yelled at her and hit her, slapped her hard in the face and said she was very bad to do that to her father."

I tried to get her to remember the episode she had just related—the second such grisly scene—but it was, understandably, too much for her. If her time sense isn't too mixed up, then these two incidents must have taken place within the space of a single afternoon—more than enough reason for anyone to forget. She came out of hypnosis and, as soon as she realized a little what had transpired, tried desperately to get back into a trance, but I prevented her as best I could and tried to calm her. After this I allowed her to return to a hypnotic state where she recounted her most recent self-injuries, in the same jumbled, garbled style that marks so much of this confusion:

"She tried to tell you—things got mixed up—she cut herself and everything stopped for awhile—things became— (pause). First crying, then write you—then anger and took coat hanger and jabbed herself in vagina. Pains come and go—then she mixes up time. Then she is terrified. Sometimes she feels pain in stomach and back. She saw a cat, and it scared her. The pain now feels like that pain way back. Mostly she is lost—a very young girl . . ."

That was enough for one day, both for her and for me. This therapy is becoming more complex and more gruesome, as we progress. I have yet to understand the interconnection of the other personalities (or even how many there are), who this monster is (though it sounds like her father), or how the whole mess will resolve itself.

ANDREA'S JOURNAL
December 15, 1979

Functioning during the day became a little easier for a few weeks as there was less inclination to panic attacks. The primary trouble centered around sleep. Nightmares were a constant occurrence, and they were often so clear that there would be much confusion the next day as to whether or not the events were real.

When questioned by Dr. Bliss about the content of the nightmares, I could remember the states of confusion, fear, and bizarre events that would accompany them. For example, my father is holding a knife in one of the nightmares. Suddenly the knife turns into a cross, and I kiss it—like penance during Lent—a symbolic act of atonement for sins. I tried to tell Dr. Bliss about the sins, but I couldn't go on—I couldn't remember any more of the nightmares and became very upset. I wanted to run from his office as fast as I could. Then I lost control and slipped into hypnosis for a length of time. I couldn't speak at all and was usually not even conscious of Dr. Bliss's presence. I was back in my own world of random flashbacks and terror. I would experience sensations such as drowning and choking, and fear for my life just as strongly as I had many years before with my father. Eventually, I would hear Dr. Bliss's voice pulling me back to reality and could slowly return to that safety.

In the past, therapy had consisted in about 80 percent day-to-day survival. We talked not about sins, but punishment—about the distortion of events that happened before they took my father away. Since this was done when I was calm and quite conscious, it never penetrated my hypnotic unconscious. (This is what Dr. Bliss says anyway.) As a result, it had no impact on the infantile experiences hidden there. Unfortunately, reluctance to go into hypnosis grew, since the effects so often lead to anxiety, panics, and a difficulty functioning.

I was usually apprehensive and half-dazed when I entered Dr. Bliss's office. Part of this was certainly due to the uncovering of my secret world, but part was due to the building itself. The hospital had all kinds of negative associations for me. Doctors, too. But I think I understand this a little better now. My father used to work in a hospital when I was a child and would take me there from time to time. The hospital was one of the places where he used to abuse me. Other sessions revealed not a fear of doctors as much as a fear of their white medical jackets, which my father would often put on to ''play doctor'' with me and inflict more abuse.

I have seen other things too. For example, about my mother and her burning of the dress. We learned this when Dr. Bliss enlisted a personality as a ''co-therapist.'' He called the person Antoinette. It was through Antoinette that he found out about the burning of the present, about her anger. After that, Andrea just went into a closet in her mind, and stopped thinking and feeling. She wasn't angry and she didn't cry, as she really should have. Instead, she believed her mother, that she was bad and needed to be punished. She desperately longed for her mother's love and attention, but constantly felt unworthy to obtain it.

Things aren't well anymore. There is a lot of fighting going on.

Andrea wasn't remembering the twin attacks by her father, and Bliss didn't press the point. There seemed real danger in pursuing that avenue too hotly, and he demurred for a time, preferring to investigate the new character that had so unexpectedly burst upon the scene during their last session—a personality Andrea called the Angry One.

Bliss didn't even have to call him, for the Angry One simply arrived, his voice grim and filled with bile.

"I try to make her dead," he proclaimed, "stabbing and burning her, but she won't go away. She is evil."

"Maybe she isn't the one who was evil. Maybe it was her father who was bad, who was sick. It wasn't Andrea's fault."

"Part fights that and says it didn't happen. Part angry."

"Why so angry?"

"Just angry. Angry at lots of people."

"Maybe for good reason," Bliss said. "For instance, you have a perfect right to be angry at Andrea's father and mother."

"No. Not them. All lies!" the Angry One bellowed. "She is the one to be punished now because she is bad and stupid." Andrea struck herself full in the face. "She is evil. She broke up the family. Made her father go away. Her mother knew she was wrong and bad."

"But doesn't it make sense to discuss the facts with Andrea and Sister Jeanine, Angry One? Maybe you'd discover that your premises are all wrong, that Andrea wasn't responsible for what happened to her father or her mother."

"Don't care! Here to punish her and will do it every day until it is done."

Bliss tried several strategies to calm the situation, to defuse the anger of the personality, but nothing seemed to work. Finally the only thing he could do was to have Sister Jeanine hypnotize Little Andrea-Ellen and let her experience some peace, since it was obviously from Little Andrea-Ellen that so much of the guilt and anger came.

Over the next few weeks, Bliss had more run-ins with the Angry One, several ending in physical assaults on herself. One time it took Bliss and another psychiatrist to restrain her, for the Angry One proved viciously strong. Bliss could only be grateful that this patient was not a man.

He tried to uncover other old memories, but Andrea resisted. Not only that, she steadfastly refused to remember those events already discovered. Not that this refusal protected her; she was hurting herself more and more, lapsing into amnesia at every opportunity.

Bliss was disturbed by this trend. Now she was completely blanking out every time she hurt herself, no longer exercising any control at all over her actions. Bliss recommended hospitalization, but Andrea refused categorically. Maintaining her single lifestyle, no matter how vulnerable she might be to self-attack, seemed of paramount importance to her. Bliss acquiesced with the utmost reluctance, feeling that his hands were tied until Andrea saw the danger for herself. Of course, he could incarcerate her in the closed ward; but he'd learned enough about Andrea's problems by then to understand the part a hospital setting played in her original trauma. He suspected that putting her in a hospital against her will might prove more detrimental than beneficial—and with someone as bright as Andrea, it would be difficult to eliminate all opportunities for suicide, no matter how careful he was. No, for the moment he would hold off and see what the week brought.

NOTE WRITTEN BY ANDREA
Monday, December 31, 1979—2 A.M.
Dear Dr. Bliss,

I have been up for a few hours now—slowly trying to

regain some semblance of control and order. Since I could not sleep, I thought it better if I tried to write and let you know what's really been going on, as I have found it quite difficult trying to communicate with you lately.

I knew it was dangerous for me to just leave your office that way last Friday—but I didn't know how dangerous. I went back to work and was back into "Super Andrea" right away. I stayed late that night, trying to work, but found I was just reshuffling papers and lost my ability to concentrate. As much as I fought it—I finally left for home.

Dr. Bliss—you need to know exactly what's been going on if we are to really work together.

The self-destructive business is quite out of hand. The latest twist on the theme has come in the form of putting Drano crystals in my vagina—this has been going on and off for about two weeks now. The variation on the theme came this weekend as I tried to find a way of getting the crystals up through the opening of my cervix to burn out and destroy my uterus. I have figured it out and had to wait until Monday to buy the necessary tool—a speculum. As a feminist, I learned the healing art of pelvic self-examination at a woman's clinic in Boston. Now I'm using it to destroy myself.

So that I wouldn't feel bad about waiting until then, I kept up the tradition this weekend. At a point—

[Something illegible—random scribbling—was beneath. It had been made by one of her personalities.]

DR. BLISS'S NOTEBOOK
January 2, 1980

We both agreed that the present arrangement was too dangerous, and I persuaded her to come into the hospital. She could work by day but spend the evenings on the closed ward—because the "Angry One" was most sinister by night.

After having Andrea admitted, we went to work, but this time I pounded away at her, trying to make her remember the forgotten stuff. I literally told her the whole tale, but it didn't register. If they are not receptive, patients can scramble their minds so that they don't understand; withdraw so they don't hear; or hear but deny it happened. Andrea did all three.

In desperation I spoke to Sister Jeanine. Now I am no longer asking Andrea to go into hypnosis because at the slightest stress she is already there. It is a remarkable experience to talk first to Andrea with her eyes open, but confused, unaware and fearful, then speak to Sister Jeanine, again with eyes open, but calm, rational, and totally knowledgeable about all the experiences. The two are so close physically, but years apart therapeutically. The hypnotic transformation which separates the two is a formidable chasm to breach.

The basic idea is that she's too fragmented to understand anything. As Sister Jeanine tells it, "Sometimes she is just mixed up in many pieces now. Things have been too out of control. Another part makes her believe it is all a game. Sometimes she would tell her mother, and her mother would slap her and say she was making it up. There is the part that makes her go to work. She started to go to work at thirteen, even when she was sick. Her mother said go back to work and stop the foolishness. Her mother changed totally after her father died. There were seven children, and she had terrible problems with her husband."

To that was added a chorus from the Angry One:

"She is bad. You think that she is good. She did bad things. Her father said she had to be punished and her mother and church said the same. She tried to be that stupid nun. She is bad inside in her vagina. Her mother said she was bad inside."

I asked Andrea if she'd heard what the Angry One had said, and she finally said yes, she had, and then surprised me again (this therapy is filled with surprises) by going on to comment on her father's bizarre behavior.

"Once, after he died, my mother started to talk with me. Then I said, how did you know he was so sick? He would take her in the car, she said, and try to strangle her. But then he would be real nice and then go for a ride and choke her again. He kept saying she slept with other men—that my brother and I weren't his children. He got wild—this isn't right—''

At that point, she lapsed into another one of her telegraphic, stream-of-consciousness monologues. "Mind just making things up now. I'll tell you the picture. Mother grabbed little girl real hard and hit her and said you are dirty, bad—don't ever go with father again—I don't think it happened, she wouldn't do that. The last time she took her to wash her out, and it burned.''

"And that's why you're still trying to wash it out?" I asked.

"That is how Angry One knew she was bad.''

It was not until the second week of the new year that Bliss was able to break through to another personality, and it proved to be one of the most malignant of all.

Andrea had been working during the day and spending her nights on the ward. It seemed to work. Little Andrea-Ellen, she reported, was feeling more secure. This, in turn, made Big Andrea feel less self-destructive. But a return to this equanimity had its inevitable side effect. Big Andrea was trying to forget everything she had learned about her father's maltreatment of her. In the attempt, she was losing touch with logic—since she had to defy logic to whitewash her father's image—and with it went her ability to hear or speak clearly. She began to report a lot of trouble understanding what Dr. Bliss or anyone else said to her—it sounded garbled, like a foreign language.

There was no question in Bliss's mind that some "force" or personality was garbling these messages, trying to keep her away from the truth, and starting January 9 he began to dig again. Using hypnosis he was able to get first in touch with the Angry One and then with Sister Jeanine. The Angry One was less belligerent this time, and crouched there, without assaulting Andrea, and talked with Bliss. He took advantage of this truce to ask the personality what he knew about Andrea's rejection of the information.

"You say it wasn't her fault," the Angry One growled. "And then they say it was her fault, and *they* were there."

Bliss summoned Sister Jeanine.

"Did you hear that? Is it true? Did the others see that it was Andrea's fault?"

"Andrea heard that. But she can't make up her mind about who is right. There is so much fighting going on. The more you talk, the more another part of her wants to hurt her. The angry part is just confused—not so angry anymore. He couldn't come up with a reason—just says it must be her fault. But Joseph wants to hurt her."

"Joseph?" Bliss asked. "There is a Joseph inside of her?"

"Yes. Of course."

He sensed his opportunity. "May I speak to him, please?"

"Well, yes," Sister Jeanine said hesitantly. "But be careful. He can be very dangerous."

"Okay, I will." Bliss waited tensely.

Abruptly Andrea's face changed completely, from a placid, unemotional countenance to one contorted with rage. It was bloodcurdling. There was something more than anger in those eyes now—there was madness.

"You tell her I was sick." The voice was far too deep and menacing for anything Andrea seemed capable of producing. It was, Bliss considered, like hearing from a person possessed. "She should have obeyed. That house and the kids screaming—Dara was disgusting. She was cold—sexually cold—wouldn't let me have sex unless I forced it. I had a right to fun too—I had a right!"

"Why did you do these things to Andrea?" Bliss asked. There was a genuine feeling of discomfort being around this character. There was so much violence just below the surface.

"I tried to make up for it," Joseph said almost petulantly. "I would buy her ice cream. Didn't I? She would hide in the closet. Sometimes she was a fun kid but then she'd hide. I had to punish her, didn't I?"

Bliss tried to talk to Joseph further, but the personality disappeared. He enlisted Sister Jeanine's aid, but she was also unable to bring him back. Suddenly Andrea was out again, her hands over her ears, shaking and crying. Gradually she came around enough to speak with reasonable coherence.

"Three other men, three other men molested her. Yes. Three others I remember. Once walking down the street, and a man said, 'I'll take you for a ride,' and she would get lost—but not as scared. Even in high school, but she could never understand. But it wasn't her fault. Someone she trusted hurt her bad."

"Who?"

"Frank—an uncle. Father's brother. I don't remember—" She paused, wide-eyed, and went on. "Grandma's house. Mother would send me there. On a farm. F ' lived with her. Something he did was real scary. Other men hurt me, but I got angry at them.

"They put Frank in a hospital—just like father. There were weekends I don't remember—" And her voice faded out. Nothing else Bliss attempted could arouse her, leaving him with more questions—like who was Uncle Frank and what did this strange episode at "the farm" really refer to?

DR. BLISS'S NOTEBOOK
January 18, 1980

I checked Andrea out of the hospital January 17. Her stay in the hospital was helpful but also troublesome. It was possible to do a physical examination, culture her urine, and treat the urinary infection, and to remove the safety pin from the vault of her vagina. Furthermore, I was able to push psychotherapy hard and uncover some important traumatic material. But Andrea is so hypersensitive and so ill-disposed toward hospitals that the usual errors and oversights common to institutions threw her into panics and produced much paranoid thinking. She ended by not being able to trust the staff—and with doubts about me.

"I got angry at you because of the physical examination," she told me. "Some things were all wrong to begin with, but then the nurses insisted on waiting for the drugs, and I was extremely anxious about getting to the Board meeting. Then the medical student said, 'You must watch out for Andrea Biaggi, who is a multiple who was raped.' Then he said, 'She is *supposed* to be allergic to penicillin.' ''

She honestly thought the students were out to murder her or to conspire in some way to keep her there against her will. It took much convincing to allay her suspicions.

Andrea continued relating incidents in her early life, usually mixing the events up so much that it was impossible for Bliss to collate them in any effective manner. Now added to the grisly details of events surrounding her father were stories, or parts of stories, concerning her uncle Frank and the farmhouse where he lived with her grandmother. Then, too, there were the stories of other men— perhaps real, perhaps fictional—whom Andrea had remembered as molesting her. All of these episodes were liberally sprinkled with guilt and self-righteous desire to punish herself for those sins. Bliss was often left utterly disoriented. When was she talking about? Then or now? To Andrea's mind, of course, there was no difference. The past was as fresh, or fresher, than any contemporary experience she might have. Dredging up the past, therefore, became an exercise in reawakening something that had never really been put to rest—and for the most part Andrea couldn't handle it.

Not that it was hard to understand why Andrea had a hard time with the material. Most of it was horrendous. It involved not just the incestuous excesses of her father, but the equally appalling madness of her Uncle Frank. As Sister Jeanine recalled one of the episodes:

"I have had flashes of what happened. She went into the room and didn't think anyone was there, and this becomes fuzzy, and he was behind the door—began to yell at her—became very angry, saying things she didn't understand—and then he must have taken her to the barn. I don't have a clear picture. And then he sexually hurt her. It was sexual abuse because he became part of Nothing. She didn't see him much. Then he began to scare her a lot—killed an animal and hung it up on a meat hook. It was a live animal with head cut off—probably a cow. It was a huge animal head. He tied her up, and put gag in her mouth. She tried to get away. Then he hung her next to animal and she thought he would cut her head off. It isn't clear, but it comes from little pieces.''

Whether this story was true or not, Bliss had no way of knowing. He certainly couldn't ask Andrea herself, who had become utterly unreachable over the last few weeks, going in and out of hypnosis very rapidly—almost, it seemed, in an attempt to avoid any confrontation whatsoever with Bliss. But then, even a psychiatrist (or particularly a psychiatrist) had to wonder whether he wasn't becoming as paranoid as his patient when he attributed such motives to her.

One thing, though, had become perfectly clear to him: there would be no real progress in therapy until Andrea could begin to accept some of the horrible things that had happened to her and start getting angry at the real perpetrators, rather than taking everything out on herself. But how was he going to convince her? The obvious answer was to write to one of her relatives who might corroborate some of what she was remembering. But which ones?

He asked her this question at their next meeting, and she was very evasive.

''No. Not my family. My brothers think I'm Super Andrea. They wouldn't put up with a crazy person. And they'd refuse to say anything.''

''Then who do you suggest?''

Andrea shrugged. ''I don't know.'' She fixed Bliss with a look. ''What's the big deal anyway? All they'd say is I'm crazy, and that all this stuff is my craziness.''

''Is that what you think, or is that what you're *afraid* they'll say?''

''Either—both.'' Pause. ''Listen, how can it be true? There's no memory in me of this stuff. And—and all that stuff about being hurt by my father. Why, some of those pictures—I was much too young. Three-four years old at the most. That couldn't be right.''

"How do you know that?" Bliss asked.

"Because. It just isn't. I can't remember anything but happy memories—"

It was very difficult to argue with someone about the content and architecture of her own internal history. There was so little hard evidence to go on and so much room for confusion. Andrea would say she couldn't possibly have remembered the events of her childhood so faithfully and, therefore, they hadn't happened. Bliss kept trying to talk with her about it, but to no avail. A stalemate.

Bliss was left to bide his time.

15

Nothing

Sunday, January 20, 1980

WHEN I left your office Friday, Dr. Bliss, I became aware that the depression and anxiety I had pushed away most of that day were back in even greater intensity. Experiencing distortions of all my senses made the walk to my car a terrifying effort. Not being able to feel the ground below me as I walked, noises triggering fear of personal danger and visual distortions of perceptions became part of all that living nightmare.

I am not one to give up easily. In fact, I would say it is my quality of persistence that has been crucial to my success as a professional. That night, however, by the time I did reach my car, I was so much like a lost, tired child that I just wanted to sit on the ground and start crying and let someone know of the terror I was experiencing.

I often imagine myself at those times as a very frightened child living in a woman's body. That would seem to give credence to your theory of multiple personalities being my problem. The problem I have with that is that if I were totally any one of those personalities at any time, then all this internal fighting would not be so great.

In day-to-day reality, it would have meant that on Friday, when I reached the parking lot feeling most like Little Andrea-Ellen, she could have just taken over, cried, and tried to get help. But I was there too, saying "just get in the car and go home." When Little Andrea-Ellen protested, Mother Mary came out in full force, cold and stern, saying, "stop being a little girl and get in that car and go home!" No one personality was operating at the time. The three of them—Andrea, Little Andrea-Ellen, and Mother Mary—drove home. The net reality was that I actually drove home, crying the entire way, with a cold sense of anger that took shape in high speeds, cutting in front of other drivers and blowing the car horn at a bicycle rider for just slowing me down, and eventually forcing him off the road.

By the time I reached my apartment—I went back into losing physical sensations—I made it up the stairs and just sat like death for awhile.

A few hours later, I had to go to a special meeting of women in my work. I dutifully pulled myself together (what an ironic expression) and drove out there with little trouble. It was an informal meeting and I just drank straight alcohol (which I usually *hate*) and played with a paperweight.

Anyhow, I changed into the clown-entertainer then, Bridget, who you haven't met yet. We all went out for dinner and to a movie that night, and Bridget's behavior (which was just short of obnoxious) was totally accepted since they thought she was drunk but, of course, she wasn't. Continually, the whole night, I was going into panic for very brief moments (silence on the outside so no one knew), then back out as the center of attention.

It all finally clashed while sitting in the movie. It wasn't the movie, but my legs just started jumping and shaking—I couldn't sit still—and there were too many people around me suddenly and I just wanted to run and run and run!

None of them realized a thing was wrong. They didn't know the truth and wouldn't have understood. I walked out to the bathroom. I wanted to leave, but I'd come with the others in a single car. Then I tried to pull back to Bridget or Super Andrea, and that wouldn't work. I kept crying and shaking and couldn't make myself stop. After that, I went blank for a while, and after that things got very calm. I finally went back in the theater acting like a

robot and fell asleep. It was like being a living corpse.
And I stayed in that state all night—unable to find any real
rest. The next two days were the same. Panics and a
continuation of the nightmare. Mostly a lot of crying, fear,
confusion, and unable to do anything. But you need to
know, Dr. Bliss, that there was never any one single
personality that just took over and ran things. That would
have been a welcome relief. Instead, there was a constant
mix, which led to cycles of sadness, anger, fear, guilt,
confusion—a desire to kill myself.

I trust you, Dr. Bliss, as an honest person and know you
really care about what is happening to me. At the same time,
you keep saying I am getting better, yet it was not until this
afternoon that I could throw away the Drano, and I fear it is
just a matter of time until the cycle has me buy another bottle.

Through Sister Jeanine's help, I've also put the pieces
together about the events at my Grandmother's home with
Frank. I'm not sure at what point that happened, but I
remembered while I was cleaning today. It does not bother
me as I cannot believe it at all. I have the images (some
very clear) but no feeling—*no* sense of reality to it.

My greatest question of you is whether it is possible to
find out if any of this actually happened. Because of that I
will give you my uncle's address, so you can write him if
you wish to find out anything. Please don't state any
details of my case other than you are my therapist and
need information on any events he may be aware of that
may help you with my case. His wife, my aunt, will filter
any other questions.

I can't believe I've written this much, yet I still feel I
haven't communicated enough of the "net effect" of this
weekend.

This is a most wrenching time in my life and I appreciate your patience.

Dr. Bliss sent a letter the next day to Andrea's uncle,
her mother's brother-in-law, Dr. Frederic Antonio:

Dear Dr. Antonio:

I have been treating Andrea Biaggi for the last several months with hypnotherapy for her psychiatric disability, which is that of multiple personalities. She had many very disturbing experiences as a child and coped by forgetting them through a process of self-hypnosis. As a result, she created personalities that have been instrumental in producing her self-destructive and self-mutilative behaviors.

She and I are both concerned about documenting the truth of her forgotten experiences, which have now come to light, and she suggested that you might know a good deal about this part of her history. In particular, I wonder whether you might know more about the family— its history of psychopathology, her father's behaviors, and those of Frank. Any information which you might transmit could be helpful.

Sincerely yours,
Eugene L. Bliss, M.D.

While Dr. Bliss waited for an answer, he was keenly aware of the growing tension in his interviews with Andrea. The nature and extent of her self-destructive behavior had increased dramatically, and she was becoming more suicidal. The week before he had hospitalized her for treatment of severe genital burns, caused by the pouring of Drano into her vagina. When Andrea was sufficiently lucid to understand what she did, panic resulted, since she no longer had any control at all over these abusive incidents. Often now, she wasn't even aware of what was happening. Then, too, there was the constant shifting back and forth, in and out of hypnosis. One moment she would be attending a committee meeting and the next she would be driving in the car, not knowing how she had gotten from one spot to the other. On weekends, moreover, there were longer lapses during which demons seemed to take possession of her body, inflicting awful injuries on it while the responsible personalities—Super Andrea, Big Andrea, and Sister Jeanine—slept. These periods terrorized her, driving her even deeper into panic and subsequent self-hypnosis. It wasn't like the nightmares and dreams of a normal person. To Andrea the experiences were real, often with a wholeness and pureness that the reality of normal life lacked; there was everything there—smell, touch, hearing, crystal-clear color and three-dimensionality—like experiencing a holograph of an event with every technical effect for simulation of reality that science fiction could create. Why not confuse the real with the unreal? For Andrea there was no difference, only a multitude of realities that alternately frightened and appalled her.

The "movies" Andrea recalled—the ones with "Lois" in them—were vividly immediate and terrifying for her. And there were so many of them now, spilling out in torrents while Bliss rushed to take down all the details—before the incident was once again forgotten and Andrea retreated behind the veil of doubt.

"Lois is in a closet," Andrea related one day near the end of January. "And it is all dark, and she curls up in a ball with dresses hanging overhead. There isn't any danger here—but it is very confusing and she is very sad. She holds on to the dresses, crying on the dresses. She is upset because her mother isn't around and the dresses are her mother's. She talks to the dresses as if they were her mother." Startled. "A noise—like when Lois was hit real hard on the head by her mother. How sad! She wanted to be so close to her mother—tried to please her, but her mother was always angry at her. Somehow she seemed to hate her—so cold and distant . . ."

Andrea paused for a moment during the session and started to cry. Bliss realized that suddenly "Lois" had become Andrea, and, perhaps briefly, Andrea was seeing her own past as it probably had been. When she spoke again, his insight was confirmed:

"She always told me how ugly I looked, and I feel so ugly now—and then I would go and hide because I believed I was so ugly, bad and awful. And that is how I've been feeling. I can't feel that you don't hate me."

"Nonsense, Andrea," Bliss replied. "That's just the little child in you, taking out her anger on you."

"No, it's more than that," Andrea said quietly. "There is a voice inside of me that keeps shouting, 'You are evil and no good!' It is Nothing. Nothing isn't a he or a she. . . . Nothing is . . . nothing. It started when I was five or six. I would wait for a car to come by so I could step out in front of it and Nothing would be there. Inside I would feel like nothing—like a monster—like all I deserved was nothing and so Nothing came."

It was another and most substantial personality. Nothing, Andrea later informed Bliss, was a dangerous, menacing person, someone committed to protecting Andrea from her past at whatever cost, even to the point of physically threatening Bliss through its intermediary, Sister Jeanine.

"Nothing is dangerous to you also," Sister Jeanine told Bliss. "Today it is just angry, fighting. Yesterday, Nothing wanted to get a knife and stab you."

Nothing was the creature Andrea had created to keep Little Andrea-Ellen in her closet, out of harm's way, just as it provided the amnesia and numbing darkness that anesthetized Andrea if there was pain. Originally the anesthesia had been used to safeguard Andrea against the pain her father inflicted on her as a child, but as the years passed it became more indiscriminate, finally numbing Andrea to the pain she was inflicting on herself, perhaps as a proxy for her father's anger. Now Nothing had grown completely out of hand, Bliss realized, and at least part of Andrea realized this also. But Nothing in part was really the remarkable capability of hypnosis to block out pain and emotion.

"Nothing is angry," Sister Jeanine reported to Bliss in a tense voice. "It is trying to hurt her. Nothing is putting Little Andrea-Ellen and me in a coffin and hammering nails in. Nothing is trying to take over again. When you said 'Look at a movie,' a light went on in the closet. Light that hurt Andrea's eyes and scared her. It was her mother yelling at her to get out—grabbing her by the arm and telling her to go to her room. Nothing came then. Nothing put her in the coffin just now. Nothing closed the coffin with nails. Nothing is trying to get me now. Nothing wants me dead, Dr. Bliss."

What followed was both dramatic and also harrowing. At that moment Super Andrea appeared, eyes flashing, and yelled at Bliss:

"You have to break Nothing away from her!"

In the next moment Andrea, or that personality now controlling Andrea's body, grabbed a long pin from Andrea's dress and began coming toward Bliss, making jabbing swipes at him. Bliss retreated a step before catching hold of her arm and physically struggling with the girl. Once again her strength was impressive. Bliss barely managed to subdue her, wrested the pin from her grasp, and reinstituted some order.

Her body relaxed reluctantly, and Sister Jeanine was out, blinking and breathing very hard:

"Nothing almost took her today. I know that when you work with Nothing it must be safe. She started losing everything. Inside of her they were stabbing . . . it was trying to destroy both her and you."

"Yes, I can see that," Bliss said. "Nothing is very violent."

"Yes, Dr. Bliss. Nothing is the most terrifying of all the things inside of her. Nothing was triggered by the terror of the light. Nothing is terror and murderous rage. Nothing is very physical and doesn't listen very well. It has tried to strangle her a number of times, using Andrea's body as a weapon."

"Why do you think Andrea created Nothing?"

"Nothing is so physical because Andrea never fought her parents," Sister Jeanine said persuasively. "Because of the Catholic religion you don't talk back, and certainly never fight back. That is why Nothing is so physical and fights."

"How can I talk with Nothing?"

"I have a picture—the only way to talk to Nothing is an empty room with arms and legs tired. Then he has to be there . . ."

Before the next session Bliss prepared himself for the coming confrontation with Nothing. First he secured another physician to help in case of trouble—a physician with good, big muscles to restrain any arms that might begin swinging. As it was, after Bliss had summoned up Nothing, the encounter was more physical than he bargained for. Nothing struck out immediately, yelling and screaming, raining down a barrage of blows on Andrea's face. It took both grown men to restrain the young, overweight woman, and even at that it was a struggle. Between bouts with Nothing, other personalities—Little Andrea-Ellen, Big Andrea, Super Andrea, Sister Jeanine, and several others—bolted through, careening about her face and then disappearing as suddenly as they had come. It was disconcerting and disorienting even for Bliss, but for Andrea it must have been totally overwhelming. Bliss kept trying to talk to Nothing, but that personality seemed to possess a vocabulary limited to grunts and wails and inarticulate growls with only a few short, violent words thrown in here and there for good measure:

"She is evil. She must die!" Nothing snarled in a bass voice. "You have kept her alive too long. I'll show you—"

Bliss tried various strategies to impose reason on the situation, to make friends with this primitive force, but it did no good. The load of hate and brutal experiences, which it was Nothing's lot to carry, had shaped a creature of elemental rage. After a while, Bliss backed off and let Nothing slide back into the subconscious pool from which it had come. But Bliss knew that if Andrea Biaggi was ever to be healed, even partially, Nothing would have to be contended with and domesticated.

On February 4, a letter from Illinois reached Dr. Bliss written by Andrea's aunt, Cecilia Antonio:

Dear Dr. Bliss:

My husband asked me to answer your letter as I would be more familiar with Andrea's history than he (Andrea's mother was my sister). I will tell you as much as I know of the family, which may be somewhat sketchy as my sister was very reluctant to talk of private family matters except when it became absolutely necessary to do so.

Andrea's paternal grandparents came to the United States from Corsica where they lived in dire poverty. There were a few Corsicans here, so they were able to get along in their new land. The grandfather worked in the local mines and had a small farm. They were very hard-working people. Mr. Biaggi was a very domineering man. They had a large family—I wasn't too familiar with the offspring. I just knew Joseph Biaggi (Andrea's father) and several of the younger sisters. Joseph was the oldest in the family. They moved to Illinois years ago where apparently the father found work and the boys had a better opportunity to find work. They had a nice home, but not too many of the children were able to finish high school.

I can't remember if it was shortly after Dara (my sister) and Joseph married or soon after that Joseph's mother died quite suddenly of an abortion. Up to that time, Joseph idolized his mother, but later, after her death, this turned to hate. The older girls took care of the family as best they could—I don't remember their ages at the time. They were away from here, and I didn't know them that well. After the mother's death the family received charity for a while, and it was during this time that a social worker visited the home and had the father arrested for incest with a younger daughter. He was tried and sent to the State Prison. I don't recall how long his sentence was, but I remember hearing the Social Department was going to make an example of him. Since Joseph was the oldest in the family, it was up to him to take charge. After his father was released from prison, he stayed with the family until his death. Andrea never knew her grandmother, and I don't know if she recalls the grandfather as she must have been very young at the time.

Joseph and Dara moved to Chicago where he got odd jobs—everything from short-order cook to demolishing old homes. He was a hard worker but couldn't keep a job too long because he refused to take orders. He always resented the fact that his wife had graduated from high school and had a secretarial job when they were married. I still feel that had he had a chance to go to a vocational school or high school, his life might have been different. He, too, was a very domineering man, very strict with the children. When they had odd jobs, he would collect all the money they earned and demand an accounting. He kept all the money and would give just enough to Dara for a bare living for herself and the children. They moved quite frequently. Outwardly Joseph was a very amiable man, liked to go out, and would do favors for others. He always worked hard and steadily at some job he thought would make him rich. He bought equipment (rototiller, new car, plumbing equipment, etc.) that always had to be paid for on time; consequently, the family was constantly in debt.

During the early 1940s, the family (there were three boys by then) moved back to our area where Joseph got a job working in the mines. But he eventually decided he'd had enough of mining and moved to northwest Illinois, where he built a home with the help of his boys and his brothers. His personality seemed to change (or maybe it wasn't disguised as it used to be); he was very preoccupied with sex. He constantly talked of his conquests, imagined or real, especially in front of my sisters and brother.

Then the four girls came along. Andrea was the oldest, and she truly was a beautiful child—blond, curly-haired, beautiful skin. I know her Dad was very jealous of her, as of the others that followed. I remember when she was very young, perhaps three or four years old, my sister told me Andrea had a bad case of vaginitis. We told her to take the little girl to the family doctor. When we asked how she was doing, she said, "Okay," and that was all. But I know that while they were growing up, their father constantly accused them of being promiscuous. He also kept accusing my sister of infidelity and insisted none of the family were his! I saw a list of the family on which he had indicated who he thought the father of each one was—the list included his brothers, and even one of his sons. While Dara was working on a hot lunch program at one of the schools, he stormed in and accused her of having an affair with the janitor—right there in front of all the people in the school!

When Andrea entered high school, she became a compulsive eater, especially candy, which she would hide; she gained considerable weight (her sisters are all slim).

To digress a bit, I'm not too sure of dates, but I think it was in the late 1950s that the family had a weekend of terror. Joseph had purchased a gun and said he was going to kill the whole family and then himself.

I can't recall which one of the boys was able to call my husband, who talked to Joseph by phone, and it must have frightened him. At any rate, my husband contacted the local police department and they contacted the city police. He was removed to a local hospital and then committed to the State Hospital for the mentally ill. He was there three years and escaped several times, which was also a very trying experience for the family.

In the meantime, Andrea and, during the past few years, her sister, Dalia, have had a lot of emotional problems. I think if the key were found to unlock all her fears, Andrea would be a beautiful person. She has a sharp mind and is able to do things which would seem insurmountable to someone else. She did tell us that while in Boston the doctors thought she had a brain tumor. What is fact and what is fiction, however, is hard to discern.

I am not sure who Andrea means by Frank. The only one I know is an old Corsican who's about 88 years old now. He was a distant cousin or maybe just a family friend. At any rate, he has been married three times and lost all his wives. I doubt if this has anything to do with Andrea.

I don't know if this letter will be of any help. It's very difficult for me to write this as we loved Dara very much. I hope Andrea can be helped.

Sincerely,
Cecilia Antonio

Bliss showed this letter to Andrea and watched as she registered first surprise then disbelief at the sentence, "I remember when she was very young, perhaps three or four years old, my sister told me Andrea had a bad case of vaginitis."

Though it didn't say so in so many words, both of them understood what the vaginitis implied. Bliss was keenly aware of the affirmation that this piece of information would give his case.

"You mean—you mean my pictures are real?" Andrea looked dazed. "It really was when I was three? I—I can't understand . . ."

"Doesn't this tell you everything you need to know?" Bliss asked. "That the images you remember aren't just hallucinations? Your father really did do those things to you?"

For a moment she seemed to pause in thought, and then spontaneously started to relive one of the incidents. Her hands and feet were restrained by her father—she was lying on a mattress with him on top of her, a wild, screaming madman punishing her with his body. She went on to relate the first time she had experienced sex voluntarily at the age of 21. Not surprisingly, much of this was also blanked out, and she only remembered seeing the face of her father on the wall beside her. It was shortly after this that she began to "hurt herself inside." A promiscuous period followed during the late sixties when everyone around her was experimenting with sex, but it had never really sat well with Andrea, perhaps because she had never been able to enjoy the experience of it with anything like normality. There were the recurring images of her father for one thing—and her guilt for another, associated always with her mother.

"The little girl is in the kitchen with her mother," Andrea reported in hypnosis, "and mother is very angry, yelling and hitting her—telling her she did something wrong—telling her she is bad and should be sent to her room. The little girl is in her room alone. First she cries, but she is confused, doesn't understand what she did wrong, why she was being punished. The mother slapped her hard in the face. The little girl feels the hurt of being slapped— starts getting very angry because she didn't do anything wrong—it wasn't fair. She got angry at her mother and then blanked out.'' Pause. ''Then the girl changed and started hitting her head against the wall—she was still angry at her mother but was hitting her own head against the wall, in the same place her mother hit her earlier—the other person kept hitting the little girl's head against the wall more and more until blood came from her head. Someone else saw the blood and she stopped—it was she, Andrea, who saw it—she was different again. Then she curled up in the bed and cried herself to sleep.''

Andrea came out of it after that, and they talked a while longer about Andrea's strange sexual past, about the indiscriminate sex and the times on the Boston Common when she had propositioned men.

''How did you rationalize all this?'' Bliss asked. ''Were you trying to expunge the memory of your father in some way?''

Andrea looked at him for a moment and blinked. ''No. It was Bridget's job to take care of the sex. She was there for sex the first time. She is the promiscuous one.'' Andrea looked suddenly surprised that she had divulged this piece of information. There was a moment that passed, and then Andrea launched herself into a frenzied trance state, speaking rapidly and in disjointed sentences.

''Only part knows it happened, but another part says 'No.' There was a third part that saw the blood. Nothing loves blood. It was Mother Mary—yes—and it became very calm like right now. As it happens here my body is experiencing it—sensations—pain, shaky, cold. Nothing can be physically angry—and hurt and I can't.''

For a moment Andrea looked at the wall of Bliss's office, and then: ''It is blank—it was from something in here Thursday I didn't want to believe—the blue bicycle— now I know. You asked me. I said I was too young, but I wasn't. I was four years old, but Andrea said it wasn't real so Little Andrea-Ellen put it away. But in the letter it said

four years old and then—flash! The blue bicycle. I remembered getting scared and wanting to put it away—running
away from the bicycle and then the bad dreams, and then
yesterday I remembered the blue bicycle.''

''What significance does this blue bicycle have for you,
Andrea?'' Bliss asked.

The voice was a monotone. ''She said she liked the blue
bicycle. She didn't have one. She asked her father if he
would buy her one. He said she would have to do things in
the garage if she wanted one. He brought her a bicycle in
the garage. She said, 'Thank you,' but he said, 'Before
you ride it, you must do things.' He fixed the attic with a
bed and took her up there and started having sex with her,
and she couldn't say anything even when she was in pain.
He put his hand over her mouth and held her arms. But
sometimes she didn't care because she wanted the blue
bicycle so much . . .''

It was the first turning point in Andrea's therapy, that
memory of the events made real using the verification of
her aunt's letter. Not that this meant Andrea ''believed''
completly that her father had abused her in this way. After
all, as Bliss realized, there was a whole committee of
personalities to be dealt with, many of them with a vested
interest in seeing that Andrea never accepted completely
the truth of her history. Perhaps by now there were four or
five personalities who had been persuaded provisionally
that the memories were correct; but what of the others who
didn't even know there was a problem yet? What of pivotal voices like Little Andrea-Ellen's, who could only feel
guilt no matter what proof was presented to the contrary?
And what about those personalities Dr. Bliss felt certain
still prowled in the background, without name or designa-
tion, unwilling to appear until their ''time'' came?

For only the briefest of intervals did Andrea's revelation
have a salutary effect on her. Within weeks, she was crazy
again. Bliss had taken a two-week vacation and had left
Andrea in good spirits—coping finally. But upon his return he found a frenzied, hysterical woman wracked by
nightmares, on the verge of suicide. She was back to

believing she was evil and received affirmation for this belief by a majority of voices in her mind. More than this, problems had arisen at work, and there were people in her organization who had begun to complain about the way she was handling her job. She felt as if she were being pushed into a corner, both by her job and by her composite mind, bullied and badgered into accepting opposite views of the same event.

It was only now, after months of therapy, that Dr. Bliss had begun to understand one of the main obstacles to any kind of progress. Not only were there a gaggle of personalities to confront and appease, but there was the problem of the memories themselves—not just their content, but their form and nature as well. Andrea, Bliss realized, didn't experience memories as most people do—as condensed sequences of events edited to eliminate all but the most salient of the sensory impressions. Instead, because of hypnosis Andrea experienced her past with the same immediacy and completeness as a contemporary event, every second recapitulated with the same freshness and feeling of an event in progress. No doubt in a normal person it would have seemed a remarkable example of eidetic memory—unanalyzed, unmitigated, unretouched recollection—but considering the dire nature of the memories and the unrelentingness of the process, it made for disorientation and anarchy. Andrea was never aware of time in the traditional sense. No matter how old the memory, it was replayed as if for the first time. This lent a biblical tone to her thought—there was no time, only timelessness; there was no past, only the present; there were no sins to be expiated in the future, only a person caught repeatedly in the act of "sinning," for whom repentance was a constantly recurring necessity. Andrea was caught in this hideous flux, a victim of her hypnotic retreats. Most objects of everyday experience suggested objects connected with another experience and another time that ran in a parallel track. Seeing a garage shunted her off onto a reexperiencing of her father's madness; a bicycle did the same; a fire reawoke memories of her mother's cruelty. An elevator, a TV, a cat, a small room, almost anything at all could drive her off onto a side spur that joined up with another time . . .

So, in endless cycle she relived her past, without wanting to, often without meaning to, but always and eternally suffering, foreseeing no way to escape from this maze, no way to latch on firmly to real time and leave the past behind.

But knowing all this about her still did nothing to cure her. Her mind was proof against simple solutions, booby-trapped at every turn to discourage treatment. The old memories were emerging; but after a short interval of exhilaration that followed each fresh discovery there occurred a return to panic and despair, characterized by ever-deepening feelings of hopelessness, a growing tendency toward self-injury, and amnesia for the events themselves.

ANDREA'S JOURNAL

Sunday, March 9, 1980

I have been sitting here trying to piece the insanity of these past days/weeks/months/years into some comprehensible form. So understand this, it is my greatest quest in these twilight times—I believe that understanding is my only way out of this madness—either that or resolve my problems in a peaceful death.

To try and communicate the experiences of these past days in words seems painfully inadequate. If I could paint, it would look like a cross between a Salvador Dali and a Hieronymus Bosch. Scenes of torture in a barren landscape, scenes of Hell amid a thousand grisly monsters. If you could hear this experience, it would be an unending echo of the special, silent scream of total terror. The physical sensations would be that of acid searing flesh until the pain became no pain and I wonder then if I am actually alive or suspended in some limbo, caught in a web suspended over Hell.

I am not crazy tonight. I am lost, confused, tired, angry, and profoundly sad. My body is in pain from the latest abuses, but more importantly, my soul-being is in despair.

I cannot, do not want to go through any more of this, yet I know I will because I cannot yet understand what is happening to me.

Events of the past few days include the death of another cat, another suicide attempt, and horrible nightmares. What I most remembered was the wanting to die—not in a Christian sense of resurrection in death—but wanting my being to cease and become a piece of cosmic dust. The only time I pray any longer is when I plead for death.

DR. BLISS'S NOTEBOOK
March 11, 1980

Nothing was remarkably tame, has lost most of his steam and vitriol. I have convinced him to become an ally. Nothing knows all of the traumatic episodes but has kept it away from her, saying that her problems were too much for her to handle. She has had so many terrible experiences, over such a long period, that Nothing can't believe she can master them. He also kept repeating that there were many other personalities, many very strong—stronger than he is—and that he could not control them.

I have had patients whose alternative personalities arose from only one or two early traumas—either a rape or an incestuous episode or some other piece of hideousness. But compared to Andrea, most of them lived a spotless childhood. She had one hell of an early life, and it is very difficult, understandably, for her to relive or recapture these experiences without the utmost pain. Nothing explained to me that Andrea has always had trouble with my white coat because her father worked in a hospital. Part of his bizarre practice was to come home, put on a white coat, and tell Andrea he was a doctor. So his sexual play with her was often presented as part of his "medical" activities. The more I hear about the father, the more he, too, seems to have been a multiple personality. His shifts of mood from an affectionate father to a malignant fiend are typical. But I have also seen a letter written by his doctor while he was at the State Hospital. It contained the statement that he claimed periods of amnesia—also typical of multiples.

Over the last few weeks Andrea has almost disappeared. Super Andrea has taken over and runs the whole show at work, and the other personalities are in command at night. Furthermore, there has been more burning, hurting herself, and suicidal depressions. Bridget has been out, and Andrea is very much afraid of pregnancy. I'm sure there is much more to her fears than this, however.

My frustration continues. While I have begun to understand many of the episodes and characters that make up Andrea's world, I have found it impossible to communicate this information to Andrea herself. Nothing seems to know all about the traumas and is remarkably knowledgeable, but Andrea has become a blob, a passive entity who believes nothing I tell her and has no control over her daily life. For all the good it does, the information I'm uncovering might as well be on the moon. Andrea seems incapable of retaining a jot of it.

Her last comment before she left for New York to attend a conference (where she is the keynote speaker) was, "This week I was going to commit suicide. Now I'll either commit suicide in New York City or come back and work with you." A cliffhanger, and if she comes back I think it will be a major turning point. It will mean that she has decided to commit herself to therapy and we can begin to move ahead with greater hope. It is suicide versus therapy!

ANDREA'S JOURNAL
March 25, 1980—11:00 P.M.

Time really began for me last week when I got on the plane to New York. I was in and out (mostly out) of reality before that point, and I remembered little.

For some reason, I did not have my presentation ready when I boarded the plane. I did manage to bring the appropriate papers with me on the plane to help put the presentation together.

I remember some conflict was still very present when I first sat on the plane. The plane was quite crowded, which was unexpected as it was early Sunday morning. I was also angry—I don't know what the problem was.

Whatever it was, just trying to remember made me quite upset again, so I've decided not to try and just keep writing about events since I feel too fragile to explore the feelings.

On the plane, at some point, Super Andrea clicked into action and put the presentation together with great ease. By the time the plane landed in New York, the task was complete.

When I did arrive at the hotel, I started to stay in my room even though I had been invited to a social that evening. Super Andrea switched back, and I went out and spent a few hours talking with other people at the conference. It was then I discovered no one was really "up" on the topic of my presentation, which allayed any fears of my presentation coming under close scrutiny by experts in the field. I slept well that night.

My presentation was in the morning after several "political" presenters, the mayor, the social services commissioner, and a congressman. I had no real beginning to my presentation, and was still formulating it while those people were speaking. So, when I started I was nervous and fumbling. Once I got into it, I switched again to someone even more confident than Super Andrea. The presentation then flowed as seldom before.

The first question began with a comment about this being the best presentation he had ever heard, and most of the other people there prefaced their questions with the same remark. After I finished, there was a standing ovation for me—an honor not afforded any other speaker during the conference.

Then there was a flurry of people wanting to talk to me, ushering me to a VIP table for lunch, and asking if I'd be available for some training sessions and what were my "fees!" A star was born for the moment.

Then came exhaustion and a second presentation in the afternoon, and soon I was slipping into a cross between Little Andrea-Ellen and Nothing, who wanted to slit my wrists.

I slipped in and out of many persons those next few

days, but there was a difference—the stronger ones were the good ones this time. I even treated myself to a train ride to Boston, which was a favorite event.

The people at the conference treated Andrea like a celebrity. Her speaking ability and her intelligence were quickly noticed and rewarded with praise. How much more remarkable was her performance when it was considered that most of this time she was flashing in and out of self-hypnosis, flushing with panic, and running through her entire repertoire of personalities at a high rate of speed.

While part of Andrea Biaggi smiled at the applauding audience, another part (or parts) of her was contemplating suicide with calm detachment. How could she trust the reactions of these people? They were cheering for someone else—not Andrea. Super Andrea maybe—but certainly not drab, sinful, blobbish Andrea.

Soon after the conference she was off to Boston to visit her priest friend—and see the neurologist again. She was still trying to find an ''easier'' way out of her dilemma— hoping that the neurological team would discover a brain tumor or some abnormality that could be treated (and cured) through surgery. A surgical procedure—a modified lobotomy—was again recommended, but she refused. For a while in Boston, she vacillated between life and death, spending hours in the subway considering whether to jump in front of a train or buy a gun. Then, abruptly, her contemplations ceased. As if a switch had been flicked off, her indecision vanished, and she realized that she didn't want to die. But living—surely the kind of living she had been doing the last twenty years of her life—was not worth surviving for. It was then that she decided to return to Salt Lake City and continue her therapy with Bliss.

DR. BLISS'S NOTEBOOK
March 24, 1980

She has returned from New York feeling better. She seems to remember some of the events uncovered during my talk with Nothing, such as her father's impersonations of a doctor. However, she related the events with a complete amnesia for the source of the information. She retains the facts in a foggy form, but without the recognition that they came from Nothing.

We have agreed that she will come into the hospital so that we can work more intensively, while she goes to her job half-time.

For the first time in quite a while, I feel some reason for optimism.

LETTER FROM ANDREA

Sunday, March 30—10 P.M.

Dear Dr. Bliss,

This is Sister Jeanine. I made a big error in talking to you. I was trying to make it easier for you by saying this could all wait for another day. After I got off the phone, Joseph, who is in quite a murderous rage right now, started laughing at me and said he would win today as I was too kind.

I fear what will happen now, so the first thing I thought of was writing you as a document of this event/this day.

As for going into the hospital, it is my firm conviction that she needs to go in and be there all day and night as Joseph is making plans to sneak things in there such as pills and razor blades to hurt herself, and thereby sabotage the safety factor of being in the hospital. It is quite a serious problem, and you should certainly be made aware of it. Super Andrea wants to work through most of the day and then come to see you and stay in the hospital during the night. She is trying to make that world as "normal" as possible so that she can continue her role as an executive director. It is a most dangerous procedure for Andrea, however, as this situation feeds into her splitting process even more.

Super Andrea sincerely believes that everything is okay—which is true when she's in command. However, she is easily overcome these days by stronger persons such as Joseph and Nothing. That is due to her real situation at work being one of extreme stress both personally and professionally. She is, in fact, being watched closely by various board members as they sense an unknown problem becoming serious. They don't know what's wrong yet, but it's only a matter of time.

Andrea herself was the one who came up with the plan of half work days. She was trying to compromise on the demands of both worlds. If she were stronger, I guess, I would go along with that, but my knowledge of Joseph's plans would seem to preclude this as an option. I regret this, as any effort to keep Andrea on top would be the ideal now.

Then, there are quite a number of other ones such as the Angry One, Bridget, and some you have not met yet who do not want her to go in the hospital. They will most certainly try to get her out at various times if she does go.

There is one in particular, the Monster, who seems to be in quite a rage and has been a key figure in her actions the past few days. There is so much hate and destruction tied to this one.

The toll, these past few days, has included another cat, internal body damage through coat hangers, and pills, alcohol abuse, all that stuff.

I am starting to get frightened myself now—the fighting is getting stronger—great danger seems present.

Andrea refused to go into hypnosis during the next few sessions with Bliss and balked at the idea of returning to the hospital.

"But I made an agreement with Nothing," Bliss said.

Andrea shook her head violently. "I shouldn't have to pay for what other things tell you."

Suddenly the unmistakable features of Nothing appeared on her face: "The Angry One has been in rage," Nothing said softly. "There are dreams about incidents. She is going in and out. Joseph has been raising hell. She hasn't been the same since she remembered the attic room. Parts laugh at her and say it never happened. She is in the room again—and hurting herself. Then she becomes Little Andrea—Andrea-Ellen—and cries when she realizes her mother is gone. Then the Angry One slips in." Nothing looked around the office and growled. "Joseph is trying to sabotage you. Joseph has been trying to stop her from coming here all day."

"Why was Joseph created?" Bliss asked.

"It was punishment. Because she was taught early she was evil and bad."

"And why were you created, Nothing?"

Nothing ignored the question. "Her father and the faces got mixed up. Joseph has been fighting not to be in the hospital. He wants to hurt her."

"Then let me talk with Joseph's mind," Bliss said after a moment's thought.

Nothing nodded its head and rumbled, "Good idea—so he can't hit her. Yes."

"Yes, you keep the body, Nothing." Bliss remembered perfectly well how violently Joseph had attacked Andrea's body before and wasn't taking chances this time.

With a hissing intake, Joseph took over Andrea's features. A lambent madness invested her eyes, giving Bliss an excellent idea of the kind of fury and insanity that Joseph Biaggi had actually possessed.

"You let me out of the attic," Joseph said dangerously. "I don't care about her. She is other people to me. She is my mother and wife."

Andrea reappeared, gasping and frantic. "None of this is true! It is just like a little kid would make up. You know?"

Then Nothing was back, grimly regarding Bliss. "She freaked out. Joseph doesn't want Andrea to get well."

Then Joseph was back, glowering at Bliss with a triumphant madness in his eyes. "Andrea created me, you know. She was a dumb little kid. She thought she was dirty and sinful and thought she was going to have a baby by me. Some kids said you get kids by kissing."

"But you died, Joseph," replied Bliss. "You can't hurt her anymore."

The personality chuckled mirthlessly. "You think? When I left she created me to keep the punishment going."

"Do you want it to keep going?"

"Yeah. Only sometimes when I know what I did I wish someone would stop me. I'm tired of it. But other times, there is all craziness. I'm the oldest here, but no one took care of me. I had to care for everyone. It isn't punishment, it is to make it so she will never be with a man again."

It took another hour, but at last Bliss succeeded in convincing enough parts of Andrea to return to the hospital so that a consensus was reached.

ANDREA'S JOURNAL
April 1, 1980

I feel now like the bomb in me has been defused. I am most grateful for human restraint instead of mechanical restraints that have been used in the past when I felt like this. There is peace, courage, and hope right now that I pray can be sustained to work these problems through to completion. I am totally in the present right now, which in itself seems nothing short of a miracle.

There is still a great deal of sadness and crying, which is understandable now to me and even feels good. I felt that all these intense emotions could only be released by physical rage against myself or someone else. I know now that the tears (that I have been fighting not to show) are strong allies in releasing some of this pain.

I have been rather angry at Dr. Bliss saying I need to get my courage together and deal with all of this. I thought I had a lot of courage just staying alive these past months. But now I am aware that this is a state of existence resulting from fear—not from courage. Fear that death would place me in hell, which I long since have pictured as eternally caught between those two worlds. There's a quote by Rollo May about courage to the effect that it is the decision to live despite all the pain. I was not really deciding to live before—just not to die.

Now I *want* to live! That is a good feeling, but a terrifying one also. I now am aware that events did happen in the past that have created this division of my being. I know that means facing not just events but the rage that resulted.

Sometimes like the past week I just get stuck in the rage and lose sight of ever getting through it. That's where I need help. I also want to learn to help myself during those times so that I seek help right away instead of reverting to my closet.

All this sounds very noble, but sustaining my commitment to myself is what remains the critical test.

It became increasingly more obvious to Bliss that Andrea wasn't understanding much of what she was divulging. The characters remained intact, and the memories remained unlearned. Only by having Andrea recall the trauma and actually relive the occasion in detail—and in all its hideousness—was there a chance that she would believe what was going on. The unfortunate and paradoxical aspect of this was that the memories were so grim that they could not help but throw her into panic and thus into self-hypnosis, thereby short-circuiting the whole process of remembering. Still, there was no substitute for the shock that such revelations occasioned, and Bliss pressed on with them.

Part of Andrea (perhaps the majority of her) was still uncertain of Dr. Bliss's methods or his genuine commitment to her recovery. It therefore became a question of faith: could she wholeheartedly give herself to the process even without knowing that it was working? As a good Catholic she had confronted similar dilemmas before and knew perfectly well the paradoxes of that system of belief. Finally, almost in despair, she girded herself to an all-out campaign under Bliss's generalship.

With the combination of hospitalization and intensive psychotherapeutic sessions, Andrea soon began to regain control over her chaotic inner world: "Joseph doesn't have the same power right now," a coooperative Nothing reported. "Last night he tried to get her to hurt herself, but he was weak. When she worked things out yesterday, he lost his power.

"She isn't Little Andrea-Ellen as much," Nothing went on. "Little Andrea-Ellen is sad but is getting a better understanding. She let Mother Mary come back and comfort her. I had her remember by recallng key places—grandma's house, barn, attic in garage, boiler room in hospital. I wanted her to picture them and realize they frightened her. She must do it gradually, though."

Bliss tried to help the process by relating to Nothing and having that personality "translate" to the other personalities, the method by which Joseph had been implanted in Andrea. He went on to explain the damage the real Joseph had done to her. The whole time, Andrea's eyes looked straight ahead, focusing on the Yale diploma in Latin on Bliss's wall, her face expressionless, the blood seemingly drained from her cheeks. At last, after his brief lecture, Nothing spoke again in its usual gruff voice: "She hears you, but they don't record. She must go back and experience it. Otherwise it doesn't help."

"Very well," Bliss said. "Andrea, I want you to return to hypnosis, to go back in time . . ." He paused for a few seconds until he saw a flush beginning on Andrea's cheeks. "Where are you now?"

Andrea's voice, sounding very weak and far away, began:

"Nothing took me back into the attic. He said I didn't have to remember what happened before . . . but I did. Yes. I see my father hit me, and then he said, 'Don't say a word.' My mother kept yelling for me. My father put on his clothes and came out. My mother asked, 'Have you seen her?' and he said, 'No.' I wanted to yell out to her to help me, but I knew she would hurt me more. I just cried and had to be quiet, and then there was anger and the anger had me in a corner in the bed, was feeling more angry—kept saying inside it wasn't fair. Anger started to hit head against bedpost, and then there was *nothing*. Then Nothing came.

"For a moment you were my father—the beard," Andrea told Bliss. "When I saw you then as my father, I wanted to kill you . . . I remember it." A pause. "When I came downstairs my mother hit me for not coming when she called." Andrea grasped her right ear and rubbed it. "I don't feel anything now. There was a lot of anger, but I feel numb now. When it started I made it go away."

There was a pause while Bliss tried to rouse her, but as always it took awhile. Andrea was looking inward, conversing with her many voices, oblivious to external stimulus. In her own good time she returned, and continued:

"I started to feel sharp pains in my vagina, cramps—after my mother hit me and got me to my room—then the pain started—Nothing was gone—he left when she hit me—so the pain was there—then Joseph came back. I wanted my vagina gone because it hurt so much. He kept doing things; I wanted it gone so I wouldn't feel anymore—so he couldn't go into me.

"You once asked if I ever masturbated, but I never did because I don't feel there. I couldn't understand why. I can keep jabbing myself because I don't feel there. I couldn't understand why I tried to hurt myself inside. The first time it happened in Boston when Bridget came out and wanted to be with men. I don't know who did it. Bridget was a streetwalker, and then Bridget would be with a man, and then she would leave. Bridget would enjoy sex, and then someone else would come—Joseph would come to punish for that. Joseph wanted to destroy that part. The first time was right after Bridget had sex. Some part had to punish Andrea for Bridget, but it wasn't Joseph. She put oven cleaner inside, wanted to burn it out and close it. Bridget is coming out more again. It feels numb again."

"So you created Bridget to have sex?" Bliss said.

"Yes. But something is wrong. Joseph wants to hurt her now. Joseph was created to punish and hurt but not to destroy—someone else is there to destroy."

"Who is it?" Bliss asked. Another character was about to make his premier appearance.

Andrea began to twist around, gasping. "There is nothing there. No one . . ."

A moment later a loud, grating voice cried out: "She is

no good! I must leave this office. Now!'' The irate personality got up, and it was only through physical restraint that Andrea was made to sit down again. Instantly, the anger evaporated, and she was once again Andrea, pale and limp, in the chair.

''I—I can't feel anymore.''

''But you must!'' Bliss insisted. ''Who is the one who wants to destroy?''

For a moment longer she trembled there, her face flushed, her eyes large and unseeing. Then, just as suddenly, a sterner countenance took control, and Nothing boomed out, ''His—his name is Philippe. He has one purpose. When she was very young he was there. His purpose was to destroy her inside and sew her up. When she was little, she had him imaginarily sew it up, but it didn't work. Even when Bridget wants to have sex, Philippe will try to destroy her. It is incredible he hasn't succeeded. She isn't fighting him that much.''

''Can I talk to Philippe?'' Bliss asked.

''Yes,'' Nothing said, and abruptly the dour frown disappeared to be replaced by a calm, almost mannered countenance that might have done credit to a raffish dandy of the last century. The eyebrows rose, the voice and manner became haughty, condescending.

''She was five,'' Philippe said in clipped tones. ''It was pretend when she was young—to make the pain go away. I've tried everything. I can't understand why it doesn't work. Her father did it to her for years. What the hell am I supposed to do with those feelings?''

It was an excellent question, one that Dr. Bliss had a hard time answering. The new character, Philippe, had hit the pivotal question, the one that underlay the whole purpose for Andrea's multiple personalities. What indeed did one do with such gross trauma? To remember it was to relive it, and even to live through it the *first* time must have taken rare courage and a strong survival instinct. To be young, helpless, unprotected by her mother and set upon at frequent intervals by a maniac who was her father— what kind of hell was that?

The emergence of Philippe did little to quell her panic. As had happened before, this new revelation caused a clamorous riot in her inner world, and all the voices howled for retribution. As a result of that session, Andrea cut her arm with a pin she had found on the closed ward. Though the wounds were superficial it indicated to what extremes she would go to inflict injury on herself after one of those episodes. It wasn't until Bliss had talked to the Angry One, the chief offender in this latest attack, that Andrea showed Bliss the place where she had hidden the pin.

As the days of intensive therapy passed, more and more came to the surface.

A ritual had developed around her father's brutal attacks—a growing cadre of personalities to buffer Andrea from the grim reality she was being forced to endure. Even when she was little and couldn't understand the process rationally, the ritual was going on. First there was Nothing to anesthetize her and remove her from the ferocity of her father's attacks. Then Philippe would come and symbolically sew her up, giving her imagined safety against the event of another attack. Then the Angry One, a small and brutalized child in her mind's eye, would throw a silent tantrum, directing the anger she felt toward her mother and father at herself. Because she could not hope to hurt her parents (even if she had consciously wanted to) she devised a means by which she could hurt herself—turning the other cheek, so to speak, in accord with correct Christian procedure.

By the time she had been ostracized from her home and family and left to fend for herself in Boston, Philippe had grown vicious. No longer a protector, he had become the chief chastiser, and—if the time ever arose—the head executioner as well. There was more to punish in Boston, after all—more years of festering anger and resentment, more emotions to keep under lock and key, more natural impulses to obstruct and curtail. Chief among these cravings was sex, a passion abhorred by both her memory of it with her father and Mother Church's proscription. Remem-

brance and religion being in accord on the issue, the
natural course of her desire had become perverted—as her
father's had—leading to self-injury and masochism. For
contact with other people, she was forced to arrogate lust
to a pair of personalities; Bridget, who handled "regular
sex" like a prostitute, and Cathleen, who was a lesbian.

"Cathleen is a lost, guilty woman," Sister Jeanine had
told Bliss. "Andrea was so afraid of men that she turned
to women. Something then happened at the Boston
Commons—I see her bedroom. She was directing a woman's program. She was with Elizabeth, but something was
wrong with Andrea. She was losing control—she was
seeing a woman therapist, and that therapist told her she
couldn't see her anymore because Andrea was too sick.
She told her that in the park, and Andrea didn't expect it.
She wanted Andrea to go back to the psychiatric ward
where she had been in restraints—but it had never helped.
She went home and told no one. A few days later, she was
in her room and feeling horrible. Elizabeth came for help,
was crying, and Andrea held her to help. She created
Cathleen then, to be a lesbian with Elizabeth. Afterward
it went on for a few days, then something happened in that
room—Elizabeth isn't there anymore. Cathleen isn't there
either. It is blank. There is a phenomenal blank like a
stone wall—"

After this, Bliss learned, Andrea somehow found herself
on the Commons, walking.

A few nights later she was back again, walking on the
Commons, looking quite consciously for a man to hurt her.
She was walking around the Commons in the darkest
places hoping someone would come up with a knife or a
gun and stab her or shoot her. And then a man grabbed her
behind a tree by the Garden, and he wanted to rape her.
She didn't care. She said to him, "I won't fight if you do
what I ask you to do." He grabbed her and pulled her
down, and then she started fighting. He told her if she
moved or screamed he would kill her—the same words as
her father. She asked the man to do something for her, and
she wouldn't fight—she asked him to kill her, please. She

begged him to take the knife and cut her stomach. The man said she was crazy and left.

She was there for a long time—she was curled up in a ball, like a little girl—and she asked Philippe to come and help her, make her stop, and he made it clear to her that he would close it up once and for all. Then Philippe had gone to the store, had bought a large amount of oven cleaner, and had calmly walked to the bus station, gone to the bathroom, and put it into her vagina.

Someone must have found her because the next thing she remembered was the emergency room and her refusal to go into the hospital and her departure.

In the weeks that followed Bliss uncovered not only more episodes from Andrea's life in Boston but also discovered several more personalities who played integral parts in fortifying the "wall" that protected Andrea from the brunt of reality. There had been only one lesbian interlude that Sister Jeanine could recall but, then again, it wasn't always easy to keep the facts straight.

Then there was Julia, who was Little Andrea-Ellen's age, and who loved flowers, trees, warm times. Her world was a little girl's world where children danced and sang, and she ran through flowering meadows with her long hair flowing in the breeze. Julia came only rarely, but when she came she filled Andrea with joy. It was so unlike the world in which Andrea seemed destined to live—a place of freedom and unspoiled pleasure.

It was Julia who had sat on the park bench with Elizabeth, her lesbian friend, and had picked some flowers for her—just as Julia did for her mother. What did a little girl know of lesbianism? It was a harmless kindness. But there was such a distance between Julia's world of innocence and the wicked, dying world where Andrea had to live. The flowers were interpreted as a proposition by her friend and had led to untoward things that called for Cathleen's intervention. These things, of course, were sinful and wrong in the eyes of the others—Little Andrea cried and the Angry One roared with fury, and then Bridget came out to walk around the Commons after midnight. It was all so complicated, involving such a chain of cause-and-effect that no single entity inside of her (not even Nothing or Sister Jeanine) could keep it all quite straight. No wonder there was confusion and despair. No wonder there was a desire to die and leave all the chaos behind. Only an indomitable will persisted as it had through the worst of her father's demented passions.

At last Bliss began to see enough of the characters and their origins that he could start integrating some back into Andrea herself. This integration involved making the character a part of Andrea's consciousness, thereby bringing to "the surface" all the memories and actions to which that personality was heir. His first candidate for integration, because of the personality's destructive nature and the need to get him out in the open, was Philippe. When Bliss suggested this to Andrea she was reluctant.

"I'm afraid to let go. Part feels like tearing room apart—doesn't believe."

"But it's true. All of it," Bliss insisted. "And it is necessary to begin integrating all the parts of you. Philippe *must* be first because he is so dangerous by himself. Do you understand?"

"Yes, I guess so." Andrea was looking at him with clear eyes, and there was no doubt that she was out of hypnosis. She took a deep breath finally. "How do we begin?"

Bliss put her rapidly into a trance and then asked both Philippe and Andrea whether they were willing to merge. Both agreed.

"All right then," Bliss said. "Andrea, are you willing to accept all of Philippe's responsibilities, feelings, and memories?"

"Yes," Andrea said. "I will." There was a pause, and then Andrea emerged spontaneously from hypnosis, smiling broadly. "It—it worked. It really worked. Is it all going to be this easy?"

Bliss was as elated as Andrea. It had all been far easier than he first anticipated.

"Of course," he said. "I don't see why not. It won't be long now."

"Yes, I can see that," Andrea said happily. "Not long at all."

ANDREA'S JOURNAL
April 4, 1980

When I was first told of the multiple personality diagnosis, it was not only a foreign concept, but quite frightening. The visual images from the movie "Sybil" of each of her personalities looking so radically different was the first block to accepting diagnosis. It took me a few (quite a few!) months before I could accept that I could have really differing personalities and yet still look the same. After getting over that hurdle, the next obstacle came from the stated goal of integration. Again, the image of "Sybil" after *eleven years* of therapy, just putting them all together one day by just sort of shaking their hands, and then they drifted into her! Anyhow it seemed such an alien experience that I doubted ever being able to achieve integration.

My integration of Philippe was so unexpected and natural that I was able to achieve it before I had time to block the process through those Sybil images. I am so thrilled that it happened that way because I believe now that any truly "conscious" effort of integration would have been thwarted by mechanical stumbling blocks created by my preconceptions.

My experience was almost spiritual in nature though most certainly it was real and actual. I wasn't even clear what Dr. Bliss wanted to do. I thought of it as some long, involved process taking years to achieve, but when Dr. Bliss said let's do it now, go into hypnosis, I just did it.

My trust level in Dr. Bliss was so high at that point I immediately complied, asking only that I be guided correctly.

I felt no fear at first in a peaceful surrender of my consciousness to hypnosis—a most rare feeling for me because hypnosis is so often fought by me. I don't even recall the words Dr. Bliss used to facilitate the experience but I vividly remember what the experience was.

At first, I faced Philippe not as an actual person but as the terrifying self-destructive acts I had undergone all these years. I was almost frozen with terror.

Then—and I believe this to be the spiritual part of the integration—Mother Mary came to rescue me so that the terror fell off of me. I want to note here the physical sensations of cold and stiffening of all my muscles that occurred at that moment. Mother Mary comforted me and brought me back to my bedroom on the day I had originally created Philippe . . . that was the key to being able to carry the process to its fruition.

I was totally back there in my room at the age of five. I could see myself creating Philippe out of need for protection against both the physical abuses of my father and the psychic abuses of my mother. I *KNEW* it was not anything "bad" that I did to create Philippe, but rather what was done *to* me that was evil. That was the crucial memory for me. Then, there was a brief sadness, almost mourning for that time and how it had crippled my life.

Then Mother Mary helped again by bringing me back to the awareness that I was now 32, both parents were dead, and not only was I no longer the five-year-old Little Andrea-Ellen, but they couldn't harm me like that any longer. A new set of physical sensations evolved then— warmth, peace, and finally joy as I came back to consciousness with a big smile (a rare event).

The entire integration took about five minutes in actual time but spanned almost *thirty years* of pain and terror to effect completion. I know that, for now at least, I no longer need Philippe and I feel safe and whole again.

DR. BLISS'S NOTEBOOK
April 6, 1980

By the time I integrated Philippe into Andrea I thought that I'd heard the worst of it—not that I didn't suspect there was a lot more trauma back there, since I assumed Joseph Biaggi had been a terribly sick man and had done all kinds of sordid things to Andrea. But I wasn't prepared for the revelations Sister Jeanine presented to me soon after the initial integration.

"It was a holiday," Sister Jeanine began, "and the family got together. They would buy huge blocks of ice, and they would use the ice pick to chip it. Andrea was trying to remember only nice occasions five years ago, but then the pleasant, memory switched to when she was three and four. She wasn't afraid of the ice pick, but her father got drunk and very angry and everyone left early and then he took her to the attic and brought the ice pick with him. He raped her with the ice pick—stabbed away inside of her with the sharp part . . .

"There was a lot of pain—

"She couldn't turn off the pain. Nothing hadn't been created yet. It was a very clear memory. She feels a lot of pain inside now. When she first remembered, she curled up and covered her ears because she was so scared. She shook violently and was sick to her stomach yesterday like she had been before.

"Then she became angry yesterday—and had lots of pain, and then things became distorted and she began to hurt herself with a pin. She scratched her stomach and arm. Yesterday she felt the pain. It was a hard thing for her to do because she felt the pain.

"This—this was so early, when she was so young, that she hadn't learned to turn it off. Her pain inside is still strong. Philippe didn't do anything painful because with him she felt nothing. The first thing that came back was that she desperately wanted to die.

"Barbara comes to mind as the suicide one. Barbara came yesterday. . . . She is isolated and she feels ugly, stupid, untalented, no reason for existing, people always yelling at her—'Why can't you do this?' or 'Why can't you act that way?' Her face is ugly with acne. She is one of the oldest personalities. I think she is responsible for suicides . . .

"Andrea wanted to die then. Barbara started when she was four, within a year of the ice pick. Her father did it many times. Just then the pain came back. There were many times when he threatened or raped her with an ice pick. She wanted to kill him once with an ice pick. She hid an ice pick once so it would be there. She tried to use it once, and he caught her—I lost it—the pain is coming harder—she brought the ice pick to kill him when she was six. He had been hurting her more. The older she got the worse he was, and he would do more scary things. She brought out the pick—raising her right hand—he had stopped using the pick by then. He is lying on her, raping her, he was hurting her a lot. She tried to stab him in the back with the ice pick, and he caught her, grabbed her wrist and twisted it. He made her drop the pick and hurt her arm and—there is a blank—he started beating her hard with his fist and then he took his rifle and put it to her head and said, 'If you ever do that again, I'll blow you to pieces,' and then he put the rifle into her vagina and said he would blow her that way, 'I'll show you now.' He pulled the hammer back on the gun. Then he pulled the trigger . . . but the gun wasn't loaded. Then he began laughing. She wished then that she had died.''

The next thing I knew, Andrea was out of hypnosis, sitting up in the chair and shaking her head vigorously. ''These things didn't happen.'' She was obviously very frightened—almost panting with fear. ''Sister Jeanine is a sneak and a goody-goody. I *hate* Sister Jeanine. She makes up all these stories. I know she does. I *know* she does.''

Then Sister Jeanine was back, calm, unmoved by Andrea's accusations. ''She is in a panic—feeling in a corner and wanting to kill herself. It is a combination of sin and terror.''

''But she must get back there,'' I insisted. ''She must know the things that made her want to kill her father if she is ever to cope with her problems.''

Nothing roared in—snarling and glaring at me. ''You must not let her feel!''

''But *you* must let her feel,'' I said. ''It's the only way she'll ever know it really happened. That she isn't to blame for the insanity of her father.''

Nothing looked puzzled for a moment. Then, ''I don't know anymore—she has good reason to call on me. Do you know that these things happened many times? And now you make them come back. There is a lot of rage.''

''But it's necessary, Nothing. We must give her back her past and let her make her own mind up about it.''

There was a long pause while Nothing considered this proposition, then finally:

"All right. But I don't like it."

The transformation took place, from Nothing's face back into Andrea's features. She was trembling but managed to maintain awareness of the situation, though I think the awareness was buffered considerably by the hypnotic state she was in.

"Let's go back," I suggested to her, and haltingly she began.

"I don't know how."

"Go back to your father raping you. You have the ice pick."

"I can't, I'm so tired—"

"You must!"

"I—I remember—remember first part . . . feeling . . . I only remember the pain inside, and then I wonder why I didn't fight—but he tied my hands—I don't remember crying. He said not to make a sound . . . he could be mean, angry, hurt, and then he was nice as if nothing was wrong. He would say I was his little girl, and no one else would ever touch me—and then about his mother—No! Andrea put her hands over her face, writhing in pain, then became silent and immobile for a moment. "I know why I tried to kill him . . . he would tie me to the bed and would be different—sometimes he would start, or he would play with me like a doll and play with other parts of my body. I was afraid because it would start. I would cry, and he would put a gag in my mouth. He would say, 'Don't cry. The more you cry, the worse it will be.' Then he would slap me. I learned you don't cry. I would get most afraid when he talked about his mother. He would call me 'Mother.' He would shove and hurt me inside—something about 'no more babies—you'll never have babies.' He was angry. It happened many times. It was his mother— something about his mother. The pick, it hurt the most. There were no tears—no feelings—and then I was in a closet, in the shelves in my room, and I would hide there.

"Then he jabbed and then he laughed and then he hit.

'Don't say anything to anyone,' he would say. A lot of pain. Couldn't tell my mother. She wouldn't believe me. Then I got angry and found a pick in the basement, and that is all I remember—

"The rest is rage." She gyrated on the chair for five minutes. "No—no more. It isn't going away . . . I had a hard time breathing. He was on top of me. I couldn't breathe. I took something—the ice pick. I tried to—No!—it didn't matter about sin anymore. I was angry at God. I said, 'I hate God, you aren't there.' I couldn't even scratch him. I never even touched him. He twisted my arm. The more he twisted, the more I fought, till hand opened and it dropped. He jabbed me with it, and then he tied me on the bed—my hands and feet. He was furious. I've never seen him so angry. He put gag in my mouth. Then he went away and got gun. He came back and took off gag . . . He got on bed and got on between my legs. He took off tape over mouth. He put gun in mouth. I wouldn't open mouth. He made mouth open—hurt so much [Andrea was holding both ears] and then shoved gun in mouth. He said, would blow her to pieces, 'I'll kill you,'—started talking about women. 'You're all the same. I'll make you pay.' Then took gun out of mouth and rammed it inside—hard. He put clip back, 'You women, like your mother, like my mother!' He pulled trigger, but nothing happened. I heard the trigger and then laughter and then I was lost for awhile. When I was back, he was gone."

I was just about to end the session, after this wracking and emotionally draining exposition, when the Angry One leapt out, transforming Andrea's features once again. True to its name, Angry One was furious.

"There are more things!" Angry One snapped. "There is more than Joseph inside her. There is one for hanging, burning, stabbing, shooting—one to take pills. Hanging goes with the cats; stabbing was father; burning was Dara. Dara burned the dress."

Sensing that Angry One was about to reveal more personalities, I said, "Who are these ones?"

Angry One answered, "The pills are Barbara. The stabbing and the gun are father Joseph. Dara is the burning. The hanging and the cats are Anton. There is a lot of fighting.'' Angry One paused for a second and then rushed on. "There is someone else who wants death. Andrea created him to kill her father. There is link to Barbara. They are twins. Bobby and Barbara. Bobby is to kill her father and Barbara was to kill her."

"But now that Joseph is dead, what does Bobby do now?" I inquired.

"Bobby gets angry at people who try to stop Andrea from killing herself."

Like some kind of Greek chorus, Andrea jumped back in, saying, "This is all crazy. You're making it all up. I don't believe it."

I suggested to her that she look inside for herself and decide. Abruptly she was under again, eyes straight ahead. "I was angry and tired of all the stuff," she said. "It hurt. I was so angry. He would do all that stuff, and my mother would never listen. Everyone told me to shut up. So I never told anyone. I got Bobby to kill him and if he couldn't, Barbara would kill me. When Bobby failed, I went to the medicine cabinet and took lots of pills."

Following the success of my last experiment with Andrea in integration, I integrated Barbara and Bobby and, when Andrea came to, she cried but expressed relief.

ANDREA'S JOURNAL
Tuesday, April 6, 1980—Midnight
I am once again astonished by the dramatic transformation caused by today's therapy session. Last night at this time, I felt like a totally worthless entity and was searching the ward for a way to commit suicide. Tonight I feel at peace with myself and once again dare to dream about the future as a whole person—a whole woman!

The experience integrating Barbara and Bobby was similar in essence to that of integrating Philippe. The major difference was realizing how much more "separated" I was with them as opposed to Philippe. I suppose that is why the process was so much more difficult with Barbara and Bobby.

I was so terribly frightened and despondent the past three days that I could not fathom a way out and only felt more frustrated when I would try and not succeed. The death wish seemed to be pulling me like water swallowing a drowning person.

Yet there was something which made me fight for my life—that allowed me not to go home for pills—something/ someone who acts as a guard, a protector. Oh yes, I believe it is Mother Mary who helped me get through those original terrifying years. I didn't link her before in all this but I did go outside right after this session to give thanks and just feel the warmth of a mother—a spiritual warmth which has been the key to my survival of all the insanity.

I am pleasantly exhausted tonight and once again feel new hope—growing stronger.

16

Integrating

JOSEPH, Dara, Philippe, Angry One, Little Andrea-Ellen, Sister Jeanine, Mother Mary, Cathleen, Barbara, Bobby, Anton, Julia, Bridget, Nothing, Super Andrea, Doris. Sixteen personalities. So far Dr. Bliss had uncovered that many in his search, had now talked to almost all of them, and had gathered from each a little of the total story of Andrea Biaggi's early life. Like an oyster secreting nacre to insulate itself against a kernel of sand, so Andrea from the age of four had created characters to protect herself against the cruelty and madness of her father, the insensitivity and apparent indifference of her mother.

First there had been Little Andrea-Ellen, Nothing, and Mother Mary—the earliest and most elemental of the personalities. Then came Philippe and Julia—Julia to collect and hold the happiness, Philippe to protect her from a consciousness of the torment that no child should have to suffer. Sister Jeanine and Super Andrea appeared later to complete the immediate family, as a means of handling the complex fabric of her traumas. In concentric rings from this first family the other personalities radiated outward, baffling and covering chinks in the armor, keeping sturdy guard against reality. Helpful as many of these personalities had been, there were others, particularly in the tertiary ring—the satellites and keepers of subdivisions within her consciousness—that did not wish her well, that had been raised to a strict code of sin and redemption as taught not only by her church but also by her family. There was no escaping the punishment, and as Bliss delved deeper into the pathology of her condition he discovered a myriad of trap doors and hatches by which the worst of her instincts could escape reason and reassert their hegemony over her. Paradox ruled in these regions where the impulse to kill her parents was transformed into a need to kill herself; where injuring herself became a means of healing herself; where the characters that reviled and attacked her were those most to be protected and concealed. The early messages that she lied, was evil, ugly, and stupid, nullified any recall. As a result, little of what had happened was really getting through. Hers was a mind that seemed to work only through contradictions. It was also a cyclic mind: one day of elation was inevitably followed by a week of turmoil; a revelation about her past led predictably to amnesia and a complete obliteration of the memory itself.

Meanwhile the stories continued through Sister Jeanine and through Nothing. Even Andrea herself. The stories expanded on the grisly incidents already reported and hinted at still more horrific episodes that happened "over the garage—in the attic." Frequently Andrea or one of her personalities added insights about her behavior, and these perceptions were often keen. She was particularly insightful when discussing the nature of her obesity and the origins of her "eating binges," which had transformed a girl who had a minor propensity toward fat into a young woman 140 pounds overweight. (At the time she was carrying 260 pounds on a 5'3" frame.)

"When Andrea was young," Sister Jeanine reported, "she would always want candy. It was after her father left—before he left, he would bring candy and be nice sometimes. She came to associate candy with her father's love. After he was gone and she felt guilty about his leaving, she would steal some pennies and buy candy or let the man at the candy store molest her for candy. Her mother would find her eating candy, then yell and scream that she was sinful and gluttonous. Andrea went on a candy binge yesterday after work—bought a bagful and felt she had to sneak them into the hospital because people would punish her. As long as she can binge on candy that means her father loves her—''

There was no way at present to attack this serious condition, Bliss knew. The obesity was so much a symptom of everything that was going on inside of her. Perhaps if once he could accomplish the integration of the other personalities, then she would begin finally to lose weight.

A more immediate success was registered when Little Andrea-Ellen began to come out of ''her closet'' and talk. Admittedly, the conversations were often incoherent affairs, with the voice of a child. But whatever the level of communication, Little Andrea-Ellen could tell Bliss plenty about what was going on ''inside'' and added considerably to an outline of Andrea Biaggi's history.

''I've been scared,'' Little Andrea-Ellen whimpered to Bliss one day. ''I hid in closet. Something white and something about ears hurting. Mother—''

''What about your mother?'' he asked.

''Holding ears, my ears hurt, hit hurt in the ears—it was my mother—the white is safe—I wanted to die, she did that a lot, and when she hit me it made everything whirl and not be right. Come close and protect me, please. Mommy and Daddy. They were fighting. First in closet and ears hurting, and then it says to die. Then Daddy had butcher knife. I told Mommy what he did with the cat. I said help, Mommy. A part wants to finish killing me now. It is Sheba—''

Momentarily Bliss was mystified but, as so often happened, emotionless Sister Jeanine stepped in to interpret the words and adumbrate:

''She was trying to tell you—I don't think it is a story. Something linking then and now.''

''Yes, Sister Jeanine?''

''Andrea-Ellen—it is the day her father threw the cat in the furnace and raped her. He warned her to say nothing, but she was so upset that she told her mother about the cat—she didn't understand the sex part. She thought her father was asleep, but he must have heard her. There was a huge fight in the kitchen, and he was yelling, 'How can you let your daughter make up such stories! You're together to get me—' Then he got a butcher knife and forced the two into a little space. Her mother and father were screaming. The knife came down to cut someone. [Sister Jeanine suddenly looked startled.] He tried to kill her—Little Andrea-Ellen—and she moved fast, and the knife went into the wall. Her mother started screaming more and fighting, and her father left. Then her mother started screaming at her—said never say a word, never tell anyone. Then all the children were crying—"

Andrea herself came out and held her ears. "She yelled at me—Mommy—and hit me hard so my ears hurt and said, 'Go into your room. Say nothing about the damn cat.' She was very angry. I didn't understand. I got dizzy. Things were swirling around, and then remembering—the cat was there. Then I got angry at Mom and the cat. They were swirled together. They became Sheba—Sheba was supposed to kill her mother. She was going to strangle her mother. She heard her mother crying a lot, and then I thought I should die for wanting to kill her. He tried to kill her too, you know, with the knife."

Andrea was obviously in a lot of emotional pain, and Bliss tried to soothe her, but the pain turned into panic as soon as he tried. There was copious crying then, and finally, in a strangled voice, she managed to get out, "I've been trying to want to live for so long, but each time a part comes together, there is another period of agony."

DR. BLISS'S NOTEBOOK
April 10, 1980

This was an incredible day. It began with an hour session, then Andrea went to work because she had an important conference. It was against my better judgment, and I should never have permitted it. Despite the integration of Philippe, Barbara, and Bobby, I knew she was very vulnerable, riding a roller coaster between elation and utter despair and, to use her phrase, "there was a lot of fighting." When she didn't return in the early afternoon, I called her home. Someone answered the phone, but it wasn't Andrea. The personality insisted that she would stay there and not return to the hospital.

I drove to her apartment, had the landlord open the door, but no one was there. I called my office, and was told that Andrea had returned. At 4:30 P.M. we began again, and at 8 P.M. all the ruffians (Joseph, Dara, and Sheba) were finally integrated. It happened only because I persisted and insisted. The resistance was formidable, and I doubt that I could have done it a year ago. The principles of therapy are simple, but the tactics and gambits come only with practice and confidence. In any event, I think we are out of the woods. The rest should be apple-pie simple. It is hard to believe that any case could be more complicated or more difficult.

ANDREA'S JOURNAL
April 11, 1980

Joseph has always been the person of greatest danger in my life. He was the mirror image of my father complete with bizarre behavior and death wishes. He was physically strong—fighting with him yesterday has left me still exhausted. He was not all evil. Often, after attacking me, he would cry and say he was sorry.

Joseph was created for two purposes. The first was his mission to torture and finally kill me. He could not do this, however, without his second mission: to make me believe that I would *never* be free of him. The more I succeeded in integrating other personalities, the more fierce his fighting to convince me I would never get better.

It is important for me to emphasize here that I had always believed Joseph's greatest strength was his murderous rage, but I now know his core strength was the imparting of despair. Creating a profound sense of despair was Joseph's way of getting death.

Joseph was, by far, the most dangerous and destructive of all the personalities. You would question why anyone would create such a person. He was created after so much pain and abuse that, even to a four-year-old, death was a way of coping.

ANDREA'S JOURNAL
April 12, 1980

I wondered yesterday what would happen to an integrated personality when put to the test by outside stresses which previously triggered them. I unfortunately had the first test today. I am still in a slight fog, so this may not be as clear as other experiences.

The trigger for today's mess came during a physical exam to which I have always had violent reactions. I was nervous but conscious during most of it. The medical student doing the exam seemed uptight too, which didn't help. Then he had me lie down so he could listen to my heart. That was the precise moment of Joseph's reemergence.

Physically, I was first very tense and anxious. Then the room began to spin.

I HATE WRITING THIS—IT MAKES IT COME BACK AGAIN AND I WANT TO TEAR THIS ROOM APART AND SLASH ANYONE WHO COMES NEAR ME—
SLASH ME!!!
(Written by Joseph)

ANDREA'S JOURNAL
April 13, 1980

After I wrote that last section last night, I panicked once again and went back into Joseph's space. It was different because I had more initial control, so I sought some staff help but they were all in meetings. Then the traditional spiral I have come to know so well seized me again, and I was lost to Joseph's despair.

One thing that was different was wanting to kill my roommate very much—a feeling I was not in touch with until the staff kept pushing me to return to my room. I began hysterically crying that I was afraid I might kill her. I slept in a different room last night and finally calmed down and gained a good strong hold which I was able to maintain today.

I knew there would be sliding-back-times, but this was far more like the worst of my past times with Joseph. Is integration working?

*   *   *

It didn't take long for Bliss to come to think of the joining process in terms of "partial integration" or "tentative integration." It was like making a skin graft: he could never be certain when one would take and when one wouldn't. It took only a hypnotic snap of the mind to reincarnate them.

Near the middle of April, Bliss integrated Nothing, which was particularly difficult. "He didn't want to leave," as Andrea put it, and she was reluctant to absorb him since he had helped her through so many bad times with his gift of numbness. But Bliss insisted, telling her that until all the personalities were fused there would be no hope of recovery. On this premise, Andrea agreed, and Nothing joined the other personalities in the integrated group.

Some time was also spent putting Joseph back in his place as an integrated entity. He had wreaked havoc over the weekend, but now Bliss tried again and felt reasonably comfortable about the results. On the heels of this, came another tale, wrenched from Joseph's memory via Sister Jeanine's interpretation. Another scene of torture: her father had taken her to the attic, to the old, rusty bed in the dust-filled room, and had begun to twist her legs, at first playfully but then, as so often happened with this unstable man, more and more brutally. By the time he had lost interest in his daughter's screaming and pleading and had left the attic room, her legs were badly bruised. She couldn't walk for hours after. But she had to get out of that room and dragged herself, hand over hand out the door, down the stairs, and back into her room where she hid, crying, in the closet. She tried to fall asleep, but the combination of her terror at the thought that her father might return and the pain in her legs kept her awake. Somewhere in the house, she knew her father was prowling—laughing, cursing, and crying to himself by turns. She never knew when he might sneak up to her room, burst in, and begin the torture again.

DR. BLISS'S NOTEBOOK
April 25, 1980

I believe the difficult work is past. These marathon sessions (this last one was four hours) are necessary but exhausting. In a sense, I am sorry to see all of those wicked characters disappear. They were powerful adversaries, and unraveling the mystery was like being Sherlock Holmes. Like Andrea, I'll miss some of the rascals. They were not exactly friends, but they did pose enormous strategic and tactical problems.

Andrea has taught me once again the power of these hypnotically implanted ideas, feelings, experiences, and personalities. She explained to me later that the physical pain in her legs after she recaptured that memory, for example, was greater than the pain of traumatic injuries she sustained when she totally wrecked her car a while ago. It is difficult to convey to other people how these physical feelings of fever, pain, cramps, headaches, etc., generated by these early implants, are equivalent to the original physical experiences in all their intensity.

I have bet Andrea that she will spontaneously lose 70 pounds during the next year (she weighs 263 now), because all the personalities will soon be integrated and there will be no Little Andrea-Ellen to sneak sweets anymore, or father Joseph to bludgeon her with the sin of her gluttony.

During the next week Bliss completed integrating Little Andrea-Ellen and Super Andrea. Andrea seemed in so much better health now, so elated and enthusiastic, that Bliss saw no reason not to discharge her from the hospital. He was premature.

DR. BLISS'S NOTEBOOK
May 13, 1980

Andrea was discharged—in retrospect, too soon. In fact, she split at the time I was writing out her discharge. For several reasons she was not able to tell me how distressed she was and was only able to hint at it. I missed the signals. The previous integration was soon proved incomplete.

She went home and soon after called me because one of the personalities (Sister Jeanine, I think) thought that Andrea was acting very suicidal. When I telephoned and there was no answer, I called the police. They went to her house, found that she had taken some pills but was neither intoxicated nor somnolent, and left her when she refused to go to the hospital.

The next morning, there was no response to my telephone calls, so I asked my secretary, Alice, to go to her home, hoping that she could induce Andrea to return to the hospital. Alice found Andrea crouched in a corner of her bedroom as Little Andrea-Ellen. She had a coat hanger in her vagina. At that point Alice called me, and I drove over to her house, spending the next two hours trying to contact Sister Jeanine, Andrea, and Little Andrea-Ellen until finally Andrea was oriented enough to return to the hospital.

The day after this incident, Bliss struck back, hoping to catch all the personalities at the same time with a counterattack. The best defense, as he had learned through working with Andrea, was often a spirited offense. After putting Andrea under he called all the personalities together:

"Are they all there? I want to talk with all the parts—you're all there, aren't you."

"Yes . . . yes . . . yes . . ." Andrea's voice fluctuated as one character after another answered.

"All right then. All parts, I want to make a suggestion. Andrea knows all about what happened in the past, and she got back the feeling. But something happened yesterday, and you all split off. I want all of you to come together as you were before, and then we will work and see what it was that upset Andrea. I want everyone to come together and to become conscious memories as you were before. All right? Let's do it."

There was a momentary pause while Andrea looked straight ahead, and then a smile appeared on her face.

"That's better?" Bliss asked her.

"Yes."

"Any problem integrating?"

"Just one—right now." She struggled for the right words. "And it was the thing that hit me last night. Whammo!"

"What was that?"

"The loneliness. I've . . . I've become much more aware of loneliness. Those personalities were like old friends. I know it's perverse, but it's true. I created my own world, my own family, so I could always pack up and move. I'm more dependent on you as a therapist now than anyone before because there's no one left to talk to. And it's lonely."

It was like putting too much strain on a pop-bead necklace. A little twisting and turning, and one or several of the personalities would pop out and start raising havoc. Bliss would try to fine tune the system, integrating and reintegrating. Each time he did it, he got closer to a final solution. If a character came out and started to cause trouble, Bliss knew there was still an incident or a problem that hadn't been confronted. More often than not it was yet another story of her parents' cruelty.

But, however slowly, Bliss felt that the obstacles to total and lasting integration were being surmounted even though he suspected that there were personalities still undetected beyond "the wall" where Little Andrea-Ellen crouched.

ANDREA'S JOURNAL
Wednesday, May 14—7 A.M.

There is a deep sadness this morning. I keep wanting to cry—to be held and rocked to comfort as a child would be. There is so much pain again. The night was filled with nightmares—old memories that still linger and haunt.

I remember leaving the hospital Monday so proud that I had integrated all my personalities. For a split second though, fear awakened again as I wondered who "Andrea" really was. I would not allow that thought to continue and quickly dismissed it as meaningless.

But here I am this morning, wanting and needing something so desperately, yet unable to really know what this is all about.

My wish right now is to be a baby again—born into a loving family—and nurtured. I want to erase my real life childhood by being reborn to different parents and just starting all over again.

Now tears come as the pain of knowing that this fantasy can never be. I am cold, empty, shaking—

ANDREA'S JOURNAL
Thursday, May 15—10 P.M.

Anger is out again—he— her—no it's just me!—Super Andrea, Andrea, Sister Jeanine—

Who else do you want to know . . . they weren't people just one hell of a lot of pain and that goddamn pain IS STILL HERE!! And you thought I was cured Monday—and so did I—I believed the whole thing for a whole day. But the pain came back—just like the old days—it's come back BAD.

But why??

You know it's not just the pain—it's the wanting to die so damn bad that I couldn't call you and tell you because I'm a failure—not a success. I am sorry, I tried to be a success—part of me—part for you as you tried so hard. You don't need to see me like this.

All that noble crap about courage is wrong. You made me hold on too long for too long.

Help.

Everything around me lately says do not be afraid of death. It is peace, rest, no more fighting. Being reborn is my only fear—having to go through this again until I get it right.

I am so tired. Scared. Battle-scarred.

Bliss had outfoxed himself. Now with every personality he could find, including Sister Jeanine, integrated, Andrea still had serious problems. And there was no Sister Jeanine to consult anymore.

He called for Sister Jeanine to return after Andrea was under, but she shook her head.

"There is something choking me. No Jeanine."

"Perhaps it's another personality," he suggested.

"No. I don't think so." Her pupils were expanding and contracting rapidly, her face flushing and blanching in turn. "All week—I've been going in and out—something wrong about my mother—something happened in here. It doesn't want me to talk about it to you—something is trying to stop me. It tries to destroy."

"Can part of you act like Sister Jeanine?" he asked. If his observer wasn't available anymore, then perhaps something else would do as well.

"I . . . I have to shut off the feelings then," she responded.

Of course, the feelings. "Great. Then turn off the feelings, Andrea."

Andrea started to shake. " . . . None of it is right. It is just a bad kid who made up stories. I just saw pictures—dumb pictures. I see my mother hitting me and yelling at me, very angry, saying, 'You are bad and made up stories, and what happens in this house shouldn't be told to anyone.' Stupid dumb kid. She also told her teacher about her mother being locked in the cellar and all the fights. 'Don't you know if anyone finds out it makes it worse?' says mother. 'I don't want you to ever say anything about this again.' Hitting, angry, crying, twisting the arm and dragged downstairs to cellar. 'You stay here,' and then the lock closed. I hated that room. It was dark, and I was scared of spiders. Sat in corner and it was cold—shivering from cold and scared, terrified, calling out. Then stopped feelings and then there was light outside and the door opened but no words, and she walked back upstairs and I didn't feel. I went to my room, lay in bed, and tried to get warm, and then I thought, 'I wish that she would keep me there until I died. People would stop yelling at me for doing things I didn't do wrong. I didn't lie.'"

Andrea flashed out of hypnosis and then, quite spontaneously, resubmerged. Gradually a smile crept across her face.

"What is it, Andrea?" Bliss asked.

"It is incredible," Andrea said. "I remember something else."

"Yes?"

"It was shortly after the exam with the doctor when it happened. Her mother must have suspected—the ice pick rape. He couldn't penetrate then—she was all bruised, but he would take her into the basement and wash her out with lye soap. He was afraid of infection—suspected mother knew. He was so crazy. Also in the basement was a furnace. She would cry and beg, 'Please, it burns, leave me alone.' Then he became very angry and said, 'Don't tell anyone. I have to do this or they will find out.' She said, 'It burns,' and he said, 'You don't know what burning is.' His eyes were wild. He . . . he took a coal from the furnace and burned her arm, and he said if she told anyone he would take a live coal and put it in her vagina. He put her in the wine cellar room and told her to think about it—how it would feel if he stuck a piece of coal inside of her. The room had no window, and the door handle was on the outside—so it had no way out."

It was out of this episode that Andrea had created another personality—St. Joan, to handle the burning. St. Joan, like the Christian figure, was ritually burned at the stake, but unlike the real figure, Andrea had created a character that could be burned again and again—and not just burn, but cause others to burn. Mostly this meant burning herself. St. Joan was formed to take care of all the traumas inflicted by her father and mother that were connected in her own mind with fire. Burning her arm or her vagina were roles assumed by St. Joan as the faithful martyr.

When Bliss integrated St. Joan during that next week he was prepared for revelations (they had often followed integration), and this was no exception, laying bare the pivotal episode that created St. Joan:

"There are pieces missing. They accused her of setting fires, but her father was wild—like he got with her mother many times. The fire was next to the garage. And he started to yell that the fire could burn down his garage. Oh—" She put her hands over her eyes. "I think she started the fire. Andrea was seven, and she hated the garage. The picture—Andrea is taking a stick on fire to burn the garage and he caught her—yes. He was very bad that day. He grabbed her arm and the stick and put out the fire and took her upstairs—I can't believe the picture—he tied her to the bed, took off her clothes and used the charcoaled stick and stuck it in her vagina—oh! It . . . it was still on fire—burned her. She . . . she was screaming this time, and her mother heard. He got frightened, let her go, she was crying, 'Daddy hurt me,' and they did have a big fight—her father said he was punishing her because she started the fire. He didn't say anything about the garage—Andrea is wild anger. Andrea is saying none of this happened.''

"Then what happened?" Bliss asked.

"Her mother came in later and punished her. Andrea kept saying, 'I didn't,' but her mother was very angry because he had been hitting her also. Her mother gave her a bloody nose—there was a lot of blood. Then her mother left.''

Immediately after this, Andrea emerged from hypnosis, shaking her head vehemently. "It didn't happen. None of it happened. It's all a lie!''

She was like a trapped animal then, frenzied and shivering, desperately refusing to admit that anything was true, but terribly upset nonetheless by what she denied.

17

Unraveling

ANDREA resigned her job in the middle of the summer under heavy pressure from a number of people in her department. There had been a good deal of departmental infighting that preceded her resignation and several women— including the board chairman—had finally pushed her into a corner. From Andrea's perspective, it was simply a case of other women coveting her position. But it was more than that. She had missed a lot of time while on the ward, and even when she had been there, she could not always keep Super Andrea front and center. There had been embarrassing lapses—other personalities had gotten out and created some mischief—and at last the board chairman had discovered that she had been a patient on a psychiatric ward. When this was revealed, a great deal was made of her instability, and despite her outstanding record as an administrator, her "emotional problems" had gone against her.

Only half of Andrea was sad about this turn of events. Much of her craved a quieter job, one involving less pressure and fewer people keeping tabs on her every move.

But the loss of her job inevitably cast her emotional life into turmoil, and the delicate balance Bliss had worked so hard to establish became even more delicate. "It doesn't help to think it out," Andrea told Bliss. "It isn't working that way. I'm just overwhelmed trying to survive from hour to hour. The task of suicide isn't finished. I'm back thinking everything can be burned away and destroyed. Little Andrea-Ellen is almost pure feelings again. She is hysterical and panicked. She must learn that you are here and not her father.''

While most of Andrea could accept that Dr. Bliss was simply a psychiatrist, the four-year-old inside couldn't get around the resemblance she saw between Bliss and her father. It was something about the face, the white jacket, the gestures. Perhaps it was none of these things really— just the fact that Andrea had begun to think of Bliss as a father surrogate and this had set up an alarm in Andrea-Ellen's mind. One father, after all, would be pretty much like another to the little girl: cruel, monstrous, demented. The normal course of transference was the last thing in the world Bliss needed, but it came naturally and inevitably.

The result of all this turmoil was that the core and heart of Andrea Biaggi—that emotional region where the ultimate truth of the story was analyzed—refused to ratify the majority of what Bliss elicited from her. Little Andrea-Ellen wouldn't believe it, and it played havoc with the integration process. In frustration, Bliss decided to bring the child back to the surface—de-integrate her, so to speak— for the purpose of identifying those problems that troubled her and trying to deal with them. But this exercise proved only partially successful, and Bliss soon found himself confronted by problems he could not even address, let alone resolve.

"Something wrong—I hate them," Andrea-Ellen cried, "The house, garage, attic—I want to kill them all, but I don't know why. I didn't do anything wrong. I don't know why they are so angry at me."

"Your father is a sick man."

"He hurt me—he yells and my mother hurts me."

"Your father upsets your mother."

"He hurts her too—she gets angry and yells." Crying harder. "She says I'm bad. I make things wrong. I try to stay by the lake but then I'm at the house." Little Andrea-Ellen drew away from Bliss, curling into a ball and glowering at him. "Go 'way! Stay' way. You bad. I'm bad."

It did no good. An unintegrated Sister Jeanine reported: "She is clinging to thinking she is bad and evil. Part of the problem is she would use Nothing during those incidents so she doesn't associate her father with them. She isn't conscious of the incidents. She can hold onto the image of a gentle father, but then she hears him say, 'You are evil. You must be punished.' She can't grasp her father as sick and brutal—the other times she is being punished for being bad and evil."

Bliss continued to employ Sister Jeanine, now keeping her out of the integration process until the end was really and truly in sight. And there seemed no cure near at hand. Just when it looked like Andrea was straightening out, when she was overcoming her terror and really beginning to feel better about herself, the curtains would fall again and she would be back in her closet with Nothing, inflicting still more damage on herself. The cycles of doubt and despair continued. In her most fundamental mind she was still wicked and sinful, and nothing Bliss seemed capable of doing could change that.

He set himself the task of working more with Little Andrea-Ellen, for it seemed that only through persuading the little girl in Andrea could he hope to convince the whole woman. But Little Andrea-Ellen was refractory, still reticent and contrary by turns, in every respect a child of four—as Andrea said, "pure feelings." The child spent most of her time now by "the lake"—a place remembered from childhood, a place where some of her happiest memories were found. Like Julia who frolicked in imaginary meadows picking flowers, Little Andrea-Ellen was an inhabitant of a mythical shore where her parents existed only as abstract role models of the perfect parents and everything could be the way it was supposed to be. Bliss tried having both Mother Mary and Sister Jeanine intervene for him, but neither was successful. Little Andrea-Ellen hated Jeanine, considering her a "snitch and a goody-goody."

Finally it was Bliss himself who contacted Little Andrea-Ellen, and the conversation served as a paradigm for all their communication.

"Why do you want to die, Little Andrea-Ellen?" he asked.

"I don't want to be home anymore. You can't make it stop. Only way is to be no more. You pretend to make it stop. You don't know what it like." She began to cry. "I hate them. I hate that house—no more. Why don't you let me drown. Mother Mary couldn't make it go away."

"But I can, with your help," Bliss offered.

"Last time you said 'I will guarantee' but it keeps coming back. I try running away. I can't unless I go into the water forever. I don't understand the world."

"Well, you've been badly treated, becoming desperate, and have lost your faith," Bliss said.

"No. I am bad. God say obey and love mother and father. I not do. Father say I bad and evil."

"But your father was a very sick man. He beat and raped you. He beat your mother."

"No." Little Andrea-Ellen shook her head and pouted. "Father would be kind. Then I would make him change. It was my fault. Me bad."

"That's not true," Bliss protested. "You must come to understand that your father was very sick and you blamed yourself for his madness."

Little Andrea-Ellen cried, wracking sobs that nearly doubled her over. "No. Not true. I made him sick . . ."

ANDREA'S JOURNAL
Sunday, July 27—10 P.M.

I try to pride myself on being intelligent and resourceful enough to transcend most of the "classic" psychiatric behaviors. However, in the past few weeks, as the first year anniversary of my mother's death is approaching, I find myself consumed with anger, guilt, and panic. At times I feel almost possessed as by a ghost—her ghost—in a terrifying sense.

My father's death marked a critical turning point in my relationship with my mother. All the pain, misunderstanding, and confusion caused between my mother and myself while my father was alive necessitated a distant relationship. But when he died we both felt released from fear so that slowly we were able to get closer, to share feelings, to learn to love each other—and, most important, to forgive.

We both never directly talked about those early years—in fact, great lengths were maintained by both of us to insure the subject never came up. I still regret that, because only my mother could have confirmed the reality of my nightmares. It might have saved me a lot of spiritual and mental trouble later if I'd only been able to understand the truth.

Two months after she resigned her position, Andrea was offered a job working with troubled children. It was a job in many ways tailored to her credentials, for despite the fact that it did not provide the kind of prestige and responsibility that her former position had offered, she was called upon to deal with children who were going through the same kind of bad times she'd experienced herself as a child. She knew where those kids "were coming from" and could empathize with their plights. Almost immediately—and despite her obesity—she was able to set up connections with them. Most of their therapists had been social worker sorts—well-meaning but basically unacquainted with how it really felt to come from a home where your parents abused and mistreated you. Andrea knew. And even if she didn't elaborate on this fact, they knew that *she* knew. In turn, the children and the job restored to her some measure of stability that the resignation from the other job had destroyed. It gave her perspective. This new objectivity allowed her to see more clearly than ever before the cyclic nature of her response to therapy and the problems that lay before her.

The problem was clear: she had to stay out of that self-hypnotic world, learn how to live and cope in the cruel world outside where people tormented you with their real problems, pettinesses, neuroses, and thoughtlessness. With all its hassles, that real world was still better than anything her memories could provide her—anything was better than that. And yet she continued to torture herself with the horrors of the past, replacing the relatively puny travails of day-to-day life with the awesome traumas of her early years.

Her greatest support seemed to come from her association with Bliss, and she would often fantasize that now she was a member of the Bliss family—a daughter in a way that she had never been for her own father and mother. To a certain extent Bliss felt compelled to cater to this need, making Andrea feel more at home than he did the majority of his patients. Then again, giving her a taste of this fantasy seemed to be giving a prescription for her loneliness and alienation. This dependence on Bliss's "father-hood" seemed to give her the courage to break with her past more completely and allowed her certain superficial liberties, such as changing her residence. But while such support therapy was good, it could not alleviate her feelings of worthlessness and wickedness completely. Nothing seemed to help those.

During the summer and fall of 1980, Andrea went out with a man she had met while on the ward. Bart seemed interested in her, and surely Andrea was interested in Bart. Only a few months had passed before she started talking about marriage and added to her other anxieties a worry about her boyfriend's intentions. Catholicism and a craving for intimacy battled one another in Andrea's mind while Bart remained an aloof figure, seeking out Andrea's support when he needed it but never really there for her when she did. In November, it was with surprise that Bliss learned that Bart had proposed—but not to Andrea. Of course Andrea's surprise, not to say shock, was even greater and brought on another series of panics and depressions.

Added to Bart's "rejection" of her was the difficult situation that was developing with her new "roommate," a middle-aged woman named Jane whom Andrea had sought out as a remedy for the loneliness she was feeling. Jane's presence made her feel even worse. Insensitive, tyrannical, utterly self-absorbed, Jane pushed Andrea deeper into depression until finally Andrea made a suicide attempt.

Again the attempt was half-hearted, and although she had swallowed every pill she possessed she was brought to the hospital in plenty of time to have her stomach pumped. Within two days she was back on her feet and moving in with another roommate who seemed more agreeable. However Andrea was no better, and over the next few months, well into 1981, she "lost time"—massive amounts of it. She was feeling dizzy, nauseated and panic-stricken. To allay her panics, Bliss tried a drug to control her anxiety, but it did nothing to settle the conflicts in her mind that Bart had created.

Of paramount importance to her since Bart's departure was the condition of her own body. As Bliss noted, Andrea was plainly disgusted with her body and wanted to change it. To do this she intended to undergo an operation for obesity that would staple off a section of her stomach and thereby cut down on her caloric intake. Bliss wasn't enthusiastic about the procedure; in fact, he opposed it, but she was adamant. She harbored the idea that if she could transform her body she could get in touch with it. Bliss was in a corner. He couldn't guarantee a cure, nor was he sure that a cure would solve the problem of the superobesity. The operation might help, but surgery for obesity was radical, still experimental. If he went along with it, he had to hazard the possibility that the operation would prove to be destructive. Despite the fact that several surgeons had reassured him about the success of the operation, Bliss wasn't comforted. Like most doctors he had a healthy respect for the limitations of new procedures.

Finally he acquiesced to Andrea's need and allowed the operation. In fact, she gave him no alternative. *She* had made the decision.

ANDREA'S JOURNAL
Thursday, December 18, 1980–10 P.M.
   It is the long night before my stomach staple operation.

I have filled the day with much activity until now. The TV is even off.

Now comes the waves of fear. Now comes the shadows of panic and the desire to run away from this hospital—from all of life.

Mostly I am conscious of a very deep sadness. I want to cry. It is the sadness of a motherless child. The people I wish most were here with me tonight are Dr. and Mrs. Bliss. They are the closest thing I have to a real family now.

I WANT SOMEONE TO CARE, not just be a friend—but as a parent! Someone who would just stay with me and see everything through with me and help me make decisions like this operation so I wouldn't feel so damn alone in this.

DR. BLISS'S NOTEBOOK
December 29, 1980

Andrea came for the first time after the operation, looking thinner. She has lost 28 pounds from the flu and post-surgery. She is wearing makeup—a gift from her roommate. "I never knew how to do it," she told me. "It felt foreign and strange, not like me. It is more like fun now." She has been on liquids alone. "I have been having food dreams—about food binges. It has been incredible—about getting Italian bread and saturating it with garlic. During the day it has been torture—with all the food around—rolls, cakes, bread. It has been difficult with the elaborate Christmas dinner when I could only have broth, juice. I felt full but it doesn't feel real—as if I haven't lost weight. Also I feel like a little kid dressing up with makeup. Not using makeup may come from my father. He would say only prostitutes used it."

Later on in the session she started talking about her parents, and for the first time, I felt, showed some real insight into her troubles.

"Andrea-Ellen survived by turning everything off and believing her mother and father were wonderful. When I wanted to die and join my mother in death it was a fantasy, not reality. It wasn't until high school that I wanted different parents, but that came from a different part. Little Andrea-Ellen clung to fantasy parents—but if you take them away there is nothing. I don't want to be alone.''

As the recognition of the facts about her parents is allowed to penetrate, Andrea needs the support from other sources, like me and my wife, to fill the void. As she gives up the fantasy of good parents, and replaces them with the reality of their aberrant behavior, she creates a vacuum.

The simple realization that her parents were not the same creatures that Little Andrea-Ellen had created seemed a routine observation, but for Andrea it proved a major breakthrough. Never before had she actually accepted that the "ideal parents" of her imagination were just that—fictions created to gloss over all the nastiness and abuse. She had forgotten their grave aberrations hypnotically and had thrown all their sins onto her own shoulders: she had become the evil one, the crazy one. It was all *her* fault. This belief had been reinforced by both her parents and her teachers. Only now was she beginning to see the truth.

In the months that followed, Andrea seemed to consolidate her gains and move ahead. In a strange way the operation catalyzed her. The periods of depression and panic continued, but now there were revelations as well—and far fewer personalities to deal with, as most had been successfully integrated. Only the basic three were around for any amount of time—Super Andrea, Andrea herself, and Little Andrea-Ellen. Of the three, the child, Little Andrea-Ellen, seemed the most essential.

Though more communicative than before, Little Andrea-Ellen continued to wallow in fictions she had created as an abused child. Slowly, however, Bliss felt as though he was drawing her out, making progress. He was exploring "the closet," that place where Little Andrea-Ellen spent most of her time, watching the pictures that the four-year-old child watched—and now, for the first time, reliving the pictures with some fidelity. As this process continued, Little Andrea-Ellen was coming to trust Bliss more and reveal more. It was during these sessions with Little Andrea-Ellen that the full story of the first cat incident came out—related under deepest hypnosis in the childlike voice of an innocent four-year old:

"I had a nightmare about the hospital last night—may I close my eyes? There is a big wall around the hospital, and Daddy took me there to work with him. I wasn't in school yet, it was before school. I was first with the nuns, and they gave me ice cream. Daddy was working, and he said you can go for a walk but don't go far. I went out by the emergency door. The sister said you can go out here and walk. I went out, walked around—I could see I was in the front. It was dark."

She abruptly was terrified—then calmer. "It wasn't dark then—only later. I used to hate that building where my father worked. I don't know no more. I see but I don't know . . . Maybe I just make it up . . . I saw a kitten, and it was crying. It was black and white, and I found it in front. I—maybe it wasn't there. If it wasn't there, then nothing else happened."

"But it was there, Little Andrea-Ellen," Bliss asserted, breaking through the barrier of doubt that always seemed to separate Andrea from the most terrifying of her memories. "I guarantee, it really happened."

The child sighed. "Then, if the wall was there, the kitten was. I remember the wall well—I can't see the cat real—it doesn't look real yet—it is far away. I don't want the kitten to be real."

"But it was. Are you afraid to make it real?"

Little Andrea-Ellen nodded her head. "What if I make the kitten real and it wasn't?"

"Look and see," Bliss suggested.

"Mother Mary says it is real." Andrea began to cry. "You must get those things back."

Little Andrea-Ellen sat silently for a moment and then continued. "I put the kitty on my shoulder. It was very little. I thought it was hungry. It was alone and needed help. I didn't want to hurt it." She cried louder. "I wanted to take it home, feed it, and take care of it. I didn't want to hurt it. Could I have some Kleenex?" She dabbed at her eyes with the piece of tissue Bliss offered. "Thanks. I—I can't see any more."

"Go into the basement."

"It was hard with the kitty to go down. The stairs went to the big room where my father worked. He had a desk. There were two chairs but Saturday Daddy was only there. I would sit on the chair and wait for him. He would say, 'Stay away from the big machines.' There was a little room with the coal in it—I don't know any more." She began to shake with terror.

"Was your father there?" Bliss pressed on.

"I don't know—why should I trust you? I trust him and—" Her eyes closed and she shook still more. "He—he was angry like wild. He scares me. He wasn't angry in the morning when he brought me. He put a dress on me in the morning and was nice to me. . . . But he was angry—he grabbed—no, no." She shook her head violently back and forth. "He grabbed me and the cat. The cat kept running. He kept yelling, 'Why are you late? Why weren't you here sooner?' Then—then he yelled at me for the kitten. I don't know anything else . . ." Andrea tried to flee back into her amnesia, but Bliss was ready for her this time.

"Yes, you do! What happened next!"

"He—he let the kitten go at first. I don't want anymore. I just made it all up!"

"We can't leave this in the middle. Go on."

"I don't want to feel. . . . How could he have done those things?"

"He was sick, Little Andrea-Ellen. Very sick."

"He kept wanting me to touch him. He kept twisting my hand. 'Come on and don't fight me.' 'Just let me get kitty—please Daddy—let me go home.' He hit me. I wouldn't do what he wanted. I kept saying I wanted the kitty. He kept hitting, but I wouldn't do it. 'All right, if you want the kitty, I'll give you it. You want this kitty?'

He was real angry. He pulled the furnace door open and threw the kitty in the furnace—then I ran up to him, and I was screaming and crying and I kept begging, 'Please take the kitty out.' He was angry, grabbed my arm. He said, 'If you want that kitty, do what I want and I'll get the kitty.' I thought he could do it. I really did. That is when I did what he wanted. First he wanted me to do things to him, and then he did things to me. He pulled me into a dark corner. I hated it, but I thought I could save the kitty. It was my fault the kitty died. He didn't save the kitty, and he hurt me a lot, and when I cried and said 'get off me, it hurts,' he said, 'If you want to save the kitty, be still.' I tried not to feel but it hurt so much . . .'' She cried copiously.

''And when he didn't save the kitty, how did you feel?'' Bliss asked.

''He put my clothes on. 'Now, Daddy, you promised the kitty.' He started to laugh. 'You dumb kid, don't you know the kitty is dead!' Then he opened the furnace to show it was dead. He said he would put me in the furnace if I told anyone. I didn't feel anything then. I didn't feel my body. I didn't cry. I wasn't afraid, and I didn't care. I didn't feel or care anymore.''

''What did your mother say when you got home?''

''I was crying and my mother came in. She was angry. They had a fight about my dirty dress. He told her I had played in the coal. I tried to tell her about the cat and Daddy, but she hit me and said, 'Stop telling lies.' She hit me again and told me to stay in my room. I hated both of them. I hated them, and I wanted to die, just wanted to die. But then it got mixed up—either the kitty had to die, or I had to—because he said he would put me in the furnace, too. I had to be punished. Punished for kitty dying. Punished for hating mother and father—Fourth Commandment—Love father and mother—I don't want this to be true . . .''

It was a pivotal moment in the therapy, and Bliss hoped that they were over the worst with the full exposure of this grisly incident.

Andrea had lost 80 pounds by the end of April 1981. She was down to 183, and the weight was still coming off at the rate of several pounds a week. Andrea felt great about this, but Bliss wasn't so sure. She was constantly dehydrated now and seemed unable to swallow either food or drink. Still, it hadn't reached the critical stage yet, and Bliss was retrieving great quantities of information from her. She seemed to be making sense of it, particularly where it involved her father's savagery and its effect on her.

Slowly, Bliss felt, Little Andrea-Ellen was growing up—an important symptom of her improving condition. Still, she was having difficulty making sense of her mother's diffident attitude: why hadn't she protected her daughter from this madman? Fear and tradition were the answers, but to a four-year-old those didn't constitute answers at all. Even to the grown woman, such pat responses offered meager compensation for the years of torture. Why couldn't her mother have done something sooner to help her children? On one level Andrea could understand; but on another, neither Andrea nor Little Andrea-Ellen would ever understand.

By June, she was 95 pounds lighter and much weaker. She complained of a persistent pain in her stomach and when Bliss insisted on a workup, the attending physician discovered that she was suffering from esophagitis and gastritis, and was developing an ulcer around the staple. Her stomach problems and her pain were enough to launch her into hypnosis at almost every turn. She would no sooner emerge from one blank spot that the realization of her pain and problems would send her careening into the "other world" again.

Her pain had become profound, and she was going in and out of hypnosis all the time. She was being tyrannized now by nightmarish scenes from another incident with her father, and Bliss brought the story to the surface.

"I was six in the first grade. Kids said people have babies from kissing so when my Dad came I wouldn't let him kiss me. He became angry and said, 'Kiss you when I want.' He kissed me on the mouth, put tongue in mouth too—I'm sick, making up things—I fought him because he had my arms. I kicked him. Then I bit him. I hated his tongue, his mouth. Then he stopped and I was crying. I told him they said I would have a baby. He said you and your mother are the same. You will have a baby if I want it.

"He said, 'I'll make sure you don't have a baby.' He takes me to garage and he has an ice pick. He put me in attic and then he tied me up. He said, 'I need to tie you, but I won't hurt you. I'll make sure you don't have babies.' He said, 'I have to take off your clothes. Daddy won't hurt you.' He took ice pick, waved it in front of me. 'You and your mother are the same. Man has his rights'—No more. I don't want to feel it—Oh no, no. He got crazy and he was going to show me and her. All women were sluts and whores. He kept waving the ice pick. He said, 'Remember this? I take care of you ever having babies. You will never have a baby by anyone.' He kept calling me Dara. 'You are a slut. Those babies weren't mine,' and he kept jabbing me with the ice pick. Then I turned off my body, and I saw blood coming out of me all over. 'Now you will know,' and he put the pick in the wall, and he left me tied up. I can't believe he would do it! I cried for help, and my mother found me. She brought me to the house. I was so cold, and she yelled at me. They had a fight. There was blood all over. She yelled at me not to tell anyone. They took me to the hospital. She said we will say you were climbing the fence and you fell and it was an accident. Then she hit me. I kept telling her make him stop and she hit me. 'Don't tell anyone!'"

Adding to her troubles, Andrea had created a new personality, an older version of Bridget to handle her need for sex. Her name was Marna.

DR. BLISS'S NOTEBOOK
June 20, 1981
Andrea has had another crazy episode, and I had a long

talk with her over the phone. In essence, and this is a digest of an hour's discussion, we have been getting at those deep-seated early feelings. The depression has been barely tolerable, but the hate—the murderous hate—has been too much. She created Marna, who put an advertisement in the newspaper for men to hurt her:

DESPERATE DEBT! Have day job but need $500 extra cash by September. 30-year-old female, attractive, intelligent, strong, willing to consider any legitimate offer.

As a prostitute she would make money, but the real purpose was twofold—to be punished according to the Ten Commandments for wanting to kill her parents, and also be sexually mutilated so that the memories could be clearer. She must learn whether these things happened or were a creation of her imagination. As yet she doesn't accept the facts, and until then there will never be any hope of a cure.

Over the last week Marna has been on a rampage, lining up dates on the telephone—making appointments for sexual brutalities. At the end she begged me to protect her against Marna.

There were plenty of sick people ready to take advantage of her, particularly now that she had slimmed down and had begun wearing makeup. She looked completely different. From the mountains of excess flesh had emerged a pretty young woman. The physical transformation was complete (whatever its cost to her health), but the mental confusion continued. She was on the streets again, just like in Boston. It was a return to the madness of more than four years before, and it terrified her to think that she had gotten no further than that in therapy.

Not only was she not coping now, but by the middle of June it had become obvious to Bliss that Andrea was starving to death. She'd lost more than 100 pounds in six months and was losing strength much too rapidly. For a while longer she resisted his entreaties to have the gastric staple removed, but at last she had to have another operation, this time a gastric reconstruction and a gall bladder removal.

She recovered slowly and by the middle of August had returned home, anxious and panic-stricken as always. Despite her loss of weight, she felt obese and dirty. She still spent a great deal of her day as other personalities, principally Super Andrea who managed the greater part of her teaching duties while the other personalities silently rioted.

Andrea's vacillations were becoming longer and more extreme as therapy progressed. For a whole week at the beginning of October 1981 she reported no nightmares, no hallucinations, no panics of any kind. But by the next week the pendulum had swung to the other side, resulting in this letter:

October 18, 1981

Dear Dr. Bliss,

I think it's time for me to write you directly.

This is me—Andrea. It always has been me. There are no other "personalities" in my life. It is always just me. Sometimes I'm just scared or angry or OK. But it has always still just been me.

I kept believing all this crap about personalities just to please you because you were the only therapist who would see me for more than one session anymore. I made up all those names just to please you—they aren't real!!!!

As you can tell, I'm angry now. I'm angry because despite all the therapy and all the holding on and all the Valium in me tonight, I'm still going very, very crazy!!!

It has been hell all day again—you must have known things were wrong when I saw you this morning. I keep being "polite"—it was your weekend off from work, and you are sick of seeing me. Then too, I decided your golf game was more important than me. I don't blame you for this morning.

I am really crazy—you must know that by now. All I've done is go from one crisis to another. I think my record for sanity has only been a few days at a time.

I feel like a caged animal ready to strike. And guess who in the hell is going to get it again—I looked for a cat to kill and leave at your office so you would know but I couldn't find any. So maybe this will let you know a tiny, tiny bit of what is going on in me for what seems to be the thousandth time!!

I don't believe about any of this crap about my "past" because I really don't remember any of it—they were all stories to make you feel happy about your damn therapy. Well, maybe it's true with some people but NOT ME!!

If it was all true—then I should be much better with all of it out. I'm not getting any better. I am getting worse— yes, *worse*. I am sadder, and angrier than I ever was in my life. I feel more than I ever did and it is all very, very shitty.

Even though I don't believe any of the work we did— you did somehow help make things worse. I don't know how. Or maybe I am just plain getting sicker in the head.

I'm not in hypnosis now nor ever was—I get "spacey" just like every other damn person I know, even *you* I've seen.

So, I thought about just never seeing you again, but my reality is this craziness. I can't seem to manage really killing myself yet, so I guess I need help at least to function or something now.

I am obviously very sick—crazy or whatever. I know it is again too much. As a doctor I hold you responsible to close up the wound you have caused. It is TOO MUCH!

Andrea's disclaimer was a discouraging turn of events for Bliss. He had thought there had been more progress. Now it was all too clear that the primary personality,

Andrea, still refused to believe or take responsibility for any of her nightmarish past. In alliance with Little Andrea-Ellen she was still resisting the idea of multiple personalities with every ounce of strength in her, against all evidence to the contrary. Bliss could only sigh and keep on going. Now into the third year, Andrea Biaggi was becoming a sisyphean task.

18

Slow Progress

ANDREA moved into yet another apartment with yet another roommate. Part of her wanted to live alone, but she realized she wasn't ready for that yet. During those hours when Super Andrea wasn't "on duty," there was still too much danger of running amuck. And that was still one of the main problems: Super Andrea was getting too much of her time, obscuring the fact that the real focus of the confusion and terror was Little Andrea-Ellen. For months now Bliss had cultivated the little girl, tried to make friends with her, tried to get beyond her distrust, and now he felt he was beginning to get through. By the first week in November, Andrea reported to Bliss that Little Andrea-Ellen was making progress.

"I've been telling her she is okay—she can like herself," Andrea said. "It isn't so much now that she is stupid and bad—she can relate more to the realities. I close my eyes and see a little girl in a big room, in a corner crying—waiting for someone to rescue her."

"Do you recognize that little girl?" Bliss asked.

"She is me! It is time for Little Andrea-Ellen to come out of her closet." She said this with such resolution that it surprised him. Once again she was back on track, trying to help rather than hinder the integration process.

A small voice piped up softly: "I would like to come out."

"Come out, Little Andrea-Ellen," Bliss said, "come out and join Andrea and grow up as much as you wish."

The little girl broke into sobs.

Then it was Andrea who was crying and stretched out her arms toward Bliss. "Could I have a hug?"

Bliss hugged her warmly and patted her on the back. "Feel better now?"

"Oh my—I don't know—yes. The little girl is better. She is in a nightgown. You come in with a white coat, but it is safety this time—not like her father. Even though the room is light, she has been in the dark so long it is a little scary. When you brought her to the door to come out, she was scared, but it is the only thing she has ever known, *I've* known, all my life. It isn't nice, that darkness, but it is safe. There is still war between Joseph and Little Andrea-Ellen."

Bliss thought a moment. "What if we get rid of Joseph?"

"How?"

"We must bury him—give him a funeral—so the little girl can know Joseph is really dead and can come out for good. All right?"

Andrea's eyes sparkled. "Yes. That might work."

Bliss put her into a deep hypnotic trance, and together they buried Joseph. Bliss followed the ceremony, knowing that for Andrea this was exactly like the original funeral—a literal replaying of the event.

Finally she looked up from her private replaying. "Can I put a flower on his grave? I never put a flower on his grave at the funeral.'

"Yes. Please do."

She made a gesture, her hands outstretched, and laid an invisible rose on top of her father's grave. It was both a real and symbolic admission of her father's death, for the first time allowing both Little Andrea-Ellen and herself to see the truth. She came out of hypnosis smiling.

"Putting a flower on my father's grave has been deferred twelve years. It was only after I could confirm his death that the child could come out of the closet. I've been in the closet for almost thirty years."

It was a declaration of independence from a lifetime of persecution and submission to old memories. Like few other moments in the course of her therapy, Andrea had made a serious step toward sanity.

ANDREA'S JOURNAL
November 7, 1981

Putting a flower on my father's grave was impossible at his funeral. His entire death had been surrounded in hues of unreality. His dying was the same type of schizophrenic experience as his living.

A major illness is traditionally the time when Italians gather—ranking equal to baptisms, weddings, and funerals. It is, most certainly, an occasion of mandatory attendance for a daughter.

I was attending college that last year of his life. For the two years between my leaving the convent and my father's death, he became increasingly angry at me, an anger filled with obsession. I came to hate family gatherings such as the holidays since they only seemed to give him an audience for his attacks. The Christmas before his death, he sat at the head of the dinner table cursing me as a "nigger-loving whore" between glasses of wine. His anger grew so intense that his swearing got out of control.

There were no words of comfort from any member of my family. I had long stopped hoping for solace from my father after his attacks. I was angry for a few minutes that night. The next day I went back to my apartment at college and began a few weeks of intense insanity.

One month later, I found myself totally split and in the middle of the first of more than a dozen stays in a psychiatric ward. I had "forgotten" about that Christmas until now. You see, it was one of my classic binds with my father: if I remembered what really happened, the anger was strong enough to kill him. Then the guilt of hating, waiting to kill him, turned my Catholic-trained conscience into an awareness of what a sinner I was. Despair would set in. My mind could no longer retain the pain and I would begin the splitting cycle all over again.

My mother would write me every week—about the weather, her flowers, her arthritis, my cousins' latest babies—but never, never about my father. It was with silent shock that I arrived home one summer day, six months after my Christmas ordeal, to find my father crippled by a stroke and infested by cancer.

Over the next months he kept on dying but always seemed to recover just at the brink. The doctors called it a medical mystery, the hospital nuns said it was a miracle, and my family silently cursed both the doctors and God for allowing him more time to torture us.

I remember: it was Sunday, a cool, crisp Illinois winter day. The cancer stench in his hospital room had permeated my entire being, and I sat in a corner trying not to smell, not to feel, not to think. There were no life-saving machines attached to his body—just a frail, emaciated body on white sheets. Fortunately he was unconscious most of the time, so I could do this daughterly duty without much fear—just disdain and disgust. Somewhere between his final Christmas and that Sunday I had managed to be hospitalized three times on various psych wards and had been drugged to numbing capacity on several occasions, finding that far less desirable than my own ability to numb myself.

So it was when I knew my time of vigil was served that I bent over to say farewell to my father. I was counting on unconsciousness. Instead, he grabbed my arm and started to speak. His voice was barely audible as he could hardly breathe, but the words were clear enough, each one a source of physical pain both to him and to me. He managed to say, "Your mother did a horrible thing. You aren't my daughter." He became unconscious and I returned to numbness. The next morning he died.

It is now 12 years later. The events of abuse with my father that created my web of insanity have become awesomely clear. The final illusion of my fantasy father shattered a few weeks ago, and I began to truly grieve. He was not the pretend father from "Father Knows Best," nor was he a heartless monster. I know now that he caused me intense physical and mental pain, but that *he* was truly insane—not me. I was enraged, not insane.

That knowledge, as simple and as basic as it appears in these words, has taken me many tortured years to discover. And it all brings back tears of loneliness and a sense of fear to my being now to write this. But I can take a deep breath, close my eyes, see the rose, and can, ever so gently, drop it on his grave. I can cry now, not for the lost rose, but for my lost father. Perhaps now we can both get some peace.

For a whole week Andrea was happy. And then the roof fell in. She was binging—eating as much candy as she could stuff down her throat. In just two weeks she had gained back seven of the pounds she had taken off at such risk to herself. She was losing time too, in huge chunks. Super Andrea was playing the main stage, keeping her job while Little Andrea-Ellen hid in the closet and the rest of her "parts" ran riot. The cycle had begun again. Her overeating and craziness fed her self-hatred, which in turn heightened the panics and made her still more disgusted with herself. All the old experiences and formulae were still swarming inside of her, unsettled, ungoverned, uncovered. Festering.

She had a new boyfriend, but instead of this being a cause for celebration she seemed mortally frightened of the developing relationship. Where sex and intimacy were involved, she quickly became distressed. Her fears and angers returned and redoubled. Her weight, her new boyfriend, her mother, dying, and cancer . . . the world teemed with problems she'd not resolved. Bliss could work only on one or two problems at a time, and most of those had to be handled obliquely and delicately. The little girl in her still screamed that she was no good, evil, wicked; Bliss had to convince both Little Andrea-Ellen and Andrea herself that this wasn't so. But how? Abstract terms have such elusive definitions, such private meanings. Their discussions on evil and goodness often ended in a meaningless exchange of views.

In an attempt to strike out toward more constructive areas of debate, Bliss settled on the big dilemma of Dara

Biaggi. Now that Andrea's father had been laid to rest, there was still the thorny question of her mother. Why had she acted the way she did? Why hadn't she defended little Andrea against the depredations of her father?

The old image of her mother as a saint (and hers as a sinner) had taken firm root in early childhood and now it was necessary to uproot this bit of apocrypha. Bliss proceeded by first putting Andrea deep into hypnosis and placing her in "the closet." Then slowly he conducted her to the door and opened it. There was her mother, waiting for her, willing to explain everything. The mother and the daughter had loved and hated each other in equal measure. They had needed each other, too, but were driven apart by the dimensions of the madness that ruled their lives. Finally, Andrea could see the basic problem clearly: they had both been victims, two people caught up in a crazy man's life. Here was the beginning of forgiveness.

She wrote in her notebook, "I had blocked out all those times when my father was in the same room, fighting with my mother—hitting her, abusing her, just as he abused me." It was a phenomenon known to hypnosis for over a century: the ability to block out a noxious vision—a "negative" hallucination.

Joseph Biaggi had done as thorough a job of torturing his wife as he had of deranging Andrea, Dalia, and the brothers. Of the whole family, only the youngest child, Lucy, had escaped because she had grown up in the house after her father had been committed.

By the end of 1981, Andrea was making good progress toward a final resolution. Symbolically she had begun cleaning the walls of the closet, which had been bloodstained and filthy for years. Little Andrea-Ellen was growing up—now five or six—and had ventured from the closet on many occasions to talk with Bliss. Even Andrea's loss of her new boyfriend did not stop the development of understanding.

"I feel like a new person," Andrea announced to Bliss. "There are times when I feel like escaping, turning it off, but I don't want to do it anymore. I can have anger and not lose it. Before, it triggered off my past. When I saw you the first time I was convinced I was hopelessly crazy. There were six or seven referrals before you, and all refused to treat me. I've had enough therapists by now to staff a hospital.''

They laughed together, and then Bliss asked if she knew where her voices were coming from. ''They began in pre-school. They weren't voices, they were my friends, my family.''

In his notes, Bliss wrote the single word, ''VICTORY!!!!''

He felt certain that now Andrea was accepting what was happening, that Little Andrea-Ellen was emerging from her hermetic life, and that the cure was just around the corner.

Bliss and his wife accepted an invitation to dinner from Andrea and that night, December 27, drank champagne, toasting the cure. It couldn't have been more affable, optimistic . . .

Or wrong.

PART III

19

Back in the Closet

JANUARY 1982 marked the beginning of a new year. With a new year came new problems. The victory that Bliss had thought was at hand was now shown to be merely a respite. For even while Andrea was drinking to her own health, her mind had been going crazy. Added to a congeries of other sensations—fear, terror, pain, anger— was now an even heavier burden of guilt: not only did she feel guilty about her parents, but now she felt agonizing guilt about Bliss as well. She had let him down, she had masqueraded as sane and good when she was really crazy and wicked. All the detritus of illusions and voices crowded back on top of her.

"What we did last time doesn't feel right," she admitted to him. "I'm either depressed and sleeping or angry and awake. Irrationally there is a strong desire to go back to the crazy world. I'm feeling abandoned and alone—very self-destructive."

The stories and the insights hadn't imprinted. Bliss had inoculated her, and it hadn't taken. She was forgetting everything again. All the beasts in her private jungle were out and governing by anarchy. Most important—since the little girl was the pivotal element in all the craziness— Little Andrea-Ellen was back in her closet and too angry with Bliss to respond.

DR. BLISS'S NOTEBOOK
February 16, 1982

I discovered why Andrea has taken a nose dive and has been in a panic with a recurrence of her "craziness." After many false starts, tracing unproductive clues, we solved the problem—at least the present one.

Andrea felt much better after we finally resolved her mother. But then Super Andrea told me that Little Andrea-Ellen could now grow up. I accepted the pronouncement blithely, not realizing that it *was* Super Andrea speaking. It seemed that only some processing, a little housecleaning, remained. It was an error on both our parts.

She became aware that all wasn't right, but she was ashamed to tell me because that meant she was a failure and not a "good" patient. Furthermore, I had demonstrated my elation at our final "victory." Well, our relationship is all fouled up now. As Andrea's switching and panic increased, triggered by Little Andrea-Ellen's inability to grow up, she went back into the hypnotic morass. She became paranoid about me—I didn't like her, I didn't like her Christmas present to me (a remarkable set of covers for my golf woods done in needlepoint), I didn't trust her anymore—and I would sever my relationship with her. I am in the midst of trying to clear up a lot of these problems, but now I'm not so sure that the path lies straight before me—or that it is a *short* path.

The panic continued and got worse. Andrea seemed to regress before Bliss's eyes. Once again she was no good, stupid, fat, ugly, bad, sinful, evil. In her mind she saw Little Andrea-Ellen hitting her head against the wall in the closet, bloodying the wall once again. With the new problems, her optimism collapsed, and she was once again certain that she was irrevocably crazy. With the renewed feeling of hopelessness came an utter repudiation of all the things she had learned about herself and her family over the last two years. She had never accepted them, not really, not in her heart of hearts, and now she was sloughing off these childhood fictions, returning to the original point. She was terminally insane and only waiting for the courage to kill herself.

Bliss bolstered her and propped her up as best he could before taking off on his vacation, but he knew no amount of prevention was going to keep her completely safe. While he was away he put her in the hands of another specialist for the time he'd be away. But he couldn't hope there would be any improvement. The most he could expect was a minimal decline.

Andrea, meanwhile, was furious at Bliss. For one thing he had as much as promised a recovery, and now she was right back where she started, or so it seemed to her. And at that critical moment he was *leaving* her, just as her parents had left her. How could she have faith in such a man?

Several times while he was away she contemplated hurting herself seriously just to show him how much she was suffering. Yes, that would show him! Instead, she contracted both the flu and a bladder infection that kept her in bed for more than two weeks. Despite these illnesses she still found the time to consume huge quantities of candy and gain an additional twenty pounds. Now she was back up to 180.

By the time Bliss returned, Andrea was a mess.

"I've been depressed, angry, binging like crazy." The breakup with her latest boyfriend had finally hit her, her job was becoming a big hassle, and she was losing more and more time. Super Andrea wasn't playing her part so well anymore, sometimes leaving Andrea to fill in at work. The first time it had happened, it had filled her with hope, but by now despair and panic had returned and she longed for her "better part" to resume its accustomed duties. These problems coming all at once added fuel to her anger, making her demanding, especially of Bliss's time. "I want you to stop me," she told him. "Stop me from being depressed, eating junk, having crazy thoughts!"

Bliss couldn't. They were hung up again as they had been so many times before. He couldn't get through to Little Andrea-Ellen, rarely even to Andrea herself. He wasn't trusted anymore; he had failed her in a number of ways, and now she wouldn't open up to him.

"There is a lot of sadness," she reported to him. "Deep. And confusion. Candy is mixed up with it. My dad used to give candy-bars to me . . . candy is being bad sexually . . ." Then she was lost again.

She asked to go back in the closet with Little Andrea-Ellen where it was safe, but Bliss didn't want her to go. It didn't matter anymore; she went all the same.

Bliss wrote in his notebook: "Like so many of these severe cases, Andrea has an incredible startle reaction like a timid animal. One sees this with deer in the wild. When she is suddenly upset—which she is most of the time now—she goes into a frightened state and immediately is in hypnosis, that other world of craziness. Right now I can't do anything to help. We've reached a deadlock, and she's back to the early years of cringing in the closet."

DR. BLISS'S NOTEBOOK
March 21, 1982

I had Andrea come to my house on Sunday because the crisis continued. The big trouble began when she learned I was going on vacation. It is still going on now.

"There is a lot of confusion and anger—like a bomb," she told me. "Then there was severe depression huddled on the couch. It was wanting to be a baby and have a mother—the Virgin Mary. A newborn baby who could then grow up happy. Then I got angry because I can't go back. Then I got overwhelmed by the thought of work—I can't handle that or the feelings with my boyfriend. I want revenge. Then there's you—anger and I can't trust you anymore. I'm no better.

"Things are out of control, wanting to revert to the old stuff. I feel I have to show you a burnt arm."

"Like with your mother?" I asked. It was a guess but it paid off.

"When I was sick, she couldn't face it. She would say I wasn't sick. There was a feeling of relief when she took my temperature and it was very high—like 104. Then

there was a feeling of peace when it was that high and real
. . ." She paused, collecting herself. "The core of the
fight is, was this all a fantasy—or real like my scarlet
fever?"

"What do you think?"

She skirted the question. "When I was working on
those gifts for you before Christmas, you were really my
parents, and I fantasized—I would have a good Christmas
with you. But the closer I got to Christmas, the more I
realized it wasn't real. The reality is, I'm not your
daughter—you're my therapist!"

I didn't try to deny this.

"It started going downhill," she resumed after another
pause, "when both of you came for dinner and I realized I
was creating a fantasy world. My boyfriend was another. I
would be okay, and I could live with you as an adopted
daughter."

"But your fantasies are very real to you," I assured her,
"the hypnosis makes them seem real."

Andrea shrugged.

I'd gotten as far as I was going to get with Andrea, at
least for that day, and so I asked to speak to Sister Jeanine
and got a nasty slap:

"I killed her," said Andrea. "I hate her."

No amount of argument could convince Andrea to give
me back an objective voice. She was adamant about Jeanine's demise and wasn't about to resurrect her for my
sake. The whole session ended in a shambles with her
crying and execrating herself for being bad, sinful, the lot.
Still, enough of the evidence is in that I can make some
conjectures. Before Christmas Andrea was able to work
effectively with me because she had installed my wife and
me as parents. This gave her courage and faith in me
because she felt secure and close. As a result she was able
to go into hypnosis in therapy despite her deep fears and
make a great discovery that her father had been almost as
brutal to her mother as to Andrea, that on a number of
occasions her mother had pushed Andrea aside to protect
her against him. In fact, her mother had often fought with

her father, at great expense to her, trying to protect Andrea. This was an important insight and allowed her to make peace with her mother and finally bury her decently. But the fantasy of the new parents, which had allowed her to retrieve this and other experiences, now became a booby trap because she increasingly realized as Christmas approached that she was not our daughter and was not a member of the Bliss family.

She turned to her boyfriend for a substitute family and began to fantasize a love affair and an early marriage. It should be realized that her fantasies are not the least bit casual but are vivid, hypnotic experiences, indistinguishable for her from real life.

It now appears that further therapy must be based upon two considerations: first, Andrea's closeness and security with me; and second, a concentration on these early attitudes toward herself, particularly the evil aspect which was so influenced by Catholicism. I thought before that the early emotions were the crux, and maybe they are, but my strong hunch now is that the core issues, still unresolved, are the concept of evil and her role in that world.

She continues to experience self-hypnotic periods, which many psychiatrists would identify as psychotic episodes, when she becomes delusional or paranoid, and hallucinates. Then she is back in the old world of self-mutilation, hate, and craziness. She keeps telling me to protect her from these experiences, but that is requesting the impossible. I have no medicine or tactic to provide that degree of safety. When Andrea becomes upset she is instantly in hypnosis . . .

DR. BLISS'S NOTEBOOK
March 29, 1982

She had a terrible couple of days, converting to Marna and picking up a man who brutalized her. She wanted to be punished. We talked over the phone last night, but I couldn't settle her down.

"I'm back in the room, but more angry," she told me.

"What seems to be the problem, Andrea?" I asked.

"I can only tell you without feelings."

"All right." In allowing her to turn off her feelings I've found another way of eliciting Sister Jeanine's help without actually asking for her by name.

"Things have become crazy, self-abusive, and bizarre." She sounded instantly calmer. "She spends 90 percent of my time out of reality. There is a lot of anger and physical pain when she allows herself to feel it. She lost faith again."

"Why the loss of faith?"

"The panic, and then it got too much. The panic came from the last session. Part of the fight is to prove that it didn't happen. None of it happened. She found someone who would physically hurt her. She tried to think that the man was her father to see if it really happened. She left her body—she did remember being sexually turned on. But it wasn't right. . . . Biting her ears used to turn her on. But this time, she sure found a real winner—someone who would *really* abuse her." She became spacey again and then, "She is crazy, bad. A fat whore. Ugly, angry, and crazy."

"Why does she insist on calling herself these things?"

"She's in trouble—especially when she gets a guy to poke glass in her until she bleeds. She wants to kill a staff member at her job. She can't cope with the job."

Even more than problems at her job and with Bliss, pain sent Andrea into hypnosis—and she was experiencing lots of pain now. The focus of the distress seemed to come from her stomach. Bliss asked a friend, a gastroenterologist, to see her. Tests were done, but they revealed nothing definite. The diagnosis was "acute pain syndrome"—one of those nebulous discomforts that had neither origin nor cure. Still, there was no denying her pain; and since it was chronic, Andrea felt the need to escape from it, to turn it off. This she could do very effectively by withdrawing her body from feeling. This, in turn, cast her into that other world where nightmares and craziness happened. It was a difficult situation. Bliss was having enough trouble controlling the course of her mental health therapy without having to cope with her physical health as well. He blamed it all on the two operations she had undergone for obesity, but it was too late now for recriminations. He would somehow have to work around the problem.

The most serious problem, and the most intractable, seemed to be getting at the source of her anger—or in this case, the sources, for he felt reasonably certain that there were many experiences that were contributing to her rage, many of which still remained undiscovered. Also, in working with the rage he had to work principally with Little Andrea-Ellen. Until the little girl could be made to grow up and accept the things that had happened to her, there would be no hope for Andrea. But really it was Andrea who had to accept and cope with the traumas.

Three other personalities who had previously caused lots of problems for her had reappeared: Joseph, Philippe, and her own private (and very Catholic) Devil. Together they were raising havoc, trying to hurt her whenever she let down her guard. And unfortunately they were having some success. She had developed a severe vaginal infection, and there could be little doubt that it was caused by more self-mutilation and the continued prowling of Marna. With Little Andrea-Ellen at the controls, and the unholy trinity of her male personalities on the loose, and Marna always waiting in the wings for a chance to abase herself sexually, Andrea was a walking disaster area.

To counter these complex problems, Bliss had her check into the hospital, both to keep an eye on her and also to conduct more intensive therapy sessions. During the first of these sessions, Andrea began reliving another of her traumatic experiences; in this one she was tied to a post in the garage, with her father angrily and sadistically burning her vagina with his cigar. The image grew stronger and more vivid. At last she grew angry at Bliss for pushing her to remember such feelings and allowed herself to fall into a deep trance devoid of pain or remembrance.

The next day Bliss was back at it again, pushing, dredging, goading her to remember. Once again she relived the cigar incident and began to see a connection between this and subsequent self-mutilations when she had used a hot iron and caustic oven cleaners to burn her vagina out.

That night Andrea tried to burn herself with some oven cleaner she had snuck into the closed ward. The burning was not bad, and the next day Bliss demanded that she bring the caustic to him. She refused, saying that it was the only thing she could do that reduced her panic. It was not the kind of answer calculated to reduce Bliss's insistence, and several hours later she came back to his office and gave him the bottle.

For the next few days she was in and out of a straitjacket as one attempt at self-mutilation followed another. The whole process was taking on a new and more compelling aspect. Past experiences suggested they were approaching some core of resistance. The more information that was dredged up, the more fervid became Andrea's need to hurt herself, as if the shadow of these incidents was intruding.

Bliss believed that, after more than two years of therapy, Andrea now knew that her father's abuses had really occurred. What remained, he thought, was the anger that she still directed at herself. To facilitate getting at that anger, they both agreed a tranquilizer was necessary; otherwise she would never be able to do it. As a precaution Andrea was put in a straitjacket, and then sodium amytal was injected intravenously. After that Bliss went at the anger head on, "flying by the seat of his pants" as he put it.

They talked about the Catholic faith and the sin attached to disobeying your parents. They probed the anger she associated with her own sins, and tried to judge the role her father and mother had had in those "sins." It took about an hour and a half, but then Andrea started latching onto the anger she felt for her parents—the rage and overflowing anger she felt for two people who had allowed so much horror. She screamed and yelled and spat out her hatred for her parents and, at the end of the session, seemed to be getting a hold on her problem. But that night she slipped silently into the throes of guilt and self-hatred once again, becoming totally catatonic.

"If she had been seen by a strange psychiatrist," Bliss wrote, "the diagnosis would have been catatonic schizophrenia or acute psychosis. Neither is true. It was acute panic with self-hypnosis—a primeval self-protective reflex, phylogenetically as ancient as arthropods."

ANDREA'S JOURNAL
Tuesday, June 1, 1982—3:30 P.M.

Feeling so sad, so empty, so cold. Time feels like it is all messed up—either too fast or too slow. I am screaming silently—the panic feels like it is far too much to cope with.

Despair permeates my coldness. I read over old hospital records last night and felt little change from ten years ago.

When I am with Dr. Bliss I feel stronger, safer. I almost believe his incredible optimism. But then, just a short time later, I am caught in this hell—suspended in futility.

I am very exhausted but cannot sleep. I am on guard constantly for someone who might harm me, yet it is clear that I am my own greatest enemy right now.

ANDREA'S JOURNAL
Tuesday, June 15—11 P.M.

This evening has been significantly calmer and as I read last week's notes, I am aware how far I have come. The calmness is not so much a sense of peace as it is a type of truce in this self war. I promised not to attempt suicide for a month, and that seems to have liberated some of this struggle.

My sense that there is something we are not confronting yet helps feed this core of self-destructive behavior. If the premise that the base reasons for these actions lies in unresolved feelings, then to continue to pursue the feelings seems right. However, material I have gleaned from previous sessions just shows the feelings were of minimal anger at my parents and primary anger at myself.

I know that I experience much anger in the present, and that expressing anger is a problem I have. Yet, I do not think it true avoidance to say this anger is not the correct focus.

Perhaps the secret lies more in the little girl needing to learn and know she can be freed of all these ghosts. But, most of all, that she is not EVIL, stupid, ugly, bad, etc . . .

I have wondered what my "core" self is—is it Little Andrea-Ellen, is it Super Andrea or is it Andrea Biaggi? The process is like watching a cocoon—what kind of caterpillar will emerge? Or will it be a butterfly? I know enough now that whatever it is, it won't be evil.

The change had come when Bliss made a pact with Andrea not to try committing suicide. That had taken considerable stress off their relationship. Then there was the continued work on Andrea's anger, and the use of amytal and the straitjacket, which in some strange way helped reduce her anxiety level. If the tranquilizer could relieve her tension, then the probing could go further and more of the damage could be uncovered. For a time this worked well, but there were many setbacks, including a physical one. Andrea's veins were so difficult to find that Bliss couldn't always inject the tranquilizer. Years of hospitalization and self-mutilation had seriously reduced the number of surface vessels.

Meanwhile, symbolically, they had been tearing down the walls of Little Andrea-Ellen's closet, bringing the little girl out into the open. This could be accomplished only because Andrea had come to accept the sincerity of Bliss's interest in her case. He had shown his commitment to her; she could do no less.

At last Andrea reported quite calmly that the closet that protected her for years had been completely demolished, but the effect of this was to cause immense sadness. Now she had no other place to go—her private home had been destroyed.

ANDREA'S JOURNAL
Thursday, June 17, 1982—10 P.M.

I began the past three weeks of therapy on the assumption that there would be difficult work but that, when it was all over, there would sort of be a fairy tale "happily-ever-after" ending.

I do feel great insight has been gained as to the reasons for both my self-destructive actions and the renewed desire to die. But there is a sadness and emptiness now that I find almost as impossible to bear—all the craziness and rage that was first there.

I seem to be experiencing a sense of loss, hence the sadness and emptiness. Yet the loss is not for my parents (as originally feared), for they were lost to me many years ago. It is not for loss of my "closet" either, since the walls have become covered with blood and there was no real solace left there anymore. The loss does not even seem to be for Little Andrea-Ellen as she is still strong. I believe the tremendous sadness and emptiness to be the loss of critical elements in my childhood, the loss of security, the loss of identity, the loss of dignity—and most of all the loss of early nurturing love.

It was easier all these years to believe I was crazy. There is comfort in an unknown genetic form of "mental illness" that so many other doctors claimed I had. This new kind of illness is harder to deal with.

For one thing it means I will have to work very hard at changing old patterns. When I experience an emotion, I will have to experience and deal with it in the present. I must learn how not to be overwhelmed by the past but accept the facts. That is not to say that present emotions cannot be overwhelming, but that the "sweet" exterior personality I have always used to face the real world is going to have to make room for a tougher one.

On August 20, Andrea broke her pledge to Bliss and took a lot of pills. Only the last minute intervention of another personality had spurred her to action in time. She ended up in the emergency room and then, after she was stabilized, they shipped her off to the ward. It was a serious attempt on her life, and she was completely at a loss to explain it.

"Monday I felt close to you and unashamed," she told Bliss. "But by last night I wanted to get a gun and finish it. I felt incurable, worthless, and hopeless. I am unimportant to anyone's life. I want you as a father more than as a therapist. I want to feel part of someone's life as an adult."

It was another example of the flipflopping that was going on now. Just as each improvement seemed to bring her closer and closer to permanent sanity, a regression would take place, hurling her further into the morass.

Using amytal and hypnosis, Bliss uncovered the cause of this latest attempt: Little Andrea-Ellen was still a little girl, primitive, almost feral in her anger. The Feral Child—that was the name Andrea gave the personality. The night before she had been acting like a four-year-old, and the terrible rage had gotten loose. Like any angry child, Little Andrea-Ellen hadn't understood the nature or the source of her anger and had directed it at herself.

Something was still in the way, as palpable as a wall. Whether it was another episode or another personality, Bliss didn't know. Andrea tried to help Bliss as best she could, but there were the usual contradictory impulses in her and she couldn't get a handle on her own distress. As the session began she felt distant from Bliss and detached from the world as a whole, mostly because of a head cold and the pain of a vaginal infection incurred the week before in a minor mutilation. This made it almost impossible for Bliss to hypnotize her in the way he wished—her aloofness and fear of being overwhelmed by the material he was seeking were an ominous combination. Finally he resorted to Amytal, and after an interval while Bliss searched for a vein in her arm that wasn't totally collapsed, she was able to relax and go deeply into hypnosis.

Then he began to work on the anger in the creature-within-a-creature that Andrea called the Feral Child. During the session Andrea was aware of a feeling of wild, almost uncontrollable anger. The rage here was greater, if possible, than that she had arrogated to the Angry One; with it came yet another assortment of pictures and images of brutality associated with her father and mother.

Bliss asked the Feral Child when she had been created.

Little Andrea-Ellen answered: "I was created at the same time I tried to kill myself when I was four. I had been sitting by the side of the road in front of my house, trying to die, crying because I couldn't accomplish my own death. I didn't want to go home because there was anger and pain back there. Yet I couldn't make myself die. That is when the Feral Child arrived—me, Little Andrea-Ellen. I accepted the rage and frustration for Andrea, took up a great stick and began smashing all the trees and bushes down the street, all the way back to my house. That same anger is always there—wanting to kill, wanting to be killed. I hate myself. I hate my parents."

Bliss asked for Andrea, and she appeared, hesitantly.

"Have you heard?" he asked.

"Yes—I guess."

"Are you willing to take on the Feral Child's rage?"

Andrea was silent for a moment, looking inward. "Yes. But the child makes it clear to me that she will be close by and ready to hurt me if I don't express her feelings, if I keep them buried."

Her memory was such a brittle thing: one second she would recall everything; the next, nothing. Perhaps no more than 50 percent of the time was she aware of the truth of the stories she had related to Bliss. The rest of the time she rejected them completely.

Almost three years had now passed since they first met, and though great strides had been made the major problems still remained. There was Little Andrea-Ellen's staunch refusal to grow up; Andrea's singular inability to retain the truth of her past life; and the woman's intense and irrational feelings of guilt, sin, anger, and outrage—all channeled by her Catholic upbringing and her mother's messages into self-destructive avenues. How to overcome these problems? The root, Bliss realized, was Andrea herself— her unwillingness to believe the facts of the case. A real understanding must dawn, with a final and complete acceptance of her past.

Several hopeful signs began to emerge in the fall of 1982. In September, for the first time she was really able to identify the basic falseness of her guilt and reject it. This admission, in turn, seemed to age Little Andrea-Ellen and bring her once again out of the closet.

"I wasn't bad, was I?" she asked Bliss. "It wasn't my fault that all that stuff happened to me."

"No, not at all," Bliss said. "You were blameless in every way for what happened to you."

"But why did it have to happen at all? What justice is there in that? Mustn't I have been a great sinner to deserve such treatment?"

"Only if you accept the principle that everything bad that happens to people is done because they are sinful. I can name several people straight out. Would you say, for example, that the saints were sinful, or Jesus Christ, because they suffered terrible punishment?"

"No."

"Then why brand yourself with this strange accusation?"

ANDREA'S JOURNAL
Thursday, September 23, 1982

The past four months of therapy were blocked by my inability to get past the memory and feeling of wanting to die at the age of four. During my visit to the family in Illinois, the place I was most strongly drawn to was the corner at the end of the block where I lived. It was at that spot that I would sit and wait for cars to come, then jump in front of them in an effort to kill myself. That memory was clear, and it was an event that was repeated several times, making the scene stronger still.

At first I thought the reason that I could not get past that memory was due to all the anger I experienced after not being able to die. Then, in the therapy session about a month ago, I was clearly able to get in touch with that anger, saw myself pick up a stick and hit all the trees and bushes on the way home. I identified that anger with a personality I called the Feral Child. After that session, I thought the entire scene was complete since I was now able to experience that anger consciously. It quickly became apparent that this early suicide attempt was not complete. My frustration grew as did the repeating compulsion to commit suicide. In early August of this year, I tried to end my life once again. Fortunately, a part of me took over to get help—it is a strong, protective part of me that I am now grateful is present. However, I lost conscious memory for about four days while that part took over—I still remember nothing of those days.

In my mind, I knew there had to be a reason for this block. However, in my heart I was very discouraged and thought that I was just being resistant to therapy, or that the memories were too overwhelming and I would never be "cured." Each day in this state only made it more difficult. I soon became unable to cope with many day-to-day realities. I was certain, for example, that my roommate hated me and did not want me living here. Although she is more uncomfortable with me because of my suicide attempt, in reality she did not have strong feelings. Paranoia became a big problem. Even at work, which has been going relatively well, I was unable to feel any sense of accomplishment and kept fearing that someone would "find me out" and have me fired.

Along with these feelings of paranoia came a variety of physical problems. I caught a cold and often thought that I was extremely feverish when, in fact, I had no fever. The simple cold had become a major illness in my mind. I had difficulty breathing from simple nasal congestion, which became exaggerated into a conviction that I would soon die. In the last week, I began to experience severe pains in my lower abdomen that were very sharp and real. I did not seek medical help since it had been my experience that doctors never find anything serious at these times. Furthermore, I become more agitated with physical exams. On the day of this session, however, I was in such extreme pain that I was seriously considering going to the emergency room for help.

Setting the stage, so to speak, for this therapy session is important as I believe it will better indicate what was accomplished by it. You must realize how extreme the problems were when I walked in that day. My mind and body had been in a critical state for several weeks. The weekend before this session found me battling a suicide attempt with a gun. Even though I "won" out over actually harming myself any further, my mind did not win. I became more and more separated from myself. That Sunday, I remember looking down at my hands and seeing them but not feeling that they were part of my body. It was a frightening sensation that I've had many times before in my life before I would go completely crazy. It was a time of unimaginable terror and suffering.

The therapy session earlier that week was of no value. I was certain Dr. Bliss, too, had given up on me. Communication was confused and labored. I left the office with a sense of futility over the entire matter. I had Friday off. That meant Thursday was the end of my work week—and the end of a necessity for relating to any sense of reality. I had pictured myself at the edge of a cliff, hanging on by my finger-tips all week long. Thursday I actually saw and felt myself fall over. I am now certain that, had Thursday's session not helped, I would have attempted suicide again that weekend and probably would have succeeded.

I knew I had to be able to get into a deep state of hypnosis if I were to have any chance that day. I would ordinarily have asked Dr. Bliss to use Amytal for the session under the circumstances. The problem was that the last time we tried to use it (about a week earlier) he failed to get into my small veins. I decided on my own to use a street drug to help me: mushrooms. I had used them before for myself and they had a strong hypnotic quality with little hallucinations. The disadvantage was that they tended to make everything more intense, which meant that I was risking a lot if they didn't help during the session. I did not tell Dr. Bliss since I didn't want him to concentrate on the drug and make it into a big issue.

The session began with me in a state of intense panic

and frustration. I think I had little hope and was certain of death. I knew I was stuck at the corner by my house at the age of four. My sense had been that there was no "event" that kept me there. I closed my eyes and reentered that space again for about the tenth time in therapy. This time, partially due to the drug, I was able to BE THERE more than before. At first I was feeling totally overwhelmed. The abuse of my parents that led me to that corner returned. The feelings of helplessness, fear, anger, and despair reentered my being. The combination of my father's physical abuse, threats, and denial of having done anything, joined by my mother's anger, her refusal to believe me, and her rejection of me. ("Go away now," she had said, "I don't want to see you anymore.") All of these things had been uncovered a few weeks before, so why was it that I was not yet free of it? Was there something else they had done or was it too much for me even in the present?

The key was my own guilt. When I went up to that street to kill myself, I felt overwhelmed and responsible, guilty. I was able to feel that I was responsible, that I should kill myself because of that. That was something I knew for a long time (that I felt responsible) but I had not really connected it with my desire to die. In that deep hypnosis, I searched my mind once again. Confess—did I do anything that made me feel responsible? With my adult mind I saw and felt my confusion at age four and understood the guilt—and I could finally, clearly see that I did not do anything wrong. Rather I perceived that I had felt guilty because of the reactions of both parents.

The relief was immediate and dramatic. The physical and mental pain both ceased. I confessed all. I was not guilty, I was not responsible for any of those events . . .

Could such a simple insight make a real difference? It is now four days later, and I am no longer in any physical pain, the nightmares that have plagued me the past two months are gone, and I feel at peace with myself. The paranoia is gone, and I am able to handle things appropriately. An added benefit seems to be dramatically increased energy.

Dr. Bliss kept telling me to keep out of hypnosis during these weeks—that it was my biggest problem. I realized after the last session that being in a state of hypnosis was so very natural for me that I had been convinced he was all wrong. What he called hypnotic states were my daily functioning states during this period—perhaps most of my life. It seems that what is needed is not a drug to block hypnosis but a more refined process of getting at the reason for being in hypnosis. In any event, the final result has been once again dramatic and liberating.

Through a *whole* month Andrea maintained her grasp on reality, without recurrences of panic or hysterical flights into hypnosis. There were still occasional anxieties but nothing significant—and that in itself seemed miraculous. She was making the conscious—and so far effective— decision not to run screaming into craziness when the tension got high. It was a difficult thing to do, and Dr. Bliss appreciated the problem. Going under, after all, had become an old and reliable habit, as automatic as the reflex of blinking her eyes or breathing. The only way to control this reflex was to quell panics and concentrate on the reasons they had formed in the first place.

"I've spent all my life punishing myself," she wrote in her notebook. "I must learn to change the habit."

As the period of recovery (what Bliss called "remission") increased from one week to two and then to three, his optimism increased. Never a man to dote on failure, he had conducted his life as an exercise in the best possible case upon the assumption that if the best can happen, it *may* happen. Now with her "clear," he hoped the end was in sight. So many problems had been addressed and confronted: the personalities, the horrendous childhood, the monumental guilt, the oppressive Catholic teachings. So much had been uncovered and revealed. It seemed reasonable to assume that this progress would accelerate and that Andrea, now confident of success, would throw herself into the task with an enthusiasm as great as his own.

The four-week recovery period, from Bliss's perspective, was all too short. Andrea was suddenly back in the closet, going in and out of panic and hypnosis. The worst part of this recidivism and the part that punctured his optimism was that she had no clear understanding of why she had landed there again. The degree of her dissociation now was profound—she had forgotten everything again and was back to thinking of her parents as ''saints'' and ''perfect.'' Nor would she budge from this position; she insisted adamantly on it and, when pressured to reconsider that precarious position, dashed headlong into trance states. The voices, the visions, the personalities were back—rank upon rank of them, all cluttering up her interior landscape with their clamor and conceits.

Bliss tried to draw her out, gingerly, as one might coax a rabbit from its hole.

''What's happened?'' he asked.

''I'm better now,'' she insisted.

''Where are you?'' The question might just as well have been *who* are you, until a childish tone took control of her voice.

''I don't know where I am.'' She sounded fretful, on the edge of a tantrum.

''Listen, Little Andrea-Ellen, why don't you come back to my world, out of the closet?''

''No! It's scary every time I try to come out.''

''How does Andrea feel about this?''

Andrea's voice came out: ''I—I can't work because it's too scary inside.''

''You've got to calm down.''

Andrea stared into space for five full minutes, glassy-eyed, eyelids fluttering, a thousand miles away.

''I'm in the closet,'' she said finally. ''It is sad and safe here. I want to turn everything off.''

''But that's not going to help. You've got to come out and face life, or you'll never be able to live normally.''

''I don't want to come out anymore. I don't like it. Hate the world and hate me.''

''Listen, Andrea, you have a very simple choice. Either

you can stay in the closet forever or come out and see the world as it really is."

"I still want to die!" Her voice was filled with despair and a plea for intervention against her self-destructive course. Then her face became more rigid. Pouting and taking up a pencil and paper she wrote in a childish hand:

I DON'T WANT TO COME OUT.
I HATE YOUR WORLD.
Put me in little room here in hospital.
No people around.
Just make it all stop. I *HATE* your world.
I not get better *ever*.

It took a full week before she was calm enough and lucid enough to reconstruct for Dr. Bliss what had happened:

"It is so very hard to stay out of hypnosis. I'm at a funny place—a pull to go back to the old world, another to stay here. A delicate balance. There is a sense of restlessness in everything—job, home, self—a lot of anger. I feel rebellious, like a teenager. I think I need 'space' to grow up. Emotionally I'm still eight. That was when my father was put in the hospital. I feel lost, like a beached whale—and I am flopping around. It's all very unstable, and I get easily overwhelmed.

"There's a part of me with you that is trying to be adult, and another part wants to have a temper tantrum because you aren't caring for her like a father should. Little Andrea-Ellen in particular is eight but verging on four—she could go either way. I am very frightened, afraid of hurting myself again."

It took a while longer before Bliss was able to extricate the thorn from her mental paw. It turned out to be something happening in the present, not the past: the marriage of her ex-boyfriend to another woman. Subconsciously she had known of the event, and that was enough to trigger her. After that, the synapses had taken over. As soon as this cause was known, she seemed to perk right up. Always hopeful, Bliss perked up as well.

ANDREA'S JOURNAL
Sunday, October 10—3 P.M.

. . . I made a very important mistake in the process of therapy that I am only now beginning to realize. I thought that once I remembered what happened to me, remembered the feelings it generated, and kept it all on a conscious level, I would be free from the problems that the events generated. I thought that the knowledge alone would set me free. I'm now clear that I also need to go through a "healing" period with all this. Knowledge certainly had to come first, but the healing process is equally important and, I might add, equally difficult.

It is also amazing to see the incredible chain of disaster that is released when I am in that state. That simple incident with my boyfriend's marriage started another intense period of dissociation. The first thing I noticed was looking at the fire in my friend's fireplace one night, beginning to concentrate on it, until it became the fire in the furnace that my father had put the cat into. After a while I couldn't stand it any longer and had to drive home. While driving I became very angry, mostly at myself, and drove dangerously. I was furious with myself for having promised Dr. Bliss that I would not attempt suicide for another six months because suddenly I wanted to die again—be free of all the pain and terror the fire immediately set off. I began to cry hysterically until I arrived home.

Once in my bedroom, the sense of terror became totally overwhelming. I lay in bed and pictured myself back in my bedroom in the small closet. The same feelings that drove me to hide in the closet at that age were driving me back into the closet space in my mind. Although I felt protected in my closet space, the sense of despair remained—intensified by time. All I knew at that moment was that I could endure no longer. Since suicide was no longer an option, I began reverting to an earlier age where I could feel no pain and terror. I literally became an infant for the next eight hours. It was a time marked with a wonderful sense of peace and safety.

I had never experienced this reversal to infancy before, although I had that fantasy for many years. I remember rocking a great deal of the time, crying softly some, and even sucking my thumb. Some hours later, I needed to go to the bathroom and didn't even think of getting up—I ended up urinating in the bed. I don't remember sleeping, but I could have.

My journey back to reality was long and tedious. I would sporadically look at the clock by my bed because of the light it emanated and the noise it made. It was just a toy to me most of the time, but later I was conscious of numbers and then their meaning. At those times I would tell myself that I had to come back to reality, but I kept refusing as the waves of feelings associated with being conscious washed over me, becoming too painful. Each wave, however, brought a little more consciousness to me. Other than my survival instinct, I'm not sure why I finally did pull back into reality. I do remember that one of my last thoughts in that twilight state was that I couldn't get the nurturing love I so desperately wanted.

Her return to reality was not complete. Over the next few months she kept slipping. The command of her consciousness was almost as tenuous as a baby's command of his muscles. She was spending more time in reality, coping with day-to-day problems, but regressed frequently and sometimes with near catastrophic results. Around the beginning of November she killed a cat and then spaced out for an entire weekend. Then she started experiencing chest and leg pains, which Bliss felt were probably psychosomatic but nonetheless real to Andrea. She was uncomfortable as "just Andrea" and still required Super Andrea to bear the brunt of her public commitments. When Bliss asked her how much of her time she felt had been spent during her life in the closet [in hypnosis] or as someone else, she answered quite seriously that she'd spent only 10 percent *at most* as herself, and 90 percent or more in other states.

By the end of the year Andrea Biaggi could look back

on her progress as only minimal. She had moved three times, gained back 35 of the pounds she'd lost (she was hovering around 200 again), had attempted suicide, had been rejected by a man she had loved, had suffered continued monetary problems, had experienced considerable trauma at her job, and had been unable to stabilize in therapy. In short, 1982 had not been a good year for her, and though she was more conscious now of her problems than she'd ever been before, that very perspective was less a reason for celebration than a point from which to critique her craziness. Also sticking in her craw (and in Bliss's, if the truth were known) was the "infamous champagne dinner" one year before, which was supposed to launch her onto a new ocean of sanity. So much for miracle cures. But the new year offered some promise, and she had made enough resolutions that, if even half of them came true, she would be the paragon of mental hygiene by the middle of March.

"All in all," she wrote in her journal, "I feel much better. My depression seems to be lifting, and I have some sense of direction again. And hope. I owe this to the genuine love and concern of Dr. Bliss, who has done everything he could to turn things around."

DR. BLISS'S NOTEBOOK
January 5, 1983

The session today was a disaster. I didn't take notes because it was a total stalemate with Andrea in a hypnotic state during the entire session. She came into the office and soon told me that she should not have come. Several times she asked to leave, said "No more hypnosis," cried, and insisted that the wall was back with all the personalities liberated.

I was tired anyway, and after two fruitless hours she was still in grim shape. I tried to return to the point where we had left off before in therapy, tried to approach the wall and see what was causing the chaos, but there was no progress. She just wouldn't cooperate. After all these years of work, I could see the whole enterprise crumbling. I went home discouraged and fatigued.

Then came the surprise. (The unexpected is commonplace with Andrea.) She telephoned early that evening in tears. A friend had called her. She had transformed into Super Andrea to take the call, and afterward during a semi-lucid moment had begun to put the pieces together.

Still in a hypnotic state but with greater clarity, she began to explain.

"All the things I was doing then, as a child, I have been feeling now. It was then that I built the thick wall. My physical pain now got involved, and it mixed things up."

In a halting fashion, over the telephone, we reviewed the last few weeks. For almost four weeks, Andrea had been virtually clear. In therapy, we had returned to the closet where Andrea had split off Little Andrea-Ellen. For the first time, Andrea had come to realize that Little Andrea-Ellen had taken the emotions and the experiences— there had been a split between the mind and the body.

Then came the medical examination to try to discover the cause of her medical disability. During the process, several disasters had occurred—being told by the doctor "nothing was wrong," and the technician drawing blood with great difficulty (Andrea's veins are awful), and then spilling some of the blood. All of this frightened her, and she reverted to a hypnotic state, returning to her past. She panicked and became lost. Back she went to the closet, separated, and was behind a great wall which no adult could penetrate—including me. Again she was with her frightful array of personalities bent upon crazy tasks. Understandably, in my office she was totally inaccessible—a reversion to our early days of therapy before any progress was made.

But another big insight was her statement that the sequence that we had been uncovering during the last months— from the home to the street scene, then to the Feral Child, and back again to the closet—was a summary or digest or condensation of all that had occurred during the four or five years of abuse. It had led to all of the splits, the erection of the wall, and the other hypnotic ploys.

At the end of our telephone conversation, Andrea was

clear and out of hypnosis. She said that she would try to separate the present from the past and try to unscramble the confusion since past and present had become hopelessly intermingled and had caused her to be crazy again. She again asked whether all that abuse had really happened, and I laughed, saying it had happened without question. Whether it is yet "real" to her—completely and unalterably so—is still in doubt.

There are limits in the mental world just as there are in the physical, and often there are surprising parallels. In the physical realm no limit is more indisputable than the speed of light. As an object approaches that limit, it becomes increasingly more difficult for it to gain still more speed until very near the absolute barrier; an almost infinite amount of energy is needed to increase the speed fractionally. A similar thing was happening in Andrea Biaggi's therapy. Many of the thorniest problems were now understood, the bulk of the hidden information was at the surface (or, at any rate, very *close* to the surface), and she was becoming more conscious of the differences that existed between reality and her nightmare world. But now, as some kind of final resolution came into view, the progress was slower, the energy required to move her ahead became much greater, and her failures became more pronounced. A good day or week was predictably followed by horrendous days and weeks. While sanity seemed closer, so also did insanity. When she wasn't getting better, she was roaming the streets as Marna, seeking out a sexual partner to abuse her, spending endless nights huddled in corners, contemplating suicide with increased yearning.

If her vacillations were greater, Bliss's knowledge of her moods and problems had increased also, together with his "tools" for dealing with those problems. He had learned how to defuse her hysterical, inarticulate outbursts to allow therapy by the simple expedient of asking Andrea for "no emotion," and he had become more adept at bringing her out of her self-imposed hypnotic retreats and rechanneling her into the more helpful states where *he* was director.

The biggest problem now—and the most intransigent—was getting Andrea to understand that her memories of the past were true. In the normal course of things she was still "cycling back" after each revelation, meticulously erasing everything that disagreed with her original fantasy that her parents had been perfect and her childhood had been very happy. Any slight disturbance in the current of her life would set the process in motion; within a period of a few minutes, a complex understanding of her traumatic past could be reduced to a childish *tabula rasa*.

As yet, Bliss had failed to discover the crucial process that would imprint the truth indelibly and thus prevent the recycling. It made sense that such a step must come, but so far he had not succeeded in discovering the exact formula by which this ratification of the whole could take place. Somewhere there was a "glitch," some piece of human circuitry that refused to cooperate. Where was it?

Could it be a recalcitrant personality—one he hadn't met yet? There was always a possibility of this, but it didn't seem very likely. He had plumbed that conglomeration to its uttermost and had come away with twenty-three "parts" in all, of which Nothing, Philippe, Little Andrea-Ellen, Sister Jeanine, Julia, and Super Andrea were the principles. The chance that still another existed seemed remote; and even if that were the case, it seemed doubtful whether such a personality could wield such utter power over the rest of the organization. No—for the most part, Bliss rejected this theory.

Then perhaps there existed an experience of some sort—a really atrocious, mind-numbing incident—vicious enough to obtrude on everything else that was happening, malignant enough to spread its venom throughout her system. But there had been so many truly horrendous episodes related already that it seemed almost impossible that some further incident remained of such compelling cruelty that it could overshadow everything else.

Then too, there might be some problems with contemporary events . . . but these were only provocations that thrust her into the past. On the whole, Bliss tended to believe that many of her physical difficulties were hindrances to progress but not complete blocks; she could manage her daily life if he could ever keep her from reverting to hypnotic states when there was panic.

There were so many variables that it was hard to know where to begin to look. As a result he spent many long hours in therapy with her—three-hour sessions that tested both of them to their limits.

DR. BLISS'S NOTEBOOK
January 22, 1983

This was one of those horrendous three-hour marathons. Our agenda was set since we knew or thought we knew what to do. I used amytal, but even a half gram intravenously—enough to put most people into a deep sleep—didn't faze her. She was so terrified that it had no effect on her at all! There followed futile efforts to get her to retrace in hypnosis the beginnings of her split.

Finally, in the office we reenacted the process. A little stagecraft is often a good thing but, as usual, there was an unexpected twist. We had been retracing a summary of all the experiences when suddenly a new one welled up. This was the worst, and for her the most horrible of all, yet it began innocuously enough.

"There is fighting, a lot of fighting between my parents," she had begun.

"Why were they fighting?" I asked.

"It is just before I ran out the street and tried to run in front of a car. Several almost hit me. One honked and swore at me . . . but didn't hit me. Then—then—"

"Yes?"

"I returned to the house. My father was gone, and my mother screamed at me. I went to my room . . . got into bed. Then all of a sudden my father was there and I screamed, but my mother had left the house. I ran into the closet, yes—I ran into the closet and tried to hide. But he knew I was there. He found me and dragged me out. He threw me on the bed and got on top of me and hurt me . . . No, it can't be true!"

"But it is, Andrea. It is. Go on."

"He has a large butcher knife—long and sharp . . . and a rifle. He is threatening to cut me—her—into pieces and is swinging knife . . . Oh! He barely misses, by inches. He is wild-eyed, wild, laughing hysterically . . . Crazy wild. He swings the knife again and again. Then he points the gun at her head—in her mouth—and pulls the trigger. Click! Click! the rifle isn't loaded, but she is a little girl, she doesn't know that. For her, each click is the end . . . and it goes on and on and on . . ."

"How long, Andrea?"

"A real long time. Longer than ever before. Her mother is gone, and there isn't anyone around to help. She screams, but no one hears her. She screams, and her father laughs some more. It is torture—torture—and no one to help her. No one. It was a near-death experience that absolutely terrified her. At the end, when he finally left, she was exhausted . . ."

She paused and seemed to lose touch with the image. By her eyes I could tell she was going in and out of hypnosis rapidly. Then she started to cry and lost it completely.

"I went back and said it couldn't happen. It couldn't happen. He couldn't do it. I don't know how I got back to my room . . . I . . . He couldn't do those things. No. I must be bad. I hated him. I couldn't believe he would do it—the gun, the knife."

Then, a moment later, the voice changed, another look took control of her face, and she said: "Lied! Bad girl! Those things he said were right. I didn't want to come out of the room anymore." It was Little Andrea-Ellen. She scowled at me, but gradually her face began to clear. Then, in a very assertive voice, Andrea said, "That happened then, not now!"

It was a major breakthrough for Andrea. That concept of a separation of the past and present was new to her. Little Andrea-Ellen was obviously growing up.

I thought it was a triumph (perhaps it was), but in the evening Andrea called in a panic. "It was too much!" she cried and became utterly incoherent.

I tried to calm her down, but wasn't successful. She was completely shattered.

The closet wasn't safe for her anymore, but neither was the outside. Having left her old realm behind, she did not yet have the strength to remain long in the new. She was truly "in between" with fewer options. She could forget everything about her past life, but then, like Rip Van Winkle, memories would reappear again as soon as she reemerged. There was less space for forgetting, more to remember. Now also there was an acute sense of the dichotomy that existed between her body and mind. She felt no coordination between the two entities, but now there was the suggestion that eventually they must be united. Her gluttony continued to offend her and it was making less and less sense in terms of an arbitrary "punishment" for imagined sins. Why should she be fat?

But had it all really happened? Dr. Bliss said yes, but a lot of the parts inside kept insisting no. How could it have happened? To prove it to herself, she wrote down a list of what she called "facts," and tried to deduce from this list whether her father had really done those things to her or not:

1) Vaginal infections from the age of four
2) Violent father
3) Father sexually obsessed
4) Father put away for four years
5) Mother distant in my youth
6) Father tried to kill us several times
7) Tried to kill myself at the age of four
8) Had a childhood spent in isolation and depression
9) Hated garages or garage attics most of my life
10) Obsessed with hurting myself, especially sexually
11) Obsessed with wanting to die
12) Hated my body as long as I can remember

As circumstantial evidence it offered pretty fair corroboration that her "memories" had spoken truthfully. But still more information was soon available.

On a trip to Chicago she managed a weekend in her hometown, where she met with most of her siblings. Little had really changed except perhaps her brothers' attitude toward her. She had gotten some time to talk with Mike, and he had laughed nervously when she brought up the topic of their past behavior toward her.

"Those were really crazy times," he had said. "Best forgotten. I guess all of us were pretty screwed up then. None of us wanted to put up with any more crap like Dad handed out, and when it looked like you'd inherited his craziness, well—"

Andrea could look around her and see quite clearly that none of the three boys had escaped that "craziness." Mike was an alcoholic working on his third marriage; Joey, also alcoholic, was a widower with three kids; and Larry was an extremely troubled man unable to deal with the problems that had ruined his personal life. Who were they, now, to call her nuts? And when they all started playing that game about how good the "old days" had been, she checked out completely. No amount of pretending would make it so for her; they were all hypocrites, and when it came to pretending they were rank amateurs compared to her. Something had obviously done a pretty thorough job of lousing up their lives.

But the real revelation came from her talk with Rose and Dalia. Dalia was crazier than ever—truly "certifiable" with paranoid delusions of being followed by the Mafia; clicking into sudden, towering rages without reason; and talking disconnectedly about their father and how "Andrea knows everything." (The implications were obvious, although Dalia never spelled it out.)

Shockingly it was Rose who put it most clearly. Andrea and Rose had never gotten much chance to talk. The age difference had seemed substantial when they were younger; Andrea had grown up in Joseph's pre-institution period, and Rose had still been a child when their father came home. But when they started talking they soon learned they had, tragically, a great deal in common.

"It happened just a few months before he died," Rose

confessed to her during one of their talks in private. "He was really weak and all—confined to the bed—but he was crazy. Sick as he was, it didn't keep him from doing it to me."

"What do you mean, 'doing it to me'," Andrea asked.

"You know. He grabbed me when I was next to his bed. I was just small, and I couldn't defend myself and he just—well—it happened."

"What happened?"

"You know." Rose shook her head. "He raped me. It was awful, just awful. It's really done wonders for my life, let me tell you."

Andrea had been the primary target for her father's brutal insanity, but both Rose and Dalia had been swallowed up in the same dementia. Strangely, it seemed to Andrea, that of the three of them she most nearly approximated sanity in her outward demeanor, though not perhaps in her physical appearance—of the entire family, she alone was fat. Dalia, by contrast, despite her madness, was a gorgeously svelte creature.

The visit had been an interesting fact-finding mission. She returned to Salt Lake City with plenty of information. There was no dearth of circumstantial evidence, but unfortunately, in Andrea's mind, it would require more than that. She needed a witness—yes, that was it! A witness. Someone who had been there to see the whole thing, whom she could trust to tell her the unvarnished truth.

20

Mental Surgery

DR. BLISS'S NOTEBOOK
March 8, 1983

SHE'D been trying to get into graduate school, to get her Ph.D., but she wasn't accepted—a big disappointment. Then too, there is a court case tomorrow for a ticket: she was stopped for reckless driving—the work of a personality.

Also, as she told me, "I'm pregnant!" A Marna product. She doesn't know the man's name.

"I didn't do it," she told me. "I wasn't even there. Can I help it if other people use my body to do crazy things?" There is both humor and desperation in this statement. She still feels that she is basically out of control, near the edge.

She wanted to abort the pregnancy herself, with a coat hanger, because she doesn't want anyone else to touch her, but I have convinced her (I hope) that there is only one way to handle this situation.

All told, she is crazier now than she was a while ago. She had been in hypnotic states 90 percent of the time. "The feelings get so strong," she told me, "that I feel I'm drowning. Then I go back and become crazy and think your work is all wrong."

What with Marna running around loose at night, the pregnancy, the court appearance, and her failure to get into graduate school, she is a mess: either possessed by one of her many personalities or withdrawn into a catatonic form of hypnosis.

I continue to try to get her out of the twilight states but it requires a delicate kind of "mental surgery." First I must remove the feelings to establish some objectivity and then slowly pry her away from the distance and aloofness that is so much a part of Little Andrea-Ellen's retreat to the closet. Of course now, with the "amputation" of her closet, Little Andrea-Ellen no longer has a small place to hide. No matter, she has found a large place in which to hide from me: she pictures herself wandering in a desert, bloody, and shooting herself. "Wandering in the desert is a room without walls," she had told me. The image she keeps of herself (and of Little Andrea-Ellen) is a female—no longer as young as she used to be—covered with blood, wandering aimlessly, lost. Now when she is desperate and alone she talks about going to the "desert" and killing herself. Perhaps this is progress, but if so it is a very grim form of it . . .

The spring of 1983 in Salt Lake City was godawful, less a spring than a continuance of the Ice Age that had over-taken the whole Wasatch Mountain basin. By April it was snowing almost every day, with temperatures in the 30s (or lower) and cloud cover so thick that most residents had forgotten what the sun even looked like. Like everyone else, Bliss was depressed by the weather. Complicating his mood was the continued poor showing of Andrea. They had reached some kind of "farthest point" beyond which she seemed incapable of probing and beyond which he was incapable of *making* her go. This obstacle was described as a great wall—Andrea could even see it clearly in front of her at times—and there seemed no earthly way around it. They both tried, but if this was some kind of final portal (or final exam), it was certainly booby-trapped in an elaborate way. Past obstructions seemed mere child's play compared to the one he faced now—like a real life, grown-up video game, complete with self-destructor buttons, blind alleys, mazes, and cul-de-sacs.

The frustration level was very high. Three-hour sessions twice a week couldn't begin to penetrate this barrier. Little

Andrea-Ellen wasn't listening, Sister Jeanine was "gone," Super Andrea was an ineffectual public-relations façade, and Andrea herself was a sightless, quivering, unresponsive, and disbelieving lump of flesh.

Days passed while the snow and winds swirled, and Andrea faded more and more. At home Bliss complained to his wife and spent time trying to figure out yet another strategy. Slowly, over the course of months and years, even his ineluctable optimism was eroding.

DR. BLISS'S NOTEBOOK

April 19, 1983

Today I made the emphatic point that she couldn't recover until she accepted the facts. The disasters happened and must be recognized and not evaded—just as an alcoholic must first admit to his illness.

It was a point I have been trying to make for eons. I determined to stick to this obvious fact: that she had not yet been able to accept the truth of her father's sexual abuses. As long as she denied this, no progress could be possible.

She had come today in a frightened, semi-hypnotic state, and I had a devil of a time calming her down. I finally became exasperated and told her point-blank that she must calm down or nothing could be done. She did finally quell the panic, but she could not suggest any way to make the events with her father real. Both parents were dead, and there were no other witnesses. I saw no way to convince her, ever, that these assaults really occurred.

I was damn discouraged, if not defeated. Circumstantial evidence was simply not enough for Andrea.

It was just at the end of the session, and nothing new had happened. It was getting late, and Andrea had to get going. In despair, I asked to speak to her mother, Dara, in hypnosis, knowing that this kind of "magic" would probably not work—and it didn't. I was unhappy enough to try anything, and it suddenly occurred to me to ask Mother Mary. I don't know why—it was just one of those impulses.

Andrea told me she had abandoned Mother Mary because she was only "a statue." I was sufficiently frustrated, however, to try anything, and I insisted. So, reluctantly, Andrea went into hypnosis and I asked for Mother Mary. I told Andrea, playing on her Catholicism, that there was a real Mother Mary and she knew the truth.

I then told Andrea that we must try. Suddenly, Andrea started crying and said to me that Mother Mary had never lied to her. That was all I needed.

I decided to gamble all the chips.

"Listen, Andrea, I have a proposition for you."

"Yes?" Crying.

"I'm willing to let Mother Mary decide everything—whether your father actually assaulted you or not. If Mother Mary says I'm right, then I'll accept her judgment. If she says all the stuff about your father is false, then I'll abide by that judgment too. A deal?"

Tentatively, "Yes."

"Okay, you go ask Mother Mary now. Remember, by your own admission, she's *never* lied to you. She'll know the absolute truth."

Slowly she went into self-hypnosis, and I held my breath. It took a few minutes for her to "consult" with this personality, but it might as well have been hours the way I felt. Just the two of us in that office, and you could cut the tension with a knife.

Then suddenly Andrea was back out and crying harder than I'd seen her cry in a long time.

"Well?" I asked.

"Mother Mary—," she sputtered, "Mother Mary says it's all true."

"So?"

"So, it must all be true, about my father, about my mother."

It's hard to describe the kind of exhilaration you feel at a moment like that. Here we'd been hacking away in the middle of this jungle for four months, not getting anywhere at all, and then suddenly, eureka! Daylight and fresh air and a clear view. But she didn't give me much time to exult. For Andrea there is either feast or famine, and this was a smorgasbord of recollections.

"And there's something else," she said, now clear as a bell. "Mother Mary made me remember something else. It was something my mother always used to say. She was a very religious woman, and she used to say that any disaster was God's will. I guess—I guess I just assumed that this was God's way of punishing me for something I'd done wrong. But now, I see that's not true."

I feel *almost* certain that this is *the* turning point. Andrea now accepts the validity of her hypnotic memories and has a new calm that augurs well. It was an absolute fluke, this new stratagem. I somehow stumbled across it by pure chance (I wish I *could* call it intuition), and when Andrea said Mother Mary never lied to her, I pushed ahead for dear life. It wasn't science or logic or anything like that—just blind luck.

ANDREA'S JOURNAL
Tuesday, April 19, 1983—10 P.M.

I feel as if I have finally broken through the wall that I have been stuck behind for the past four months!!! This has been such an exhausting, frustrating, agonizing period that I had once again begun to believe that I could not make it through—could not ever get better. I almost feel as if I had wrestled with the Devil himself, only this time I think I've won!

I've known for quite some time that I was stuck in therapy. Nothing was getting through. I just couldn't bring myself to believe that all those memories I had experienced in hypnosis had really happened.

The crucial session was riddled with all sorts of problems. The drug that was supposed to help me relax and allow me to get deeper didn't work. Its failure made me paranoid, and I thought Dr. Bliss never even gave it to me. Trust is always a major factor. When I remembered something, the immediate reaction was of being totally overwhelmed, of profound pain and grief. Dr. Bliss kept pushing me, but it only seemed to increase the emotional distance I was beginning to feel toward him. At the end, I experienced being part of the wall where I went to hide—once again, being totally overwhelmed. I kept thinking, "It couldn't have happened, it couldn't have happened," and finally, "It didn't happen, it didn't happen."

I have spent the past four months, in essence, stuck in that place fighting not only the past, but also the present—my friends, church, my job. I isolated myself in a hermitage. My relationship with Dr. Bliss changed dramatically as well.

At the beginning of the year, I was trying to hold to being close to him, but the problem was that he was on vacation for that first month. I kept writing in an effort to keep that sense of closeness, but increasingly I lost it.

Using Marna to try to find the answer turned into a major focus, but also a major disaster: I got myself pregnant by the time Dr. Bliss returned, which only complicated all of this much more. It took almost a month after he returned to find out if I was really pregnant, then to try and make a decision about what to do, then to have the abortion. As much as I rationally knew that it was the only choice, my Catholic heritage struck again, and I could not find any sense of peace—only reinforcement of the idea that I was BAD. All this set the scene for the past month, which was one of a total loss of control and a tremendous sense of panic.

All of this formed the backdrop that led to today's session. I had an extreme sense of panic and loss of control once again. I had been changing personalities rapidly and yet somewhat artificially for the past four days. I was aware of a great sense of anger at one time, and then a great sense of depression at another. Since I had made an agreement with Dr. Bliss that I would not hurt myself or attempt suicide, there seemed to be no way out of this panic. The majority of the session was spent in panic and total frustration. Even Dr. Bliss felt caught by it and finally decided that we were getting nowhere and maybe today wasn't the day to work. I started to leave with a sense of dread as I knew I could not hold out much longer in that state.

Just as I was getting up to leave, Dr. Bliss tried a new tactic. We had been trying to come up with some way that I would be able to say that all the sexual incidents really happened. I couldn't say they did, and I couldn't say they didn't, and it was in that place—back at the wall—that I felt trapped. During that time, one of the things I couldn't figure out was how I could remember some things, such as my father trying to kill all of us with a knife, but I couldn't remember any of the sexual incidents.

It was Dr. Bliss's decision to try to find out what was blocking me through Mother Mary. At first, I thought the entire idea was ridiculous and another blind alley. I have had the sense for a long time that the major problem was mixed somewhere between religion and my mother. I had no idea how, but just that sense. I had abandoned Mother Mary a long time ago as I thought her too connected with the statues in church that became my substitute family. I didn't want anything artificial anymore. Dr. Bliss pushed me to try anyway, even though I thought it was barking up the wrong tree.

To my amazement, it took only a few short minutes to know that we were suddenly going in the *right* direction. When I went to get in touch with that part of me (Mother Mary) I immediately saw myself sitting at the kitchen table, about five or six years old, with my mother. She was showing me and my other sisters a book she had carefully guarded on the lives of the saints. (We had very few books in our home, so any book was special.) She opened it to the section on St. Maria Goretti—that horrible picture from the book was etched clearly in my memory. That person, Maria Goretti, had become part of our lives, I remembered. It was then that I finally made the connection between my father trying to kill all of us with a knife and my mother talking to us about Maria. She was a young Italian girl who had given her life rather than give up her virginity to a rapist. My mother took great pains to read us the story in detail and have us look at the picture. I had thought, in my child's mind, that she felt I would have been better dead, knifed, than be forced to participate in any sexual activities with my father. "This is God's will," she would say, and I would take it to mean that it was God's way that a woman (a young girl actually) like me or Maria Goretti would be better off dead than do anything sexual with a man who wasn't her husband. I don't think that I really knew what a virgin was at the time—but I was certain of the lesson she was trying to teach.

I came out of hypnosis, and all of a sudden everything began to fall into place and make sense. I also began to remember that my mother stopped going to church every Sunday around that time, which was very unusual for her because she was a very devout Catholic. But then I remembered you cannot go to Church (under their rules) if you are in a state of mortal sin, which is what my mother must have believed herself to be in from that point on in her life. During the entire time that we've been working on all this in therapy, I've been unable to really know why a mother would let those things happen without stopping them. I could try to rationalize it as the pressure of a poor woman with seven children, but that really never quite sat with me. All of a sudden, however, thinking of my mother's motivation for not stopping all of this as a type of religious atonement made sense. "God's will" would help one bear all things—even a child's pain or a family's destruction. As ridiculous as that may all sound to an educated person, I was brought up with that teaching and I could understand it. I finally knew why religion was so much a part of this craziness. It seems ironic now that it was through Mother Mary—my good sense of religion—that I was able to get in touch with all that insanity.

As complicated as all this may seem on the surface, it is relatively simple to me. For my mother and myself, life centered around religion—the power and force behind a Catholic Italian family as it has been for generations. Religion allowed my mother to suffer anything, even death for herself and her children if that was God's will. Religion had me convinced, as a little girl, that I was indeed BAD if I did not run from my father, even if I couldn't run. The story of Maria Goretti was not an isolated example of that teaching, but it was most certainly a vivid one.

The reason this knowledge freed me from the wall is also simple. One of the main reasons I have had difficulty remembering for so long (and the reason that I kept forgetting when I did remember) was tied to my mother. It was she who said that those things didn't happen or that I was lying. I believed her because that too was tied to religion—honor thy father and thy mother NO MATTER WHAT. I had to be able to really see and remember that she had said those things before I could free myself. This session allowed me to really say she did that, and the reason WHY she did those things. It had to be a reason that made sense—a better reason than poverty or too many children or even fear. That reason was religion.

It has now been eight hours since the therapy session. I have felt so much freer than I have in ages—the sense of breaking through the wall is clear and complete for me. Upon reflection, there is one more dimension to the past four months that I find interesting. All of the self-destructive acts, etc., were not the same as they had been before. Then one piece of this kept returning. Yesterday I lost it, and got so angry that I slammed the door. The glass in the door shattered and it scared the hell out of me. I thought it was one more act of insanity along with all that's been happening lately. Suddenly, however, it occurred to me that this wasn't an act of craziness but an act of rebellion and anger—an adolescent act. I have a theory that the past four months have been different because instead of approaching life like a child, I was now approaching it as an angry and rebellious teenager, which I had never been before.

Perhaps now I can be an adult.

21

Coming Full Circle

IN the months that followed, Andrea made giant strides toward recovery.

Her comprehension of what her parents had done to her opened up the floodgates. Spread out before her conscious mind was her life history, and while the information was horrendous enough to send her back into hypnosis, she now fought the urge. And those painful perspectives of her past led to vital insights. One of the first was that she wasn't a harlot. That label had been inflicted on her, like so much else, by her mother who had frequently called her all manner of things to avoid the truth of her husband's enormities. No excuse could be given for a woman, no matter how small and defenseless, who allowed herself to be abused in such a way without killing herself.

By surviving, Andrea could see now, she had committed the ultimate offense and the damnations of her dead mother had swirled in her mind ever since, embodied in a chorus of outraged personalities who stoned her for sins she had no means of preventing. It was from this that her omnipresent image of the harlot being stoned had come.

ANDREA'S JOURNAL
October 6, 1983

I write this as a postscript to my story. The reader of this book must wonder how someone picks up the pieces from such a traumatic past and puts it all back together again. During most of my therapy, I wondered the same thing.

I have now been able to unravel most of the secrets of my past. The sources of the trouble are clear to me at last. I would have thought that was all I needed to do: find out where the terror lay and then a sense of peace would descend on me. But I was wrong.

The first step out of my nightmare world was remembering, that is true. And it was the longest part of therapy. The images were always there, though often behind the screen. Breaking down that screen was the second phase of the work. That meant getting back the feelings that went with the memories. That was really the worst part of the trip for me. After that I thought we were home free—that once I could accept and adapt to all the new memories and feelings, then at last I'd be free of the panics and hypnotic episodes. Again I was wrong. I continued to have episodes, breaking apart at regular intervals, and it took more months of frustrating work before the truth was really revealed. I couldn't simply accept or accommodate to all the events that had wrenched my life apart. I had to learn how to change the thirty years of thinking and acting that went along with it.

The repeated sexual and physical abuses by my father separated me from my body. The rejection and confused messages from my mother separated me from my mind. The two, united with the instructions of the Catholic Church, convinced me that even my soul was doomed. My being during most of my life was Nothing—the first and strongest of my personalities. For thirty years, Nothing was me!

Despite knowing what had gone into making me insane, despite regaining the feelings associated with those memories, the old cycles of insanity continued. Events in the present, at times, brought back the feelings of the past. Too often, those feelings would keep me hypnotically lost in the past because the feelings were overwhelming. I would panic and lose control. This would also lead to a loss of faith in therapy as I continued to experience many of the same horrors that had brought me to therapy in the first place.

The images through all these stages were vivid and

symbolic. During the first stage of remembering, I kept seeing myself surrounded by thick, old concrete walls, almost like a medieval church without windows. Those walls were shattered by the end of that first stage, revealing a naked child covered with blood, lacerated by feelings. When I experienced hope, I wanted to build a new image—a solar home with unbreakable glass surrounded by wildflowers and filled with people and love. I knew what I wanted, but not how to achieve it.

I kept thinking the answers to my problems remained in the hypnotic spaces inside my head. Was there a memory left uncovered? Was there some critical message I hadn't unearthed yet? The only help I had was from Mother Mary, and I usually dismissed her as too religious, too much of a goody-goody like Sister Jeanine. By ignoring both Mother Mary and Sister Jeanine, I only increased Nothing's power.

It is only over the last few months that I have begun to change all this. The final step was *change*. Despite what I know now about my childhood, when a crisis began I wanted to run back into the old space in my head and turn off the pain and panic. Somehow I had to change that reflex. And now I am beginning to. None of my stages in therapy have been easy, but this last stage, the stage of learning how to react differently to fright, brings hope and a new feeling for a new life.

ANDREA'S JOURNAL
November 1, 1983

When I left the hospital after today's therapy session there was a rainbow greeting me. A symbolic end to one of our most important sessions.

When I came into the room I was feeling a bit exhausted from a busy work day. The chair felt comfortable and comforting—I felt safer in that room and more at ease than I had for some time. When Dr. Bliss first asked me what I wanted to work on, I thought it might be nice just to have a "no content" easy kind of time together.

With my head resting on the back of the stuffed chair (a

posture I rarely took in that room), I remembered I had been bothered by recurrent urges to go back on the streets as Marna. Marna was created to help remember what happened and to punish me in the same way as my father did. Dr. Bliss helped make a further link to my current problems with religion. Swiftly and surely it all came together. Marna was created out of a sense of being evil—she was the continuation of my father's punishment.

The new awareness, the breakthrough, came in the realization that my sense of being evil was the core of my sense of being Nothing. I recalled my first conscious image in therapy as the harlot in the Bible who was stoned to death in the city center for her sins. I had always thought that was my destiny, my deserved punishment. I had also looked to be rescued from that scene, like the woman in the Bible was by Christ. Now I knew something new— now I KNEW I was never the harlot to begin with! I was just the victim. But thirty-plus years ago, a little girl became convinced of her wickedness through the combined physical punishments of her father and the mental rejection of her mother. Even though I initially knew I wasn't responsible for my father's insane attacks, my rage and desire for them both to die was most certainly a sign of my wickedness as the Catholic tradition had trained me to believe.

We had finally come full circle in therapy. The original image gave way to the knowledge now of what really happened. What the reality was. That knowledge was a big key. It meant not only remembering the attacks of my father, but the kind of things my mother used to say that supported the religious condemnation. It was remembering the rage I had felt and realizing it was a valid response to all that happened. The false image of being a harlot standing in the center of my feelings could finally be removed, and the real Andrea, the present Andrea, could replace that image. The largest stone of my new house was put into the foundation.

Could such a significant breakthrough be so simple? Why had it taken four years to reach this point? Could I trust myself and my analysis? These were questions I contemplated while Dr. Bliss took a short break from his office to get some water. Before he returned I knew the answer: the analysis was right. The background work to this day was long and terribly painful, but it had finally paid off. We had indeed come full circle.

With Dr. Bliss back in the room, I entered a deep hypnotic state to formalize the knowledge by changing the image in that deep core of me. The image of the harlot quickly crumbled like the stone of an old, useless wall! I crossed the bridge that had become symbolic of security in dealing with these feelings of Nothingness. I was greeted by my old nurturing friend who held me in her arms and confirmed my accomplishment. The key word I sensed was REMEMBER. Remembering what had really taken place thirty years ago would allow me to keep the real image in place and begin to sense some peace, some healing. I came back out of hypnosis in a state of absolute joy.

Six hours have passed since this session. I know that I will not be free from all emotional pain from this point forward, but I now believe I can deal with real life problems in a more realistic way. I don't need to feel crazy anymore; I don't need to feel like Nothing anymore; I don't have to feel like a condemned harlot. The sense of peace this evening, unlike other times of ''cease-fire,'' feels like the end of my internal war.

For Andrea, the end of the harlot was a critical revelation. But there was still one more memory needing disinterment, one so central to her problems that, without its discovery, there could be no more than a cease-fire.

The break came quite suddenly, as often happened now. It occurred around the end of November 1983, as Dr. Bliss was talking with Andrea, who was under no more than the lightest hypnosis. Suddenly she started to squirm around, not as if possessed, merely uncomfortable.

''What's wrong?'' Bliss asked.

''Nothing much . . . just this odd feeling.''

"Like what?"

"Sometimes I mix you up with my mother, and then I feel abandoned. When I figured out I wasn't a whore, I could feel closer to you. But it wasn't firm. I felt like an orphan or a foster child. But not like your real child. But then I see you as my mother all of a sudden and I feel distanced from you—sadness, anger, rage. That is what is wrong."

"Why the rage?"

"I don't know . . ." Her eyes closed and she was concentrating. "I hear myself yelling 'get away . . . don't hurt me, please!' I see crosses and statues, being punished, and tremendous rage. Nothing is at the core, but this anger is like burning down a church, committing revenge, killing a cat. Yes, that's it! Killing a cat. That has to do with my mother. She . . . she punished me because my dress was dirty . . . because my father had done something to me and I was crying." She paused.

"Yes, go on," Bliss said.

"I think she hurt me real hard—spanking with a belt. No. No, something worse, something more intolerable than spankings." She blinked and opened her eyes very wide to look at Bliss. "I remember now. I can see it from a distance. I see both of us being very upset. My father did something again. I was physically hurt—bleeding, crying—and was going to her for help. She was upset too. He'd hurt her too. She was hysterical, then angry with me. Pulling me to her, shaking me . . . I—I don't want to remember. I don't want to feel!" She shook her head and started to go deep into hypnosis.

Bliss was there before she could submerge, pushing her back into consciousness, keeping her from going under. "What happened?" he demanded. "You have to tell me what happened."

"I don't know what to do now . . . I don't know what to do . . ." She was getting spacey, but he wouldn't let her go.

"You can't do that anymore, Andrea. I won't let you. *You* won't let yourself!"

And suddenly her eyes flew open. She was perfectly clear, a look of astonishment on her face. "I—I remember it all. I was screaming and she was shaking me. I was saying 'No more, please, send him away!' and she was screaming at me—'You are evil, bad, you want to destroy the family!'—that's what she was screaming at me. And then she started to choke me, and I couldn't fight her off because she was too big, and then I fell to the floor and she was still screaming at me that I was bad and evil, and then all of a sudden she stopped choking me and she started to cry. Then she said, 'Oh, my God! Go to your room. I don't want to see you anymore!' And I went into my room, into the closet, and stayed there for a long, long time."

"Is that why you get those choking feelings?" Bliss asked.

"Yes. I'm caught, can't feel now."

"You aren't five years old anymore, Andrea," Bliss insisted.

"Caught!" She started to choke, gasping for breath, then crying, gradually calming down. As the sobbing stopped, her face took on a look of surprise and comprehension. "That's a big part of my wanting to die. Yes, it must be. I deserved to die, but if she was wrong, she was the only one I could go to for help. And she wouldn't help me. I stayed quiet, away from her. Didn't want to make her angry."

"Anything to avoid your mother's anger," Bliss suggested.

"Yes, I suppose so." She was still remote. "I'm finding it so hard to believe—that she tried to strangle me, that she said all those things to me. I'm caught between two worlds. I have to know it was real."

"Then go back into hypnosis and ask."

Andrea was gone only a moment, and when she re-emerged she asked Bliss to hold her hand. He did.

"It was the truth. I thought I was going to die—I couldn't breathe. I thought she was going to kill me. After that I was afraid to be near her. The strangling of the cats is that too! It was always a survival—either the cat or me. If it was only my father I would have burned the cats. I always felt the cats were more linked to my mother. Either I would die or the cat.''

ANDREA'S JOURNAL
December 3, 1983

I remember taking the ink blot test over ten years ago. At first I thought it was a total waste of time. After several cards had passed, one struck me. I saw a father and mother pulling apart a little girl. The girl was in the middle, and each had an arm and was pulling. The center of the girl was literally torn apart. That picture was so vivid, so real. I tried to dismiss it, but that experience still remains.

Through the past four years of therapy, I've been able to unravel the secret memories of physical and sexual abuse by my father and the emotional attacks by my mother. My father's actions were brutal but direct. His actions began to explain my bizarre sexual self-destructive acts. I knew my mother was involved, but I thought only by not protecting me and verbally berating me. Yet, after all our work, even when I could sense myself coming full circle by being able to change my self-image from the whore being stoned, I was still unable to avoid crises.

There was one gnawing piece left. I even went out and killed another cat. I felt distant and angry with Dr. Bliss. After days in that state, I knew I had to trust someone, and Dr. Bliss seemed the only answer.

The resistance was phenomenal as some part of me fought to keep the memory from getting out in the open. What finally broke the resistance was the realization that Dr. Bliss was getting mixed up with my mother—that all the anger and mistrust I couldn't understand was being directed at him as if he actually were my mother. With that clear I was able to regain control over my head and went on to the heart of the problem. It went relatively swiftly. When I returned to the pivotal scene I realized what had come before it—another of my father's attacks. I could no longer take the physical and emotional trauma he was inflicting and, despite his threats to kill me if I told, I knew I had to go to my mother for help—a natural reaction of a child.

My mother became outraged. Not at my father for what he'd done to me, but at me. She told me I was never to tell anyone those lies and that I was a bad and evil girl for even thinking of them. I kept pleading for her to help me—my sense of despair was intense. That made her even more angry. I started to cry and begged her for help.

That must have triggered her own sense of helplessness and despair because she suddenly began to strangle me. She kept her hands tightly clenched around my throat and gripped me so hard that I finally fell to the floor, almost passing out. She then began to cry and moan, "Oh, my God! Oh, my God!" When she finally composed herself, she angrily ordered me to my room. She said she never wanted to see me again. I immediately went to my room and returned to my tiny closet.

The damage wasn't over. In the closet the physical and emotional pain became unbearable. I tried to block the physical pain inflicted by both my father and mother, tried to retain my anger toward both of them. But I kept hearing and concentrating on my mother's words—that I was bad, evil, wicked, that she never wanted to see me again. My desire to die was intensified, both to escape the nightmare world where I found myself and also to punish myself for the evil in me.

I realize now that this incident must have marked the time when my mother and I became very distant.

The session was both highly significant and very painful. It did, however, mark a more complete mapping of my nightmare childhood. The work of reconstruction remains, but the source of all this insanity has been made clearer to me than ever before with the addition of this final piece of the puzzle.

Epilogue

OLD habits are not easy to break, and Andrea's were no exception. Every time she encountered a difficult situation or felt under tension, there was the impulse to dive back into hypnosis, to take up once again with her "Old Gang" of personalities, to chastise herself for the sins and evils of which she felt a familiar part.

But more and more, she resisted the temptation. That alter world that she had lived with for so many years slowly gave way to an understanding that reality, for all its suffering and sadness, was a more forgiving and salutary place than any she had inhabited inside her head.

Memories did not come flooding back because, finally, they no longer ebbed. At first consciously, later more reflexively, she has retained her memories of that past world and is learning to live with them. For Andrea it will never be easy to live with those memories—most are horrid and all are painful, and a full understanding of the extremity of her father's madness and her mother's pious helplessness can never bring much comfort to her life. Before she was a person without a past; now, for better or for worse (and it must be predominantly for the best) she is a person with a history: sordid, disfigured, bloodcurdling, but it nonetheless belongs to someone made whole by the knowledge of it.

Now that Andrea Biaggi is able to admit that much about her former behavior is controllable, can it be said with perfect honesty that she is "cured"? The question begs for some definition of the word "cure," and neither Dr. Bliss nor Andrea can give a totally satisfactory answer. The truth perhaps is that much of her self-destructive behavior and her "splitting" into personalities is over. The constant and intractable trauma, the panics and terrors, the wild anger and lost weekends—these are probably things of the past.

But totally cured, in the strict textbook sense of the word? Probably not. There will always be moments for Andrea when she will long for the peace and security of a deep hypnotic state; she may reminisce with longing about the "family" inside her head. She may lose time and act inappropriately—but then, most of us, no matter how much we might deem ourselves paragons of mental health, drift occasionally and do inappropriate things.

The best hope is that she will be able to prosper in this world, using the considerable intelligence and talent she possesses. Also, if she is lucky, she will find someone to share his life with her, if that is what she finally decides she wants. Survival is a compromise with reality, and over the years Andrea Biaggi has indicated how extraordinary a survivor she is. Now, given the pleasanter climes of a future that can offer far less trauma than her past, there is every reason to believe that she can enjoy a more complete life than she has ever known before.

Cured? Perhaps not. But stabilized, if she's careful; back in control, if she's vigilant; and happy, if life is good to her.

About the Author

Jonathan Bliss has worked on a science series for Time-Life Books and has researched widely in the sciences and medicine. **Eugene Bliss, M.D.,** is a graduate of Yale and New York Medical College. He has worked at the Menninger Institute, taught at Yale, and is currently Professor of Psychiatry at the University of Utah Medical School.